The Complete Universal Orlando

ISBN 978-0-9903716-1-8

Writing and research: Julie Neal
Photography: Mike Neal
Additional writing, photography and research: Micaela Neal

Produced by Coconut Press Media Inc. Published by Keen Communications, LLC. Manufactured in the United States of America. Distributed by Publishers Group West. Copyright © 2016 by Coconut Press Media Inc. All rights reserved. Reproduction in whole or part without written permission from the publisher is prohibited except short excerpts used in editorial reviews. Requests to the publisher for permission should be addressed to Keen Communications, PO Box 43673, Birmingham, AL 35243, 205-322-0439, fax 205-326-1012, or contact@keencommunication.com.

Our thanks to Laura Dossett, Jimmy Clarity, Michelle Russo, Jack Costello, Kristin at Guest Services, Mark Williams, J.T. Wilkinson, and all the Universal team members who assisted us.

To Oliver. Good boy.

The Complete
Universal Orlando®

Julie and Mike Neal

About this book

Congratulations. You have purchased the best book there is about one of the best theme-park resorts in the world. Yes that's not very modest, but we really think it's true. The more you look at this book, the more you will enjoy your visit. But before you start flipping through it, please take a minute and read these two pages. They explain the book and help you get the most out of it.

You should know: our ratings are weird. We rate every attraction from one to five stars. But that doesn't mean a five-star ride is better than a four-star ride. It means a five-star ride lives up to its promise better than a four-star ride. As for the attractions we think are best, we give those checkmarks.

A handbook. Really. This book is written, as the catchphrase on the back cover says,

to be "a handbook on how to have fun." That means it focuses on helping you enjoy each attraction, regardless of how good it is.

It's also deep. To get the most out of Universal Orlando, we think it helps to fully understand it. That's why there's a chapter on Universal Pictures history, another on Universal Orlando history, another just on its characters. That's why there are 24 scoring tips for the Men in Black Alien Attack ride, and 49 Fun Finds for it.

Are you a Harry Potter fan? Read the last chapter, our Wizarding World of Harry Potter Field Guide. Don't know about Harry? Read the introduction to that chapter.

Something else you should know. The authors went crazy on this one. Already residents of Orlando, we moved to Universal to create the book. We actually lived on its property, in an apartment directly behind the Men in Black ride (our dog *hated* the fireworks). We spent two years roaming Universal's parks and other areas, literally hundreds of days. We voiced our impressions of roller coasters and other rides directly into our phones as soon as we hopped off them, to make sure we captured each experience well. We photographed Universal at dawn, at dusk, at midnight. As for our 22-year-old daughter Micaela... well, flip back to that field guide.

Contents

It can be done.

How Universal fought off a century of setbacks to reach the top of its game

ITS FOUNDER CAME TO THE UNITED STATES at the age of 17 with just $50 in his pocket. When he started making movies, he went toe-to-toe with Thomas Edison, and came out the winner. He made his studio the country's leading film producer, without going into debt. After failing at an attempt to work with censors and a supplier botched his cartoon deal with Walt Disney, he turned to his son, who showed him new ways to succeed. Later his studio stayed in business despite years of turmoil, and eventually returned to the top.

"It can be done." That was his motto. His name was Carl Laemmle ("LEM-lee"), and his company was Universal. This is the story of those challenges, those failures and successes, a tale filled with determination, hard work, innovative thinking... and more aliens, monsters and magical creatures than you'd think it could possibly deserve.

An American Dream. His wife had just died, and he had made a decision. Going against her wishes, Julius Laemmle would let their 16-year-old son leave their tiny village of Laupheim, Germany, and go to America. Eight of their 13 children had never gotten a chance at life, dying of scarlet fever, so why stop the short, stocky Carl from having a good shot at it? The boy liked his life in Laupheim, especially catching trout in its

Carl Laemmle, the founder of Universal.

streams, but had dreamt of moving to the United States for years. His older brother Joseph had already done it, and in letters home made it sound like a place where people could do whatever they wanted.

He had another reason too. Years later his son shared it with Motion Picture Magazine: "He wanted to see an Indian. He read a lot about the American Indian and about cowboys and Wild West riders and Buffalo Bill."

Happy birthday, son. Carl's dreams came true a few months later, when for his 17th birthday his dad gave him a $22 ticket on a steamship to New York (steerage class, like Leonardo DiCaprio had in 1997's "Titanic") as well as $50 in spending money. Worth about $1,500 today, the gift came from the entire village, as neighbors pitched in for the ticket and a bank loaned his dad the cash. On Feb. 13, 1884, young Carl Laemmle arrived in New York Harbor, barely able to speak English. Peering through the fog toward Liberty Island, he didn't see the Statue of Liberty—it wasn't there yet. Instead he saw steam shovels, digging the foundations for its pedestal.

Like so many other immigrants, Laemmle spent time at a number of odd jobs. Eventually he settled down in Oshkosh, Wis., as an office manager and bookkeeper at dry goods stores (stores that sold fabric, clothing, sundries and other "dry" consumer items that weren't hardware). He also married, had a daughter (Rebecca, named for his mom) and saved his money. Finally, when his savings reached $4,000 (about $85,000 today), he set out to fulfill what he thought was his ultimate dream.

To own a dry goods store.

In Chicago. Where his brother lived.

There's no business like... But as he searched the Windy City for a good spot for his shop, he noticed a new type of business that was popping up all over it: nickelodeons. Set up in converted storefronts, these small, simple theaters didn't have live performers, but rather a new phenomenon, "moving pictures." Typically only 10 to 15 minutes long, these silent films were most often melodramas, but there were also "actualities" (documentaries) and "scenics" (views from moving trains). Admission was five cents, way less than the price of a ticket to a live theater, which at the time averaged $1.

Laemmle was amazed. People were lining up in the snow, even in Chicago's working-class areas where the theaters were anything but clean. Buying a bag of beans from a grocer, he stood outside one nickelodeon for more

"'Tween Two Loves," 1911.

than an hour, placing a bean in a jar whenever someone bought a ticket. And as he counted people and figured out what the rent would be, he realized he had the wrong dream.

Within days he had spent $3,600—nearly all his savings—to rent a vacant store and turn it into a theater, installing a screen, projector and 190 camp seats he purchased from an undertaker. To attract women (and hence, families), he painted the building white and called it The White Theater. It was an instant hit. On its first day, it brought in $200, enough to cover its expenses for a week. A month later he rented a second building, painted it white and opened The Family Theater.

Lighting up Thomas Edison. Frustrated with the shoddy service of his film supplier, Laemmle soon formed the Laemmle Film Service, a movie distributor. Offering first-run films delivered in good shape and on time, by 1909 it had become the largest independent distributor in the country. In other words, the largest one that wasn't part of Thomas Edison's Motion Picture Patents Co., which controlled 70 percent of the market.

Also known as the Edison Trust, the Motion Picture Patents Co. had been formed by the famed inventor—he'd created the phonograph and functional light bulb 30 years earlier—supposedly to protect his patents on devices used in cameras and projectors.

But it did far more than that. Consisting of Edison and the heads of the young industry's 10 largest studios (which had names like Biograph, Essanay and Vitagraph) it decreed that no other person or company could make, distribute or project a movie with any piece of equipment that contained an Edison device. Federal laws were written to back it up, and courts enforced them. Needless to say, the true goal of the Trust was to give Edison complete control of the fledgling industry.

Confronting Laemmle about his distribution service, Edison demanded he either sell it to the Trust or shut it down.

Old Flimmyboy. Laemmle did neither. Instead, he mocked the inventor and his pompous bullying, placing ads in trade papers that cleverly skewered Edison yet never mentioned him by name, in order to avoid a libel suit. Headlined "Gen. Flimco's Last Stand," one read: *"Old Flimmyboy, surrounded by Independent Indians, has about as much chance as a snowball in Hades. Shot full of holes, punctured and perforated from peanut-head to pants, he is milking one final bluff by shooting threatening letters to exhibitors…. We are making arrangements for the General's burial. While the band is*

Universal City opens, 1915.

*mournfully playing over the grave, you will
be making arrangements to hook up with Old
Dr. Laemmle, who will cure you of all such
diseases as 'Repeaters,' 'Dropsy of the Film'
and 'Rainstorms.' Send for Dr. Laemmle's film
list today. The Laemmle Film Service. 196–196
Lake Street, Chicago. The Biggest and Best
Film Renter in the World.*"

Edison sued him anyway. And lost.

But Laemmle was just getting started.
In 1912 he moved to Edison's home turf of
Fort Lee, N.J.—the Hollywood of its day—
and using equipment from Europe opened
his own movie studio. He called it the
Independent Moving Pictures Co.—or IMP,
a play on his short stature. Its first film was
"Hiawatha," a Western based on the legend
of a famous American Indian.

Edison sued Laemmle again—246 times.

Stealing Mary Pickford. This time his
counterpunch was ingenious. Realizing that
movie audiences might respond to something more than the title of a film, he secretly
met with some of the Trust's most popular
actors, including Biograph's Mary Pickford.
Besides a raise in pay, he offered them billing
and screen credit for their work, a practice
Edison had refused to do. The 18-year-old
Pickford, who at the time was known only
as "Little Mary," was one of the first to agree.

Other independents followed Laemmle's
lead. Soon the Trust lost nearly all of its
actors as well as its directors, and began
to crumble from the inside out. Two years
later a court ruled it a "corrupt and unlawful
association." All of its studios closed.

Pickford made 39 movies for Laemmle and
went on to become a top star of the silent
era. "Those were strange days and we were
strange folks," she later recalled at a banquet
marking Laemmle's 60th birthday. "But there
remains the memory of the man who gave
most of us opportunities, and all of us valuable
assistance at a time when we needed it sorely."

Universal Pipe Fittings. Some studios are
named after their founders, such as Disney.
Columbia is named for the mythical torch-
bearing woman who personified the United
States before being replaced by Uncle Sam.

Universal's name has less profound roots.

"Gentlemen, I have it. Universal. The
Universal Film Manufacturing Co." Looking
out an office window at the traffic down
below, that's what Carl Laemmle called out
during a meeting in Manhattan in 1912 with
the heads of the other independents, who
were joining with him to create one large
studio but having trouble naming it. His
name was ideal, Laemmle argued, as what

could be more universal than a business that provided mass quantities of entertainment for the enjoyment of the masses? The others agreed. Later one asked how he thought of the name. Easy, he said. While he was looking out the window, a truck passed by. On its side were the words "Universal Pipe Fittings."

Hundreds of movies, no debt. "I am proud to say I've never used a dollar of Wall Street Money," Laemmle boasted to the press in 1924. His pride made sense. He had built the world's No. 1 movie studio without going into debt, succeeding instead by having innovative ideas and the nerve to put them into action.

A film factory. From 1912 to 1925 Universal was the country's top film producer. In 1915 alone it made more than 250 movies—shorts, serials and features—an average of 5 per week. What made such output possible was the studio's factory-like approach to filmmaking. Instead of each movie having a large crew filled with specialists, specialized departments worked on several films at once. Singular departments handled all the studio's costumes and make-up, scripting and editing... there was even a group of cowboys and another of Indians who spent their days riding in and out of one film after another. Only a small crew was dedicated to any particular picture, which made it easy to shoot quickly.

Opened in 1915, the factory itself was Universal City, a 230-acre facility Laemmle had purchased a few miles outside Los Angeles. The developed area had Western and New York backlots, six indoor stages (including one that could shoot 16 films at once), barracks for cavalrymen, a bunk house for cowboys, a zoo, a hospital and classrooms—even an Indian village populated by 50 members of the Chimallo tribe. Brought in from New Mexico, they were encouraged to, as one newspaper put it, "pursue their life and adorn themselves as grotesquely as possible." "The biggest outdoor motion picture studio in the world," the total property came with the rights to film on 12,000 adjacent acres, including a forest and mountain range.

As a result, Universal knocked out bread-and-butter melodramas, serials and "oaters" (Westerns) at a cost-per-flick that paled to movies produced the conventional way. By 1918 the studio had 6,000 employees, and Universal City had 300 residents.

Female directors. Laemmle shocked the industry by hiring women to direct many of his films, five years before they had the right to vote. His highest-paid director was Lois Weber, whose films boldly explored social issues from a female perspective.

What would happen if a naked woman strolled through the congregation of a

An indoor stage, 1915.

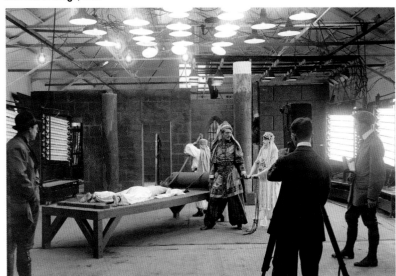

"Foolish Wives," 1922.

wealthy church? According to Weber's 1915 movie "Hypocrites," the churchgoers would reveal their true souls—souls filled with a lust for sex, money and power. Complete with four full-frontal scenes of a nude woman— the industry's first—the film earned back 10 times its cost. Banned in Pennsylvania, Weber's next film became the studio's No. 1 movie of 1916. A plea for birth control, "Where Are My Children" grossed more than $3 million, selling 6 million tickets.

One of the first directors to experiment with sound, Weber was also the first director to use a split-screen to show simultaneous action. Altogether she directed 135 movies for the studio. At her peak she earned $5,000 a week, more than any other Universal director.

"I would trust Miss Weber with any sum of money to make any picture that she wanted to make," Laemmle told the trade paper Motion Picture Weekly. "I would be sure that she would bring it back."

Faith in a teenager. He made another bold decision a few years later, when he hired a frail young man to be his head of production.

In 1917, Irving Thalberg was a sickly 18-year-old who had barely made it through high school. Born with a heart defect, his school days had been filled with chest pains, dizziness and fatigue; during his senior year

he came down with rheumatic fever and had to finish his studies from home. Unable to attend college, he taught himself how to type, and took shorthand and Spanish classes at a vocational school. Then he placed an ad in a local paper: "Situation Wanted: Secretary, stenographer. Spanish, English, high school education, no experience. $15 a week."

Laemmle saw the ad and hired Thalberg, at $25 a week. Among other duties, he screened films with his boss and transcribed his comments. Despite the boy's physical issues, Laemmle was totally impressed. Thalberg had a charming confidence in himself, and when he typed up his notes would add comments which understood the problems with filmmaking and explained them well.

When Thalberg turned 19, Laemmle named him manager of Universal City—in essence, the person in charge of things when Laemmle wasn't there. A year later Laemmle made him production manager, the person in charge of the studio's entire slate of films whether Laemmle was there or not.

The frail young man was challenged immediately. Just a few days into the job, arrogant auteur Erich Von Stroheim sent him a note stating that the film he was shooting would take longer than planned. Laemmle had hired him to produce "Foolish Wives," the story of a Monte Carlo con man who swindles women while he seduces them; when he meets an American diplomat he beds the envoy's wife as his two lovers distract the hapless hubby.

To get everything just how he wanted, Stroheim had cast himself in the lead, ignored his $350,000 budget and built a lavish Monte Carlo outdoor set. As recalled in the biography "Stroheim" by Arthur Lennigby, Thalberg immediately drove to the set and confronted the director. "I have seen all the film, and you have all you need."

The bulky Austrian towered over him.

"I have not finished yet."

"Yes, you have."

Stroheim sneered down at him. Finally, he barked out his response. "If you were not my superior, I should punch you in the face!"

Though Variety declared the 1922 movie a "sensational sex melodrama," it lost money.

Soon Thalberg told Laemmle of his own idea for a film. It would be based on one of his favorite horror stories, but it wouldn't be a horror movie, it would be a spectacle, with sets that included the Cathedral of Notre Dame. For the title role Thalberg suggested Lon Chaney, a little-known Universal contract player. Laemmle liked the idea, and in 1923 "The Hunchback of Notre Dame" became his most profitable movie to date.

Two years later Chaney starred in "The Phantom of the Opera." Though its elaborate sets and vast number of extras boosted its cost to $700,000, it brought in $2 million at the box office, an enormous sum at a time when the average movie ticket was 50 cents.

Known as the Boy Wonder, Thalberg later helped create rival studio MGM, and became its head of production at age 26. He died of pneumonia in 1936, at age 37.

Film packages. Laemmle also had a unique way of renting films to theaters—unlike other studios at the time, he offered them in packages. His Complete Service Plan included a cartoon or comedy short, an episode of a serial and a feature film. Other deals gave theaters a different film to show every day of the week.

Studio tours. Laemmle earned some extra money, and lots of publicity, by having Universal City be open to the public. For a 25-cent admission fee (a chicken lunch was an extra nickel), visitors could wander its grounds and watch outdoor scenes being filmed from shaded grandstands. Since the

"The Phantom of the Opera," 1924.

Universal founder Carl Laemmle chats with comedian Will Rogers at a Hollywood gathering celebrating Laemmle's 25th anniversary in motion pictures in 1931. Behind them are, from left, Hays Code namesake William Hays, MGM head of production Irving Thalberg, famed director Cecil B. DeMille and silent-film superstar Mary Pickford. In the foreground, Laemmle's son Carl Jr. holds a scroll the industry gave his dad to mark the occasion.

movies were silent, audiences were encouraged to cheer heroes and boo villains. "See your favorite screen stars do their work," barked an ad for the tour. "See how we make the people laugh or cry or sit on the edge of their chairs the world over!" An average of 500 people did so daily until the tours stopped in 1930, when the advent of "talkies" made quiet sets a necessity.

'Too damn clean.' Laemmle's fortunes began to turn in the 1920s, when he embraced a set of film standards created by censor Will Hays. Though much of the country had loved the racy content of early silent films, it also caused an uproar. Some cities and states passed laws that required that a movie had to be approved by a local government before a theater could show it; some churches were calling for federal censorship. To head that off Hollywood decided to self-censor its films, and created the Motion Picture Producers and Distributors of America to do it. For its first president then-U.S. President Warren Harding recommended Hays, the manager of his 1920 election campaign who

as postmaster general had recently cracked down on the mailing of racy photographs.

The Formula. In 1924, Hays released a set of filmmaking standards he dubbed "The Formula." Among other things, it prohibited a movie from portraying "the ridicule of religion" or the use of liquor or illegal drugs "when not required by the plot." It also banned nudity, "excessive and lustful kissing," "suggestive dancing" and other behaviors that might "stimulate the lower and baser element." Though the New York Times called the standards "an ultimatum to the moving picture industry to clean up films and keep them clean," they were voluntary guidelines. Studios could follow them, or not.

Clean and wholesome. Laemmle followed the guidelines. "One thing you can be sure of, when you start out to see a Universal Picture, you will know it is clean—and good," he wrote in an ad he placed in The Saturday Evening Post, at the time the country's most popular magazine. "You will know that you can take your children without fear that they will be shocked or made familiar with the world's follies before their time... So I give

Of mice, men and a rabbit

BESIDES HIS STRUGGLES with live-action films, Carl Laemmle faced another problem in the late 1920s. Cartoons. Thanks to the actions of his supplier, wholesaler Charles Mintz, Laemmle lost his relationship with the small studio that created them: The Walt Disney Co.

The relationship started off fine. Beginning in 1927, Universal cartoons featured a happy-go-lucky hare Laemmle himself had come up with, one his staff had named Oswald the Lucky Rabbit.* He chose the Disney studio to create the shorts, as its zippy approach to work gave him a new one every two weeks. And the cartoons were good. Their humor came from sight gags as well as storylines, and their art had a keen sense of perspective.

The rabbit wasn't the biggest star in the cartoon world; that honor belonged to Paramount's Felix the Cat. But Disney delivered the cartoons on time, and Laemmle's exhibitors liked them. And Oswald *was* popular, so much so that Laemmle licensed products that bore his image; the first one was a chocolate-covered marshmallow candy bar.

Things turned sour less than a year later. Deciding to make the cartoons himself, in February 1928 Mintz secretly hired away nearly all of Disney's animators. Audiences yawned at the results. They lacked the storytelling skills of Walt Disney as well as the artistic sense of Ub Iwerks, a Hungarian immigrant who had stayed with Disney and had been Oswald's main animator.

Laemmle soon cut his ties with Mintz, leaving Universal with no cartoons at all.

That fall Walt Disney created a synchronized-sound cartoon, "Steamboat Willie," which starred a new, Oswald-like mouse. After its premiere at the Universal-owned Colony Theater in New York, Walt Disney and Laemmle shook hands on a deal that would have them work directly with each other. The Disney studio would make 30 Mickey Mouse cartoons a year, and Universal would distribute them.

Universal's lawyers, however, wouldn't agree to the deal, as it violated a clause in the studio's contract with Mintz that they felt it still had to honor.

*Since Oswald was a rabbit, Universal chose his name by pulling a piece of paper out of a hat. Dozens of slips had suggestions from secretaries in the studio's publicity department.

Exasperated, Laemmle decided Universal would create its own Oswald cartoons and tapped, of all people, his part-time chauffeur to make them. And though budding animator Walter Lantz was up to the challenge—his 1933 Oswald short "The Merry Old Soul" was nominated for an Oscar—the rabbit's popularity never returned. Today Lantz is best remembered for a bird he created a decade later, Woody Woodpecker. As for Oswald, he languished for almost 80 years, forgotten by all but the most ardent animation fans.

Then, in one of the oddest moments in cartoon history, in 2006 Universal traded the rabbit to Disney in exchange for sportscaster Al Michaels. Famous for his "Do you believe in miracles?... YES!" call of the ending of the 1980 Olympic hockey game between the U.S. and the Soviet Union, Michaels had worked for Disney's ABC television network for ages but wanted to move to Universal-affiliated NBC to work its NFL games.

Afterward, Michaels quipped: "I'm just glad to spread joy around the world. And I'm glad that Oswald wasn't reduced to playing the role of a rabbit at a dog track... I'm going to be a trivia answer someday."

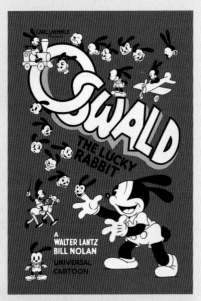

Oswald the Lucky Rabbit, 1929.

you my solemn pledge to keep Universal pictures clean and wholesome."

Unclean and popular. Meanwhile, other studios ignored The Formula. In fact, of the top 10 movies of 1927, none followed its guidelines. Four of them starred Paramount's Clara Bow, known as the "It" girl because of her sex appeal. In "Wings," the year's No. 1 film, she flashed her breasts.

Universal's top film that year? An earnest adaptation of "Uncle Tom's Cabin" (complete with a synchronized music score and sound effects) which tried to show that even something as destructive as the enslavement of human beings could be overcome by love. It placed 12th. And lost money.

Frustrated that "unclean pictures" were playing to packed theaters while most of his "clean" ones were flashing to empty seats, Laemmle sent out a questionnaire titled "What Do You Want?" to 22,000 theater owners, asking what type of films they preferred.

The 'wisdom of the majority.' "I fully expected that 95 percent of the answers would favor clean, wholesome pictures," he testified before the Federal Motion Picture Commission. "I stated my own likes and dislikes but explained that my own opinion didn't cut much figure, and I wanted an honest expression from exhibitors. I got it! At least half, maybe 60 percent, want the pictures to be risqué... Universal does not pose as a guardian of public morals or public taste. For that reason we may put out a picture that is off-color now and then. It is easy to make them. Personally, I am against them from soda to hock, but if the demand for them is so overwhelmingly great we will bow to the superior wisdom of the majority."

According to Motion Picture Weekly, he then confided to an associate: "The public now knows that we stand for clean pictures, and that invariably they are too damn clean. So they stay away on account of it."

A few years later The Formula evolved into the Motion Picture Production Code, an industry policy that required that a movie have a Certificate of Approval from Hays' censors before it could be released. In the 1960s that system was replaced by one still used today, which rWates films with the letters "G," "PG" (initially "M," then "GP"),"PG-13," "R" and "NC-17" (at first "X").

Like father, like son. What a birthday present! Just like Carl Laemmle's dad had shocked him on his 17th birthday, Laemmle startled his son on his 21st birthday—in this case by naming him head of production of the world's top movie studio. His son's name was Julius, though everyone called him Carl Jr.

Immediately he faced problems.

"Dracula," 1931.

"The Invisible Man," 1933.

The first was sound. Three months into his job, rival studio Warner Brothers released the world's first all-talking feature, "Lights of New York." Made for $23,000, it grossed $1.3 million, a record rate of return of more than 5,000 percent. "Talking pictures" soon became all the rage in the major cities, so despite being tight on cash—and the fact that Universal's best customers were rural theaters not equipped for sound—Carl Jr. spent thousands on equipment and retrofitted stages to convert the studio to sound.

His second problem: the Great Depression. It hit just one year into his tenure, before he could reap any rewards from his new investments. Universal started to lose money.

Through no real fault of his own, at age 22 Carl Jr. had become a Hollywood laughingstock. Trade papers portrayed him as the poster child for Hollywood nepotism—a point that to some extent was deserved. His dad had not seriously considered anyone else for the job and after World War I had put a total of 70 relatives on the Universal payroll, many of them refugees from Germany. At the time, a Hollywood saying coined by humorist Ogden Nash joked "Uncle Carl Laemmle has a very large faemmle."

Bored with his father's focus on cowboys and Indians, in 1930 Carl Jr. convinced his dad to buy the rights to "All Quiet on the Western Front," a German novel which revealed the disillusionment of that country's soldiers after World War I. The resulting movie marked a breakthrough for Universal. It won the Academy Award for Best Picture, giving the studio its first Oscar. Very controversial at the time, it was the first American movie to look at war from an enemy's point of view.

Next he developed two film genres that didn't cost a lot to produce, yet combined gripping storylines with eye-popping visuals. Together they would give Universal a lasting legacy. The first was the monster movie.

"I never drink... wine." With his hypnotic stare, flowing cape and heavy Hungarian accent, Bela Lugosi simply *became* the vampire Count Dracula. When "Dracula" premiered in New York on February 12, 1931, newspapers reported that members of the audience fainted in shock—a tale concocted by Universal's publicity department. The film was the studio's top film of the year.

The flat top... the bolt neck... in Carl Jr.'s next film, 1931's "Frankenstein," make-up artist Jack Pierce defined the look of the mad scientist's monster, which until then had only been a character in a book. Little-known studio contract player Boris Karloff portrayed

"The Bride of Frankenstein," 1935.

him as both a sympathetic outcast and rampaging beast. "Frankenstein" was also a hit.

"I didn't believe in 'Frankenstein,'" Carl Sr. told Universal Weekly, a newsletter to exhibitors. "I said to Junior, 'It's morbid. None of our officers are for it. People don't want that sort of thing.' Only Junior wanted it. Only Junior stood up for it. And he said to me 'Yes, they do, Pop. They do want that sort of thing. Just give me a chance and I'll show you.' Well, he discovered Boris Karloff and showed me. He showed us all. You see, my boy knows more than all the others. He has an insight."

Carl Jr. quickly made more monster flicks. In 1932's "The Mummy," Karloff plays an accidentally resurrected pharaoh driven by loneliness, who obsesses over a woman who resembles his deceased lover. In 1933's "The Invisbile Man," Claude Rains is a witty British chemist who turns himself transparent and then wreaks havoc just to be a jerk. Toying with the camp appeal of a monster's mate, 1935's "The Bride of Frankenstein" balances horrific drama and high kitsch. Universal's first female monster, the main character (Elsa Lanchester) is a creepy chick with electro-shock hair and a wide-eyed stare—who still seems to show up in every neighborhood each Halloween.

"Ooohh... Flash!" Featuring rugged good guys, menacing bad guys and sweet damsels in distress, a serial was a lengthy melodrama that played out over a dozen or so episodes. Designed to be seen in a theater just before a feature film, each installment ran about 20 minutes and ended with a cliff-hanger; a new adventure premiered each week. Carl Sr. had made cowboy-and-Indian serials since 1914.

His son's idea was to do one in outer space. Specifically "Flash Gordon," the story of a dashing college athlete who, when he learns that a planet is about to crash into Earth, finds a rocket ship and flies up to stop it, only to discover it's being controlled by the evil Ming the Merciless and his scheming daughter. To save money, Carl Jr. reused many Universal sets and props; the watchtower from "Frankenstein" became Ming's palace. Filming was fast; all 13 episodes were shot in 6 weeks, an average of 85 shots a day. An inspiration for today's "Star Wars" saga, "Flash Gordon" also featured an opening scroll, a cloud city and deflector shields.

Unlike his dad's Westerns, Carl Jr.'s serial also had a strong dose of fanservice, as its primary characters exposed plenty of skin. A dashing Yale polo player, Steven "Flash" Gordon (Buster Crabbe) wore a snug pair of shorts and was often bare-chested.

Meanwhile, his girlfriend Dale Arden (Jean Rogers) and bad-girl Princess Aura (Priscilla Lawson) rocked tight crop tops.

The actors weren't hired for their dramatic skills. Crabbe was an athlete, the winner of the 1932 Olympic gold medal for 400-meter freestyle swimming. Rogers had come to Hollywood after winning a beauty contest in her native Boston that was sponsored by Paramount Pictures. Carl Jr. discovered Lawson while on vacation in Florida, sitting in the audience as she was crowned 1935's Miss Miami Beach.

When asked about her experience years later by FilmFax magazine, Rogers recalled that the costumes and sets "were fantastic… and I have to say my costume was a little brief. I don't think the Hays Office paid much attention to what went on in serials." She said playing Dale wasn't difficult. "All I had to say was 'Flash, where are you going?' and 'Ooohh, Flash!'"

Finally… a meeting with Wall Street.

As the Great Depression started to ease, Carl Jr. was quickly establishing himself as a worthy occupant of his office. But he wouldn't get credit for it. In the spring of 1936, his dad borrowed money for the first time ever—pledging his equity in the studio to a New York investment company so his son could finish an elaborate production that was way over budget, the first sound version of the Broadway musical "Showboat."

Once the film wrapped, Carl Sr. agreed to meet in his Universal City office with an aspiring screenwriter, German immigrant Henry Koster. He pitched Laemmle an idea for a comedy about three sisters who bring their parents back together just as they're about to get divorced. Laemmle liked it. They shook hands. "Look around for a few days," Laemmle said, according to "Henry Koster," a biography by Irene Atkins. "Go through the stages. Then come back here and we'll discuss what we're going to do."

Koster looked around for two days. But when he returned to Laemmle's office, the Universal founder wasn't there. Instead, movers were. Before "Showboat" (or "Flash Gordon") could be released, the investors that granted Laemmle the loan had called it in, as he had missed its due date. The next day, on April 2, 1936, both he and his son had been uncermoniously kicked out of their offices by the studio's new owner, J. Cheever Cowdin, president of the Standard Capital Corp.

Carl Jr.'s role as the boy with the insight—the young man behind the sad soldiers, the scary monsters and the sexy space battles—was forgotten.

He never worked on a film again.

"Flash Gordon," 1936.

Kooky characters. Scheming sisters, calculating swindlers, harebrained hillbillies… even a wise-ass mule. Universal's hits surrounding World War II let the country escape the world around it and have a good laugh. They weren't the finest films ever made, but then again they weren't trying to be.

Three teens and a tart. Can a wealthy Swedish girl reunite her divorced parents before dad marries a golddigger? She can if she's Deanna Durbin, the 14-year-old who starred in Henry Koster's chipper comedy-musical "Three Smart Girls." Durbin became a box-office sensation as plucky Penny Craig, who heads to New York and hires an alcoholic aristocrat to steal the strumpet away, unaware that her two older sisters have paid another man to do the same thing. Soon there's plenty of wholesome havoc, as the men go after the teens instead of the tart.

Released a few days before Christmas in 1936, "Three Smart Girls" was the hit of the holidays, a Christmas gift to the studio from their departed founder. Shot in just 30 days on a shoestring budget, it quickly led to five sequels, all of which also made money. With additional help from Carl Jr.'s "Showboat" musical and "Flash Gordon" serials Universal soon recovered from its debts, and in 1939 earned a profit of a million dollars, its first in a decade.

Catfight at the OK Corral. "All I want is to be a cowboy and wear my own pants." That's what a young man confides to his wife after he loses his trousers in a poker match to tough saloon girl Marlene Dietrich in the 1939 comedic Western "Destry Rides Again." The film was a comeback for the German femme fatale, who had found fame in the early '30s but had never played anything for laughs.

"Hey you! Give me those pants. And from now on, leave my husband alone," the poor man's wife calls to Dietrich.

"I don't want your husband, Mrs. Callahan. All I want is his money. And his pants."

"And how'd you get 'em? By making eyes at him while you cheated, you gilded lily!"

"But Mrs. Callahan, you know he would rather be cheated by me than married to you."

An ensuing catfight gives the women access to bottles, chairs, glasses, tables and unlimited amounts of each other's hair. In the end Jimmy Stewart, the new deputy of lawless Bloody Gulch, dumps water on them.

Cuthbert and Flowerbelle. He would write his own screenplays. That's what W.C. Fields told Universal it would take to get him to sign a three-picture deal with the studio. Well, that plus $15,000 for each story and $150,000 for each acting job—serious money during the Depression but still a decent deal for three screenplays and three star

"Three Smart Girls," 1936.

"My Little Chickadee," 1940.

Photos © Universal Pictures

turns by a major celebrity. Universal said OK. The result was three more hits for the studio—1939's "You Can't Cheat an Honest Man," 1940's "The Bank Dick" and 1940's "My Little Chickadee," the one-and-only teaming of Fields with legendary vamp Mae West.

In "Chickadee" he's Cuthbert J. Twillie, a well-mannered gentleman whom golddigger Flowerbelle Lee (West) mistakes for a loaded aristocrat and tricks into a phony marriage—only to later learn he's just a common con man. In retaliation, she turns the lights off in their honeymoon room and tricks him into cuddling up to a goat—to which he inquires "Darling, have you changed your perfume?"

Fields then negotiated a fourth film with Universal—a movie about himself in which he tries to sell a screenplay—which he would not only write but also pick his supporting players. Censors had a field day with the script, objecting not only to its many "vulgar and suggestive scenes and dialogue" and "jocular references to drinking and liquor" but also "the name 'Fuchschwantz,' because of its sound," "the line 'tighter than Dick's hat band'" and "any and all dialogue about and showing of bananas and pineapples."

Co-starring two of Fields' close friends—vaudeville comedian Leon Errol and prissy character actor Franklin Pangborn—as well as Marx Brothers' foil Margaret Dumont and Fields' mistress Carlotta Monti, the result was the surreal 1941 farce "Never Give a Sucker an Even Break." "We are not sure that this is even a movie," the New York Times confessed. "Some parts you will find incomprehensibly silly. Probably you also will laugh your head off."

Boogie Woogie boys. *Abbott:* "Throw your chest out! Go on! Throw your chest out!" *Costello:* "I'm not done with it yet!" When Universal signed the comedy team of Bud Abbott and Lou Costello to three military comedies, they had perfected their shtick over two decades in vaudeville, Broadway and radio. 1941's "Buck Privates" (quoted above), "In the Navy" and "Keep 'Em Flying" all co-starred the harmonic singing trio The Andrews Sisters ("Buck Privates" debuted their song "Boogie Woogie Bugle Boy") and were all hits. By the time the U.S. entered World War II Abbott and Costello were the country's top box-office stars, more popular than rivals Bob Hope and Bing Crosby, a position they maintained throughout the war. Thanks to them, Universal's annual profits increased every year of war, reaching $4 million in 1945.

The studio's string of hits was interrupted in the mid-forties when it was taken over by its largest stockholder. Though "he knew

THE COMPLETE UNIVERSAL ORLANDO **23**

virtually nothing about films and rarely went to the cinema" according to English newspaper The Daily Mail, British flour magnate J. Arthur Rank was determined to "turn popular culture into a gigantic advertisement for British virtues." Renaming the studio Universal-International Pictures, Rank had it focus on classier fare, including the distribution of English films produced by his Rank Organisation. These included a 1946 version of the Charles Dickens' novel "Great Expectations" directed by David Lean, and a 1948 production of William Shakespeare's "Hamlet" starring Laurence Olivier. Both won awards ("Hamlet" won the Oscar for Best Picture), but studio profits plummeted and Rank nearly went broke. Soon he let Universal—or rather, Universal-International—return to what it did best.

Which meant… two wacky comedy series! One about farmers, the other a farm animal.

Pa, Ma and Paris-ites. *Ma:* "Pa, you're lazier than that old hound dog we used to have." *Pa:* "Which one?" *Ma:* "The one that used to lean against the wall when she barked." That joke and thousands like it fuel the antics of hollering hillbilly Ma (Marjorie Main) and soft-spoken shiftless Pa (Percy Kilbride), a farm couple with 15 children and a knack for winning contests that send them off on a series of adventures. In 1949's "Ma and Pa Kettle," Pa wins a futuristic dream house filled with modern gadgets he can't figure out, including rows of beds which fold up into a wall at the push of a button; in 1953's "Ma and Pa Kettle on Vacation" the couple wins a free trip to Paris, where Ma can't wait to "be acting like those Paris-ites" and Pa tries to buy racy postcards. Universal made 10 Kettle comedies between 1949 and 1957. Each took just a few weeks to film and earned about 10 times its cost, a total of more than $35 million.

Smart ass. A mule gives a teenage girl speech lessons and makeover tips to help her hook up with its 28-year-old owner. That's the plot, or at least one of the plots, of 1953's "Francis Covers the Big Town," one of seven talking-mule flicks Universal produced between 1949 and 1956. They made the studio bales of box-office hay; the first film cost $150,000 but made $3 million. Besides being able to talk, the smart… well, ass… has the uncanny ability to help get its owner—befuddled Donald O'Connor—just about anything he needs. In "Big Town" Francis gets him a girl, a job as a reporter (by chatting with police horses to learn scoops on crime stories) and cleared of murder charges by testifying at a trial. He also lands his own lady love—a zebra.

To help ensure its success, each Francis film featured a studio starlet; "Big Town" had vivacious Yvette Dugay; 1954's "Francis Joins

"Buck Privates," 1941.

"Francis Covers the Big Town," 1953.

the WACS" showed off Universal's answer to Marilyn Monroe, bad-girl bombshell Mamie Van Doren. Nearly every studio contract actor appeared in at least one Francis movie, including future Vulcan Leonard Nimoy. In the middle of the series O'Connor took a break to co-star in MGM's big-budget "Singin' in the Rain." When he had to leave in the middle of shooting to get back to his Francis duties, his role in that classic musical's "Broadway Melody" number was cut.

In reality Francis was Molly, a female mule. To make it look like she was talking an offscreen trainer tugged a thread tied to her mouth, which made her move her lips.

Drive-in desires. A fear of science, and of what it might discover beyond the atomic bomb. A fear of outer space, a place no one had been, but everyone was sure was home to a growing number of Unidentified Flying Objects. And drive-ins, outdoor theaters where people watched movies projected onto huge white boards from the privacy of their cars, with small speakers hanging from their windows. These trends helped define the 1950s, and Universal cashed in on them all.

Slimy spacemen. Hey, there's Kang! There's Kodos! Watching "It Came from Outer Space" today, you can't help but notice how much its slimy one-eyed aliens look like those in the "Treehouse of Horror" episodes of "The Simpsons," a gooey guy and girl who have their own ride at Universal Studios Florida. But back in 1953, this was serious stuff. Based on a story by acclaimed science-fiction author Ray Bradbury ("The Martian Chronicles," "Fahrenheit 451"), the movie differs from other films of its time—its aliens are sympathetic, landing in the American desert only to repair their damaged spaceship. The way they go about it, though, isn't exactly neighborly— they kidnap local townsfolk to do their work, then morph their gooey bodies into clones of their captives so they can shop for supplies unnoticed. Universal's first 3-D movie, "It Came from Outer Space" cost $800,000 to produce and brought in $1.6 million.

How to pick up girls. He's the strong, silent type. A lonely guy who thinks the way to pick up a woman is to literally pick her up, preferably after sneaking up on her from behind, or better yet from underneath her as she swims in a lagoon. And yet for some reason that doesn't work. Maybe it's her habit of screaming every time he approaches her, or perhaps it's because she's already got a guy, a clean-cut scientist. But most likely the Mr. Romeo in 1954's "The Creature from the Black Lagoon" strikes out is because he's a fish. A

fish-man. Or if you're the literal type, a Florida State college kid in a fish-man suit, a part-time lifeguard at North Florida's Wakulla Springs where the movie's underwater scenes were shot. The film kicked off an unexpected career for 20-year-old Ricou Browning. After playing the Creature in three films, he went on to direct the underwater scenes of many productions—everything from the 1960s television show "Flipper" to, at age 80, a 2010 episode of the HBO series "Boardwalk Empire."

Extra cheese, please. By 1956, the number of American drive-ins reached 11,000—the same number of Starbucks today. As teenagers began to discover how ideal they were for dates, Universal learned it could make money on just about any film that promised to scare—or stir—a young couple into each other's arms, even if its story was ludicrous and its sets looked like cardboard. Standards were so low that when the director of the 1956 flick "Curucu, Beast of the Amazon" finished his shooting in rural Brazil and still had lots of unused film left, he didn't fly back home. Instead, he quickly came up with a second screenplay ("Love-Slaves of the Amazons") and shot it with the same cast and crew. Other Universal kitsch included 1957's "The Deadly Mantis" (a monstrous mutant insect munches on people like popcorn), 1958's "The Thing That Couldn't Die" (the severed head of a devil worshipper just says no) and 1958's "Monster on the Campus" (a mild-mannered research professor morphs into a blood-thirsty ape). All of these films made money; "The Deadly Mantis" brought in more than $1 million.

You must remember this... or not. Fans of the 1942 movie "Casablanca" would probably never guess that one of its stars had a hand in Universal's campy crime caper "Girls on the Loose," but only if they've never seen it. Directed by Paul Henreid—noble Victor Laszlo in "Casablanca"—it shares the classic movie's dark, shadowy imagery and, in a way, its lofty romance. Here it's one of a bad dame gone good, as four high-heeled payroll snatchers drink, smoke and bed delivery boys until the youngest one falls for the cop who's chasing them. Leader-of-the-pack Mara Corday appeared later that year as Playboy magazine's Miss October. Henreid also directed more than 80 episodes of the 1955–1965 Universal television series, "Alfred Hitchcock Presents."

"It Came From Outer Space," 1953. At left, "Creature from the Black Lagoon," 1954.

"The Birds," 1962. At left, "Leave it to Beaver," 1959.

The godfather. In 1995, President Bill Clinton presented him with the Presidential Medal of Freedom, the highest civilian honor in the U.S. In 1996, he was inducted into the Television Hall of Fame. In 1998, screen legend Charlton Heston called him "the godfather of the film industry." After his death in 2002, the New York Times proclaimed him "arguably the most powerful and influential Hollywood titan in the four decades after World War II... the last of the legendary movie moguls."

His name was Lew Wasserman. In the late 1950s he took over Universal by ingeniously merging it with his talent agency—MCA, which represented most of the industry's biggest names. Finally with easy access to stars and a new, skilled leader, the studio achieved a level of success—and respect—that it hadn't seen since the silent era. It succeeded on two fronts—movies, of course, but also "the small screen."

Television. By the mid-1950s, television viewing had become a standard part of American life. Though only 9 percent of U.S. homes had a TV set in 1950, 72 percent did by 1956. That same year attendance at movie theaters fell by 20 percent, the steepest one-year drop-off ever. Though other studio heads scoffed at the idea, Wasserman pushed Universal into television big-time; in his view

the wealth of backlots and sound stages at Universal City were perfect for it. Within a few years, nearly half of all prime-time shows were being filmed at Universal City, including such long-running series as "Leave it to Beaver" and "Wagon Train."

Motion pictures. As for films, Wasserman kicked off his reign with two lighthearted service comedies. In 1958's "The Perfect Furlough," sex-starved corporal Tony Curtis wins a three-week leave in Paris with a pin-up queen, only to be supervised by strict lieutenant Janet Leigh (Curtis' real-life wife). Curtis and Cary Grant rescue a bevy of beautiful nurses in the following year's "Operation Petticoat," then battle for space with them in the sub's tight quarters.

The studio also found success that year with another romantic comedy. In "Pillow Talk," innocent Doris Day shares a telephone line with charming playboy Rock Hudson and learns all his seductive routines, yet still falls for the one he uses on her. The saucy comedy was a smash hit, bringing in a then-staggering box-office sum of $19 million. Deemed "culturally, historically or aesthetically" significant by the National Film Registry, a copy of it was preserved by the Library of Congress in 2009. "Operation Petticoat" and "Pillow Talk" carried Universal to record

Steven's private film school

"MY NAME IS STEVEN SPIELBERG. I know one of the executives here." The teenager was lying—having just finished high school, he didn't know anyone at Universal and had no business wandering its backlots and sound stages. But he acted like he belonged there, and always wore a suit. Plus, he had made friends with a security guard, who would always vouch for him. So throughout the summer of 1965, the 18-year-old was able to treat Universal City as his own private film school. Ten years later, he would direct its first major blockbuster, and go on to become its most successful director ever.

"I snuck onto the Universal Studios lot dressed as an executive," Spielberg told the magazine TV Guide. "I was there for three months, my whole summer vacation. I couldn't get on movie sets because they always had closed sets—they had guards out there—but I got on every TV show. Everybody asked me what I was doing there and I would always say, 'Well, I know somebody in the executive offices.' I so wanted to be a director." He couldn't have been there at a better time. Since the studio was producing television shows as well as movies, the backlots were bustling with people; blending in was easy.

Filmmaking 101. He watched shows being shot, including the sitcom "The Munsters" (1964–1966). He also watched an editor cut a few minutes out of the sitcom "Leave it to Beaver" (1957–1963), preparing it for syndication to local stations that needed extra time for commercials. While cutting down the Western series "Wagon Train" (1957–1965), another editor let Spielberg make a few cuts himself. Technically, this was his first professional job in the industry.

Independent study. After enrolling at California State University in nearby Long Beach, Spielberg got an internship at Universal in 1968. Meeting some executives, he asked them to take a look at some films he had made with a home-movie camera. They declined. Undeterred, he rented a 35mm camera and shot a "real" movie, a short story about a boy and girl who hitchhike across the desert to the Pacific; he dubbed it "Amblin'."

This time, he found an audience: Sid Sheinberg, the 33-year-old president of Universal Television. Impressed by the movie, he offered Spielberg exactly what he craved: a job as a director. He dropped out of college and signed a 7-year contract that would pay him a weekly salary of $275 (today about $1900). It made him the youngest person ever to land a long-term directing deal.

A television director. Screen legend Joan Crawford starred in Spielberg's first directing assignment, a segment of an NBC series pilot called "Rod Serling's Night Gallery" (1969-1973). The series would be an anthology, with each episode consisting of three unrelated short stories. His story, "Eyes," concerned a wealthy blind woman who gets an eye transplant to restore her vision, but for only 12 hours. Filled with ideas, he filmed it with a combination of wide shots, close-ups, stills and moving dolly shots. He even threw in a series of jump cuts—edits that create the effect of jumping forward in time by omitting all but the critical moments in an otherwise continuous action. A few months later, when he directed an episode of the medical drama "Marcus Welby, M.D." (1969-1976), he worked in a few rack zooms—changing the focus point of a still shot as it moves from one actor to another.

In 1971, Spielberg filmed an action scene of the first episode of the detective drama "Columbo" (1971-1978) using a hand-held camera, at the time an experimental technique used mostly in France. Later that year, he used a tense mix of rack zooms, car-mounted point-of-view shots and crane shots to convey the story of the first TV movie, "Duel" (driving across a desert, a mild-mannered salesman is suddenly stalked by the driver of a giant truck).

A movie director. In 1973 Universal gave Spielberg his first feature—the comedy-adventure "The Sugarland Express" (shown at left). By then, he had gained a reputation for emphasizing particular combinations of lens choices and camera angles, and this film gave rise to another one: a wide-angle establishing shot filmed very low to the ground. He also co-wrote the screenplay. Based on a true story, it told the tale of a poor mom (Goldie Hawn) who reunites her family by sneaking her husband (William Atherton) out of jail and taking her son from his foster home; she then becomes a folk hero as she's chased by a fleet of police and news crews.

A year later he filmed "Jaws." Soon came "E.T.," "Jurassic Park" and "Schindler's List" and many more. Today Spielberg is the top-grossing director of all time. He's also an active consultant to Universal Orlando, and has been involved with its theme parks since the beginning.

In 2002 he re-enrolled in college and got his degree at Cal State Long Beach. On graduation day he sat among the 500 other graduates of its College of the Arts in a rented cap and gown, and when his name was called walked across the stage and received his diploma.

Six-year-old actress Drew Barrymore with Spielberg during the filming of "E.T.", 1981.

A mistake it made. An epic it made not.

EVERY COMPANY MAKES MISTAKES. In the early seventies, Universal made a big one. In 1971, it made a deal with USC film-school graduate George Lucas to make a teen comedy-drama titled "American Graffiti"; it also got first-right-of-refusal for a subsequent sci-fi flick he hadn't quite figured out or even named yet.

For "American Graffiti," Lucas re-created the small-town America of 1962, where four high-school graduates spend their last night together before heading off to college. They consist of clean-cut Steve (Ron Howard), closet rebel Curt (Richard Dreyfuss), his cheerleader sister Laurie (Cindy Williams) and bespectacled nerd Terry (Charles Martin Smith, secretly channeling Lucas himself). The film opens at Mel's Drive-in, a cruising hot spot. Universal hired Francis Ford Coppola ("The Godfather") to produce it.

Today the film is considered a classic, a subtle masterpiece of time, place and mood. But when Lucas previewed it to Universal execs they had a far different reaction.

"This movie is not fit to show an audience."

That's what one told him, according to a 1980 Rolling Stone interview with Lucas. The studio accepted its wall-to-wall use of period music (the licensing fees were substantial), but wanted several scenes recut, others rewritten, its name changed (preferably to "Another Slow Night in Modesto" or "Coppola's Rock Around the Block") and wanted to downgrade it to a TV movie.

With Coppola's help, Lucas convinced Universal to drop most of those demands and at least test it as a theatrical film, with an initial release only in New York and Los Angeles.

Meanwhile, Lucas needed money. Since he had taken two years to make the film, the 28-year-old had spent his $20,000 advance. To make ends meet he had taken out a bank loan and it was time to pay it back. "So I thought, 'I'll whip a treatment on my little space thing,'" recalls Lucas. "I did a 15-page treatment… I showed it to them and they said no."

A year later, "American Graffiti," which had cost Universal just $1.3 million to produce, had grossed $55 million. By then Lucas no longer had financial problems, and had written out his "little space thing" into a nine-part epic he titled "Star Wars." He showed it to execs at 20th Century Fox—they said yes.

"Are you ever going to forgive Universal?" Rolling Stone asked.

Lucas smiled. "I hold grudges."

He never worked with the studio again.

profits in 1959, assuring that its new focus on star-driven films would continue.

"Spartacus." And it did continue the following fall, with the September 1960 release of this historical epic, in which enraged slave Charlton Heston leads a violent revolt against the decadent Roman empire. The most expensive film in Universal history at the time, it cost $12 million to produce but brought back $30 million—the No. 1 box office hit of the year. Secretly hired by director Stanley Kubrick, screenwriter Dalton Trumbo had been blacklisted for his alleged Communist ties; in Trumbo's defense, president-elect John F. Kennedy crossed American Legion picket lines to view the film.

"Psycho." Confused identities, voyeurism, the deadly effects of money... they all converge in Universal's first film by "master of suspense" director Alfred Hitchcock. Often focused on birds, eyes, hands and mirrors, it tells a disturbing tale about Phoenix secretary Marion Crane (Janet Leigh). After stealing $40,000 from her employer, she travels on back roads to avoid police until a heavy storm spooks her into stopping at the Bates Motel, a ramshackle place run by a polite, highly strung young man (Anthony Perkins) who seems to have a strained relationship with his mother. Once Marion checks into her room, she decides to take a relaxing hot shower; what follows is one of the most memorable scenes in film history. "Psycho" cost $800,000 to make, and earned back $40 million.

The beat goes on. More interested in developing the studio than micromanaging it, Wasserman didn't force its films to follow his personal tastes. So as the 1960s, then the 1970s, then the 1980s went by, other Universal hits spanned a gamut of genres.

"To Kill a Mockingbird." Based on the Pulitzer Prize-winning novel by Harper Lee, this 1962 drama still stands today as one of Universal's finest achievements. In it, a young brother and sister in the sleepy 1930s town of Maycomb, Alabama are exposed to the evils of racism when their father (actor Gregory Peck, in what is widely recognized as his finest role) defends a black man against fabricated rape charges. Like "Pillow Talk," it was also honored by the National Film Registry; the American Film Institute named Peck's Atticus Finch the "greatest movie hero of the 20th century."

"The Birds." Flocks of wild birds attack children and eventually a whole town in this 1963 Hitchcock thriller. Its stunning special effects—which included mixing animated and live birds into multiple shots—were

"Jurassic Park," 1993.

handled by Ub Iwerks, the animator who drew Oswald the Lucky Rabbit and Mickey Mouse for Walt Disney.

"Airport." The winner of five Academy Awards including Best Picture, this star-studded 1970 melodrama portrays what happens when a troubled demolition expert (character actor Van Heflin) intends to blow up an airplane—a jet whose captain (Dean Martin) has just learned that his stewardess mistress (Jacqueline Bisset) is pregnant, a jet which maybe can't land at the snowed-in airport managed by Mel Bakersfeld (Burt Lancaster), a jet with a devious elderly stowaway (Helen Hayes). The industry's first disaster film, "Airport" was produced for $10 million and earned back nearly 10 times that.

"Halloween." After killing his older sister, young Michael Myers (various actors) is committed to a sanitarium, only to escape 15 years later. As his former psychiatrist tries to stop him, he dons a hockey mask as he stalks and kills people on All Hallow's Eve. The 1978 movie was the first modern slasher film.

"On Golden Pond." With the help of his understanding wife Ethel Thayer (Katharine Hepburn), crotchety old professor Norman Thayer (Henry Fonda) repairs his long-strained relationship with his daughter Chelsea (Fonda's real-life daughter Jane) and bonds with his grandson Billy (Doug McKeon) during a summer vacation in idyllic New England. The 1981 movie was the only one to feature both Henry and Jane Fonda, and reflected their own internal tensions.

"Fast Times at Ridgemont High." This 1982 coming-of-age film brought a fresh perspective to teen comedies by tracking the lives of three characters. Innocent Stacy Hamilton (Jennifer Jason Leigh) follows the flawed dating advice of her uninhibited friend Linda Barrett (Phoebe Cates). Stacy's brother Brad (Judge Reinhold) has a crush on Linda, which she learns of in the most embarrassing way. And then there's scene-stealing stoner Jeff Spicoli (Sean Penn), who has a pizza delivered to his desk in his history class, only to face the ire of strict teacher Mr. Hand (Ray Walston).

"Back to the Future." When an experiment by eccentric scientist Doc Brown (Christopher Lloyd) accidentally sends teenager Marty McFly (Michael J. Fox) back in time, Marty finds himself on a most unusual mission in this 1985 sci-fi classic: to make sure his parents fall in love, so that he can exist.

Other films during the Wasserman era included "Jaws," "Jurassic Park" and many other Steven Spielberg blockbusters, as well as "Smokey and the Bandit" (1977), "Animal House" (1978), "The Deer Hunter" (1978), "The Blues Brothers" (1980), and "Field of Dreams" (1989).

"Ted," 2012.

"Despicable Me," 2010. Steve Carrell voices Felonius Gru.

Back to the future. As Universal first learned in the 1930s, sometimes it's a film's characters that make all the difference.

Dominic Toretto (2001's "The Fast and the Furious"): "I live my life a quarter-mile at a time. Nothing else matters: not the mortgage, not the store, not my team. For those 10 seconds or less, I'm free."

Felonius Gru (2010's "Despicable Me"): "Okay, we need to set some rules. Rule number one: You will not touch ANYTHING. Rule number two: You will not bother me while I'm working. Rule number three: You will not cry, or whine, or laugh, or giggle, or sneeze or barf or fart! So no, no, no annoying sounds."

Fat Amy (2012's "Pitch Perfect"): "I can sing, but I'm also good at modern dance, olden dance, and mermaid dancing which is a little different. You usually start on the ground."

Ted (2012's "Ted"): "John, I look like something you give to your kid when you tell 'em Grandma died."

Christian Grey (2015's "Fifty Shades of Grey"): "I don't do romance. My tastes are very singular. You wouldn't understand."

After years of costly flops, Universal saw its 2012 rude-and-crude comedy "Ted" became a surprise smash. Produced for $50 million it grossed more than $550 million. "This one was a fresh viewpoint, it had a unique concept and was executed very well," Universal's co-president of production Peter Cramer told TheWrap. "Everybody likes something fresh, something new," added Nikki Rocco, the studio's head of domestic distribution. Seth MacFarlane, the creator of the television series "Family Guy," wrote and directed the film, and voiced its title character, a bong-smoking teddy bear with a bad attitude.

The studio's been on a tear ever since, finding success with big-budget blockbusters ("Fast & Furious," "Despicable Me") as well as small-scale sleeper hits ("Pitch Perfect").

The year 2015 was the studio's best ever. Led by the return of one of its classic franchises—the Spielberg blockbuster "Jurassic World"—it also included many smaller hits. Some were original concepts, such as "Fifty Shades of Grey," "Straight Outta Compton" and "Trainwreck." Others were based on previous films. "Pitch Perfect 2" grossed more during its first weekend ($69 million) than the original made in its entire run ($65 million).

Laemmle's legacy. Over its century of life, Universal has had nine different owners. Most of them nearly drove it into bankruptcy. But still, like a cat, it found a way to have nine lives. Because whenever it struggled, what always rang true was the motto of its founder Carl Laemmle: "It Can Be Done."

Extraordinary.

A studio tour. That's all it was going to be. Thanks to Disney it's something much more.

Holy Moly! "Florida's the new Hollywood!" proclaimed Jack Valenti, the president of the Motion Pictures Association of America, as he kicked things off at the 1990 grand opening of Universal Studios Florida. A long line of white limos inched down the park's Hollywood Boulevard, bringing movie stars to a red-carpet walkway. Charlton Heston, Moses himself in the 1956 epic "The Ten Commandments," passed judgment: "This Universal Studios Florida will be extraordinary." Steven Spielberg cut the ceremonial ribbon with a giant pair of scissors, in front of reporters from around the world.

And then… it all flopped. Florida the New Hollywood? Nope. Universal Studios "extraordinary"? Not yet. In the history of Universal, nothing it had ever done had gotten off to a worse start than its Florida theme park. Today it's still not what it was going to be, and not what it was when it started. But these days it is becoming, as Moses himself predicted, something extraordinary.

The New Hollywood. Before the park opened the outlook for Florida being a "New Hollywood" seemed bright, as the state had an established filmmaking history. Before World War I, 30 silent-film studios set up camp in the Sunshine State, attracted by its clear winter light and tropical landscapes. During the thirties, Tarzan swung through the "African" jungles of North Florida's Silver Springs and Wakulla Springs. In 1960, when Connie Francis sang the title song of spring break flick "Where the Boys Are," everyone knew the answer: on the warm sunny beaches of South Florida's Fort Lauderdale.

Hollywood East. Then came "Hollywood East"—a slogan created by the Orlando Chamber of Commerce in 1977 that signaled a serious effort to make filmmaking one of the city's major industries. After all, why wouldn't it be? Orlando's land was cheap, its non-union labor was cheap, it had that great year-round light, and encompassed, claimed the Chamber, "a variety of locales that can easily pass for any major urban center, tropical jungle or even the Old West." To up the ante, the city set up a one-stop permitting office and offered studios some useful services free of charge, such as "police assistance for traffic or crowd control" and "the use of our fire department for the supervision of pyrotechnic effects."

The result: "Hollywood East" happened. Soon several films were being shot around Orlando, including Universal's 1978 "Jaws 2" and 1980 comedy "Caddyshack." By 1986 34 major motion pictures had been filmed in the area, as well as 2,400 television commercials and dozens of music videos. The Florida Motion Picture and Television Bureau estimated that film production in the state would soon top $1 billion a year, about a quarter of California's earnings. The Los Angeles Times reported that some Hollywood execs feared that their stars were so fed up with the area's infamous smog and traffic that they'd take the first opportunity to fly off to Florida.

A clash with Disney. In 1979, Universal bought 400 acres of land in Orlando, and in 1981 announced it would soon build Universal City Florida. Like its California namesake, this movie and television studio would include sound stages, backlots and, for tourists, a version of Universal's signature tram tour.

A boulevard, a tram tour, a canyon. The studio's public entrance would be a 1940s

---

Preceding spread: Steven Spielberg cuts the ribbon to open Universal Studios Florida on June 7, 1990. To his left is Jay Stein, the driving force behind the project (holding the microphone); Sid Sheinberg, the Universal executive who gave Spielberg his first break; animator Walter Lantz, the creator of the resort's mascot Woody Woodpecker; Lew Wasserman, longtime Universal chair (blue sport coat) and Bob Graham, Florida U.S. senator. Others in the front row include Jack Valenti, longtime president of the Motion Picture Association (holding the E.T. segment of the banner) and actor Robert Wagner (white sport coat). At the left are Linda Blair, star of "The Exorcist" (blue dress); actress Morgan Fairchild (behind Blair); Richard Brooks and Michael Moriarty of "Law and Order" (behind Fairchild); Ernest Borgnine, star of "McHale's Navy" (behind Moriarty); and screen legend Jimmy Stewart (to the right of Borgnine). Also on stage are actors Beau Bridges (eyes closed, wearing shorts), Tippi Hedren (behind Wagner's left shoulder), Janet Leigh (smiling, behind Spielberg's arm), Ben Vereen (eyes shut, behind Hedren), "E.T." star Henry Thomas (behind Leigh), Craig T. Nelson, star of "Coach" (behind Sheinberg, in sunglasses), Dennis Franz, star of "NYPD Blue" (at Nelson's left) and animator Joseph Barbera (with glasses, behind Thomas).

SEE WHAT MOVIES ARE MADE OF.

What makes the Universal Studios Tour the most unique experience in Southern California? It's the only place where you can actually see movies like the stars do—from behind the scenes!

Your day begins with a tram ride through our huge 420-acre movie backlot. You'll see 640 outdoor sets, buildings and facades, representing some of the most famous movie sets and locations ever created. Your journey includes an unforgettable encounter with some of Hollywood's greatest special effects, like the "Jaws"® attack, the parting of the Red Sea, a collapsing bridge and a chilling alpine avalanche. And just when you think you've seen it all, there's more action around the corner.

We'll take you to a sound stage where you'll learn the secrets of how movie makers create space battles and other spectacular feats.

In our fabulous Entertainment Center, you'll experience five live shows each depicting a different dimension of film making. You can discover your hidden talents when you star in our SCREEN TEST COMEDY THEATRE, witness the action-packed STUNT SHOW, be dazzled by real movie

ANIMAL ACTORS, experience the awesome CONAN—A SWORD & SORCERY SPECTACULAR, and learn how WOODY WOODPECKER comes alive on the screen.

It's a full day of movie magic, live shows, shopping and dining. So, come be a part of the stuff dreams are made of at Universal Studios Tour.

UNIVERSAL STUDIOS TOUR® AN MCA COMPANY

Celebrating Our 20th Year

An ad for California's Universal Studios Tour, which was to be replicated in Florida, 1984.

The King Kong Encounter planned for the studio tour at Universal City Florida, 1985.

version of California's famous Hollywood Boulevard, lined with façades of Tinseltown landmarks. The tram tour would include a stop at "Hollywood Canyon," an outdoor special-effects set where an earthquake would strike and a large truck would crash into an oil tanker, triggering a fire and flash flood.

Looking for a partner in the project, Universal invited the top brass of Paramount Studios to Universal City for a two-hour presentation, complete with slideshows, blueprints and detailed color renderings.

Paramount passed. But, as Universal execs later recalled to the Los Angeles Times, Paramount president Michael Eisner took a keen interest in the idea. "He asked very intelligent questions," development executive Peter Kingston told the paper. "I was very impressed by his grasp of the subject and equally his interest in the subject."

A boulevard, a tram tour, a canyon. Four years later, Eisner left Paramount to become president of the Walt Disney Co. At his first stockholder meeting, he announced that Disney would open a studio-based theme park in Florida named Disney-MGM Studios (today's Disney's Hollywood Studios).

Looking over the park's promotional material, Universal Studios Tour chief Jay Stein noticed what he told the Times were "remarkable similarities" between Disney's plans and what Universal had shown Eisner; that "65 to 70 percent" of Disney's studio park was simply a copy of Universal's idea. The entrance to Disney's park would also take visitors down a 1940s Hollywood Boulevard and its main attraction would also be a tram tour, one which would stop at "Catastrophe Canyon," an outdoor set where an earthquake would strike, an oil truck would catch fire and a flash flood would rush in.

Universal's Sid Sheinberg said Eisner's actions had given him "a horrible sense of personal and corporate betrayal." Universal execs showed the paper the slideshows and renderings it had earlier shown Paramount.

In response Eisner said he'd stolen no one's plans, and besides, Universal's presentation to Paramount had taken place "many, many years ago." And he went further. "When I arrived at this company [Disney], the studio tour was already on the drawing boards and had been for many years," he told the paper. Later he told Newsweek magazine that it was Walt Disney himself who first conceived of a studio tour, back in the 1930s. Eisner added that the studio being harmed was actually Disney, as Universal was going "to feed off the millions of visitors who are already traveling to Orlando to visit our parks." In a statement,

The Kongfrontation ride built at Universal Studios Florida, 1990.

a Disney spokesman denied "categorically: (a) that Disney ever stole, borrowed or misappropriated anyone else's ideas for the Disney-MGM Studios—or that Disney will ever do so, or would have to do so; and (b) that Michael Eisner saw or discussed any plans or drawings of anyone else's studio tour proposals before or after he came to Disney."

"When you work as hard as we did to get this program and studio tour off the ground," Universal's Jay Stein told the Times, "and then you see someone come along and take your idea… and say that it was conceived by his imagineers… that just makes me angry."

Fish or cut bait. As Disney went forward with its studio park, Universal changed its plans. Dropping the idea of Universal City Florida, it instead put together Universal Studios Florida. A traditional theme park with no tram tour, the revised area would keep its Hollywood Boulevard and New York streets, but have individual attractions and shows—some using more advanced technology than those at Walt Disney World—that visitors could experience at their own pace. It would also have more walkways than first planned, and more restaurants. And it would still have a production center, though instead of using the facilities itself, Universal would lease most of it to the Nickelodeon cable network. In exchange, the network would operate a tour of the sound stages for park guests and promote the park in the programs it filmed there. These programs included various incarnations of Nickelodeon's popular "Double Dare" game show, the messy "Slime Time Live" audience-participation show and the live-action series "All That," "Clarissa Explains It All" and "Keenan and Kel."

"Disney took what we had, and we had to fish or cut bait," Stein said. "We had to reprogram and repackage and rethink everything that we had originally contemplated. We really had to go back to ground zero." Universal upped the budget for the project from $200 million to $500 million, and delayed its opening date two years.

Meanwhile, on April 29, 1989, a pouring rain delayed for two hours the star-studded opening of Disney-MGM Studios. Interviewed by the Orlando Sentinel, its host, Hollywood columnist Army Archerd, quipped, "It's a first!"

A grand opening with 'nothing grand.'

"Oh my God, look at him!" squealed a 21-year-old woman near a Sentinel reporter, catching a glimpse of Sylvester Stallone. "My God, it's Rambo!" After the opening-day ceremony of Universal Studios Florida on June 7, 1990, Stallone and other movie stars took off on golf

Back to the Future The Ride, 1991.

carts, zipping around its walkways to give visitors some Hollywood-style thrills.

But even Rambo couldn't save the park from what happened next. Within minutes of its opening, its Jaws and Kongfrontation rides both broke down for the day. Later the power blew out at the Earthquake attraction; when it returned a spike in its current closed it down too. Since construction problems had already delayed the opening of the park's Back to the Future The Ride, the only ride left open was E.T. Adventure. Soon the wait to go on it reached two hours.

The park drew just 10,000 visitors that day, half what Universal expected. Needless to say, many of them weren't impressed. "Big disappointment," a 14-year-old boy told the Sentinel. "There was nothing grand about this grand opening."

About 1,000 guests asked for their money back, or a free pass to return when the rides were working, which Universal gave them. The next morning, it announced a similar deal for the public at large: buy a ticket for this summer, and get a free one for later. "We've got fantastic rides and shows," said General Manager Tom Williams, "and we'll continue to work on them until the bugs are out." The park's Jaws attraction didn't re-open for two years.

Hollywood East, Rest in Peace. Sadly, Orlando's filmmaking fortunes didn't last. Even with all it had to offer, it lacked the one thing a real Hollywood needs: stars. Nearly every noteworthy actor and production pro stayed put in the rolling hills of balmy Southern California, preferring them to the flat-as-a-pancake sweatbox that is Central Florida, even with L.A.'s smog and traffic.

In fact, as of 1993 only two major names had moved to the area: Muppets creator Jim Henson, who purchased a vintage lakefront cottage outside Orlando in 1988 but died before he could move in, and actor Wesley Snipes, who was born in Orlando and went to school in the city. Even when Orlando itself gave rise to a star—such as Kenan Thompson, who found fame on the teen sitcom "Kenan & Kel"—he or she always moved on to greener pastures.

For the industry, the cost of flying actors and crews out to the Sunshine State and providing them with housing there just wasn't worth it. By the year 2000, Orlando was producing little more than reality shows and commercials. Disney shut down its Florida studio operations in 2004.

Universal struggled. In 1999 it had added a second park, Islands of Adventure, a group of themed areas focused on thrill rides that were instantly popular; at the same time it debuted the entertainment complex CityWalk and its first resort hotel, the 750-room Loews Portofino Bay. But as the years went by, its success started to slip. Nickelodeon Studios closed in 2005. As Walt Disney World attendance continued to go up, Universal attendance started going down—from an average of 7 million visitors in each of its parks in 2000, to 6.5 million in 2002, to 6 million in 2005, to 5.8 million in 2007.

And then there came a child. A chosen one. A boy scarred of forehead and orphaned of parent. And yo he brought forth a wand, and he waveth it. And as new lands arose, the prophecy of Moses began to be realized.

Harry Potter and the Fat Chance. "I want more"—that's what Disney's Ariel sings in the 1989 film "The Little Mermaid" It's also what author J.K. Rowling said to Disney, as she met with the company in the spring of 2007 about incorporating her Harry Potter stories into Walt Disney World. Disney was offering her a lot of money, but like its teenage mermaid, the wealthy Rowling already had gadgets and gizmos aplenty, and wanted something beyond the material world—in her case, control. As the New York Times reported, "Rowling wanted veto power on matters big (the look of the Hogwarts castle) and small (the font on the restaurant menus)."

She wanted control over her characters. She would not, for example, agree to have local young men dress up and pose as Harry Potter to greet guests and sign autographs. She also wanted her characters to exist only in their world—not on floats rolling down

E.T. Adventure, 1990. Above: Nickelodeon's "Slime Time Live," 2003.

Diagon Alley opened in 2014.

Main Street U.S.A. or in some song-and-dance revue in front of Cinderella Castle.

She wanted control over her stories—the right to sign off on the plots of the rides.

Finally, Rowling wanted control over her environments. When guests visited her worlds, they wouldn't glance around and see other parts of the park—no one in Hogsmeade was ever going to look down a walkway and exclaim "Hey look! It's Donald Duck!" And there would be no selling of logo-adorned bottles of soft drinks. Instead, there would only be beverages that made sense to be there, like butterbeer and pumpkin juice.

Unaware of the particulars of these meetings, many local theme-park fans believed that even though Rowling was talking with Universal, Disney would soon welcome her into its fold. Universal simply didn't have the money, or the resources, or the willingness, to seriously compete for such a catch.

In April of 2007, respected local blogger John Frost—owner and editor of The Disney Blog, one of the most accurate and insightful sources of Orlando theme-park news—wrote that "it looks like Disney has taken the big prize back from Universal and will now be the only company licensed to put Harry Potter-themed attractions in their parks."

Less than two months later, on May 31, 2007, Frost's headline read "Silence Spell Shattered, Harry Potter coming to Universal." In a press release, Universal announced that its Wizarding World of Harry Potter "will feature immersive rides and interactive attractions, as well as experiential shops and restaurants."

"We've tried to include something from every book," explained Alan Gilmore, an art director from the films who helped with the area's design. "We had free range to be as grand and as excessive as we could be."

The Hogwarts Express locomotive being lowered onto its track, 2014.

"The plans I've seen look incredibly exciting," added Rowling, "and I don't think fans of the books or films will be disappointed."

The announcement was the shot heard 'round Orlando. People were staggered: Disney lost Potter to Universal? But Disney has so much clout. So much money. How could that have possibly happened? The answer was simple. It happened because Disney didn't have the willingness to give up control—at least not the amount Rowling wanted.

The result was fantastic. "Breathtaking," Rowling said, as reported by the New York Times, roaming the completed Hogsmeade section of Universal's Islands of Adventure, just before its opening day in 2010. A young man walking next to her nodded in agreement: actor Daniel Radcliffe, Harry himself.

Within a year of Hogsmeade's opening, Universal Orlando's overall attendance had surged by 2 million people.

It can be done. Since that time, Universal Orlando has become a theme-park powerhouse. It's opened a second Harry Potter area, Diagon Alley, which dwarfs Hogsmeade in ambition and scope. It's also debuted or refurbished an average of one other attraction each year—all of which have been hits. They include Despicable Me Minion Mayhem, The Amazing Adventures of Spider-Man and Transformers The Ride 3-D. The resort has also revamped its CityWalk area, built two more hotels, expanded its workforce by more than 60 percent (from 13,000 to more than 21,000) and been showered with awards from industry trade groups. Attendance has gone up every year, sometimes by double digits.

As for the future, "We're going to keep our foot on the pedal as far as it will go," says Universal Parks and Resorts Chair Tom Williams. "Any chance we get to pour the gas directly into the carburetor, we'll do that, too."

What's New

THERE'S A BUILDING BOOM at Universal. Driving toward it on Interstate 4 you can't help but notice the construction cranes, piles of dirt and pillars of concrete. What's going on? Success. Or rather an aftermath of success, as Universal's investment in J.K. Rowling and her Harry Potter stories has paid off with millions of new visitors and billions of new dollars, which the resort is investing in more new rides, hotels, even a water park.

Skull Island: Reign of Kong. It's the colossal ape as you've never seen him. Not getting captured and chained by man, not swatting at planes from the Empire State Building, but rather on his home island, a treacherous world where he controls everything—including your fate after you dare to explore it. Opened during the summer of 2016 at Islands of Adventure, the multi-dimensional experience starts off as an outdoor truck ride, but soon becomes an indoor adventure through forbidden temples, caves and crevices—their dangers brought to life with elaborate physical sets, huge wraparound 3-D screens and a massive animatronic King Kong.

Loews Sapphire Falls Resort. Meant to recall the Caribbean, this casual hotel wraps its 1,000 rooms around a tropical lagoon and waterfall. Amenities include a white-sand beach. It opened in July 2016, between the Royal Pacific and Cabana Bay Beach hotels.

Raptor Encounter. Is it a real raptor? Probably not. But the intense, yellow-eyed creature sure acts the part. The unique meet-and-greet debuted in the Jurassic Park area of Islands of Adventure in 2015.

NBC Sports Grill & Brew. Opened in 2015, this CityWalk restaurant expands the idea of a sports bar with a wide-ranging menu and upbeat ambient music. One hundred screens give every seat a decent view of the top games and events of the moment. As for the brew, there are more than 100 brands, including craft and regional varieties. The eatery sits in front of the Universal Studios park, in the space that was previously home to the NASCAR Grille.

Other news. A new queue, launch system and vehicles are among the improvements that came to the popular Incredible Hulk roller coaster when it reopened in mid-2016, after a 9-month refurbishment... Badtz-Maru. Chococat. Keroppi. My Melody. Purin. Ring a bell? If so, you'll love the new Hello Kitty store at the Universal Studios park, which offers merchandise based on the penguin, black cat, frog, rabbit and dog characters created by Japan's Sanrio Co. as well as a cute-a-copia of Hello Kitty stuff; shoppers can even create their own versions of her signature hair bow. Hello Kitty herself is on-hand too, posing for pics. Opened in 2016, the store is at the front of the park in the building that previously held Lucy: A Tribute. The Betty Boop shop next door was also redone... The Hard Rock Hotel has added some new memorabilia to its collection, including items from James Brown, Lady Gaga, Michael Jackson and Elvis Presley... Goodies at the new Sugarplum's Sweetshop in Diagon Alley include Exploding Bon Bons, Fizzing Whizzbees and Pepper Imps...Universal installed four electric-car charging stations to its valet parking area in 2015. Two are Tesla chargers, two are Clipper Creek; they all charge most electric vehicles... An Auntie Anne's pretzel cart arrived in CityWalk in 2015, on the walkway to the Universal Studios park.

Coming in 2017. Universal Orlando will soon open its own water park, add more hotel rooms and debut more new rides.

Volcano Bay. "An experience that we hope will change the way guests think about water theme parks." That's what Universal says it's creating with Volcano Bay, a 53-acre water park currently under construction just south of the Cabana Bay Beach Resort. Anchored by a central volcano, the family-friendly park will feature "radically innovative" takes on a wave pool, water slides, lazy river and other attractions set in a tropical island world. As a consequence, nearby water park Wet 'n Wild, which is owned by Universal, will close at the end of 2016.

Cabana Bay expansion. Two new towers will soon add 400 rooms to this retro resort hotel. They'll be at the south end of the budget complex, next to its Continental and Americana towers. Some rooms will overlook the new Volcano Bay water park next door.

Bob Costas joins other NBC sportscasters Hines Ward, Cris Collinsworth and Michele Tafoya to dedicate the NBC Sports Grill & Brew. Above left, the Volcano Bay water park.

Set to open in 2017, the new towers will bring the number of rooms at Cabana Bay to 2,200, increasing the total number of hotel rooms at Universal to 5,600.

Race Through New York. Building on the success of the Simpsons and Despicable Me Minion Mayhem simulation rides, Universal is creating another one that is more about just having fun than stopping some evil force from taking over the world. In this case, your adventure begins as you step into NBC's fabled Studio 6B, where "The Tonight Show" debuted

Race Through New York opens in 2017, as does Fast & Furious Supercharged (above).

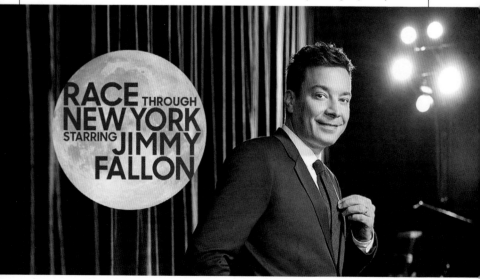

in the 1950s and is currently recorded. You're there for a special taping, in which Jimmy Fallon challenges you to a race: a twisting, turning dash through the streets and skies of The Big Apple. Expect to also encounter announcer Steve Higgins and house band The Roots. The 4-D ride replaces the Twister attraction in the Universal Studios park.

Fast & Furious: Supercharged. Racing down the streets and freeways of Los Angeles at a perceived 120 mph, you'll dodge cars, explosions, flamethrowers, machine guns, missiles and shrapnel in this open motion simulator, which will literally shake, rattle and roll in sync with the action on a wraparound 3-D screen. Other sensory effects such as fire, smoke, water, wind and 108 decibels of sound promise to immerse you in a thrilling adventure. On the ride you'll interact with five stars of the franchise (Vin Diesel, Michelle Rodriguez, Tyrese Gibson, Luke Evans and Dwayne Johnson); in the queue you'll see some of the cars used in the movies. The Universal Studios ride takes the place of the Disaster attraction and the Beetlejuice Graveyard Revue.

Nintendo attractions. Video-game stars such as Mario and Donkey Kong—maybe even Pokémon's Pikachu—will star in new attractions coming to Universal Orlando in the next few years.

The ultimate Interstate 4. Throughout the new few years expect the traffic around Universal to be somewhat of a headache, as construction crews take on what the Florida Dept. of Transportation has dubbed the I-4 Ultimate Improvement Project. Starting directly in front of Universal and stretching 21 miles east through downtown Orlando, it will add a separate four-lane "dynamic-tolled" expressway down the median of the interstate. Pricing will go up or down based on the number of vehicles using the lanes to keep traffic moving at a minimum of 50 mph.

The project also adds illuminated fountains and signature decorative pylons to dress up what for ages has been an ugly gash through The City Beautiful. Officials say it will be finished in 2021; at that time the road's speed limit will increase from 50 to 55 mph.

Universal Orlando area. Drivers coming to the resort from the west (i.e., Disney) will exit (finally!) on the right side of I-4 on a sweeping double-lane ramp; those coming from the east will have their choice of exits. Drivers leaving Universal will have (again, finally!) direct access to I-4 regardless of whether they're headed east or west. In front of the main entrance to Universal—at the intersection of Kirkman Road and Major Road—a pedestrian bridge will make it easy for visitors staying at nearby hotels to walk to the resort.

Six years of construction will transform Orlando's Interstate 4 into the "ultimate" highway.

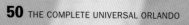

Six Secrets

1. You can always get in early. The theme parks always open before their stated times. Sometimes it's 10 minutes early, at times 30 minutes early, depending on the time of year and how crowded it is that morning. Each day one of the parks opens an hour earlier than that for visitors staying at a Universal hotel.

2. The longest waiting lines aren't where you think. Not at the Harry Potter rides, not at the roller coasters. They're at Despicable Me Minion Mayhem, a family-friendly attraction just inside the entrance to Universal Studios Florida theme park.

3. Some great experiences rarely if ever have long lines. At Universal Studios Florida these include meeting Transformer Bumblebee (a transformed Chevy Camaro, he talks to you through songs on his radio), catching a Celestina Warbeck show or a late-afternoon Despicable Me, Hop or SpongeBob show at the Character Party Zone, and for kids the water slide at Fievel's Playland. At Islands of Adventure check out the unpredictable, compelling Raptor Encounter.

4. There are good places to eat. And by good, we don't mean just the most expensive spots. At CityWalk, check out Cowfish (table service) or Red Oven Pizza and the Bread Box (counter service, made to order). At Universal Studios Florida try Finnegan's (table service), the Leaky Cauldron anytime except the lunch rush (counter service, also made to order) or the Bumblebee Man taco truck. At Islands of Adventure consider Confisco Grille (table service), Thunder Falls Terrace (counter service) and two outdoor stands, the Fire Eater's Grill and Doc Sugrue's Desert Kebab House.

5. You can get free food. There's a bargain at Universal: its fast-food Dining Plan card. For $20 it gives you a meal (an entree, side dish, and drink; worth up to $18 or so), a snack (worth up to about $5) and a soft drink (typically $3 or $4). In other words, if you take advantage of it you'll always get at least a free snack out of the deal.

6. You never have to buy a drink. Ice water is free at every theme-park restaurant, fast-food spot and snack stand. Just ask for it.

Universal Studios Florida

RIDE THE MOVIES. That was the slogan of this park back in the 1990s, and it still rings true today. Because for the most part that's what it is still is—a collection of rides and motion simulators that immerse you in the action of particular movies, or sometimes television shows. Half the park appears to be a studio backlot—its walkways roads, its buildings famous ones found in Hollywood, New York and San Francisco. Filmmakers occasionally use these areas, sometimes directly in front of park visitors. Off-limits to the public, a working production studio hides along the left side and behind the park; it has six soundstages. Two table-service restaurants and nearly 20 counter-service spots together have more than 3,000 seats; more than two dozen snack carts line the park's walkways.

Best of the park. Want thrills? It's got them. Want laughs? Those too. True, Islands of Adventure has more thrill rides, but the Studios park has its share, including two big-time coasters. As for funny, The Simpsons Ride and Springfield area slap you silly with it, Despicable Me Minion Mayhem and Men in Black Alien Attack take a dryer approach.

Diagon Alley. Clinging to the roof of Gringotts Wizarding Bank, an awesome fire-breathing dragon lurks above you in Diagon Alley, this park's Wizarding World of Harry Potter area. But that's just the most obvious highlight. Diagon Alley is Universal's crowning achievement, an immersive experience unlike any at any other theme park. It encompasses five distinct areas: Diagon Alley itself, Knockturn Alley, Carkitt Market, Horizont Alley and—the only one visible from the rest of the park—regular London itself. Potter fans can spend hours at Diagon Alley; besides its headline attraction (Harry Potter and the Escape from Gringotts), every shop and food spot offers some magical diversion.

Springfield. Down a Duff beer. Pig out on a huge Lard Lad donut. Get insulted by a gigantic Kang (or is that Kodos?). Even though it's

Fifth Avenue is the main drag of the park's New York area, which has many streets and alleys.

really just a walkway, there's plenty to do in Springfield besides go on its rides.

Best attractions. *Best rides:* The coasters Hollywood Rip Ride Rockit and Revenge of the Mummy, also Escape from Gringotts. *Best simulators:* The Simpsons Ride and Despicable Me Minion Mayhem. Transformers The Ride 3-D is technically better but nothing transforms. *Best shows:* Celestina Warbeck and the Banshees, the Blues Brothers and Universal Orlando's Horror Make-Up Show.

Hidden gems. Meeting the Transformer Bumblebee; he talks to you through songs on his radio. The late-afternoon Despicable Me "You Should Be Dancing"), Hop ("Lollipop") and SpongeBob ("Rock Lobster") Character Party Zone shows. The Men in Black queue. For kids, the water slide at Fievel's Playland.

Compared to Islands of Adventure. You'll be inside more at this park—compared to its sister park Universal Studios Florida has more simulators and more theatrical shows. There's a more elaborate Harry Potter area and more entertainment including many street performers, a parade and (often) fireworks… but fewer thrill rides.

Attractions at a glance. The park has about 20 rides and shows; here they're rated from one to five stars (★) based on how well they live up to their promise (not how well they compare to each other). The authors' top choices have a checkmark (✔).

Animal Actors on Location. ★★ Live show turns to chaos when everything goes wrong. *Woody Woodpecker's KidZone.*

The Blues Brothers Show. ★★★★ ✔ Live singers portray Elwood and Jake. *New York.*

Character Party Zone. ★★★★★ ✔ Parade characters, dancers and musicians greet and groove with park-goers. *Production Central.*

Curious George Goes to Town. ★★★ Water play. *Woody Woodpecker's KidZone.*

A Day in the Park with Barney. ★★★★★ Live indoor sing-a-long; adjacent indoor playground. *Woody Woodpecker's KidZone.*

Diagon Alley live shows. ★★★★★ ✔ Mrs. Weasley's favorite singer, Celestina Warbeck is marvelous, as are her sultry Banshees. In other shows, actors use marionettes to bring to life stories from "The Tales of Beedle the Bard." *Diagon Alley. 20-minute shows.*

Despicable Me Minion Mayhem. ★★★★★ ✔ 3-D movie has in-theater effects, moving seats. *Production Central.*

E.T. Adventure. ★★★ Classic dark bicycle ride returns E.T. to his home planet. *Woody Woodpecker's KidZone.*

Fear Factor Live. ★★★★ Park visitors compete in scary contests. *World Expo.*

Fievel's Playland. ★★★ Kiddie spot has huge props. *Woody Woodpecker's KidZone.*

Hollywood Boulevard is lined with re-created landmarks, including Schwab's Pharmacy.

Harry Potter and the Escape from Gringotts. ★★★★★ ✔ The breakthrough indoor thrill ride combines coaster with simulator; takes you under the bank. *Diagon Alley.*

Hogwarts Express. ★★★★★ ✔ Train ride to Hogsmeade area of Islands of Adventure (requires a two-park ticket). *Diagon Alley.*

Hollywood Rip Ride Rockit. ★★★★★ ✔ High-speed roller coaster lets you pick your soundtrack. *Production Central.*

Kang & Kodos' Twirl 'n' Hurl. ★★★★ ✔ Witty hub-and-spoke ride. *World Expo.*

Men in Black Alien Attack. ★★★★★ ✔ Fun shooting gallery has elaborate detailing, with many inside jokes. *World Expo.*

Revenge of the Mummy. ★★★★★ ✔ Indoor coaster has elaborate scenes and special effects, goes backward. *New York.*

Shrek 4-D. ★★★ 3-D movie with in-theater effects. *Production Central.*

The Simpsons Ride. ★★★★★ ✔ Coaster simulator crashes through Krustyland theme park. Hilarious. *World Expo.*

Terminator 2 3-D. ★★★★ ✔ Live show combines actors, robots, 3-D film. *Hollywood.*

Transformers The Ride 3-D. ★★★★★ ✔ Motion simulator travels through scenes, screens portray 3-D war. *Production Central.*

Universal Orlando's Horror Make-Up Show. ★★★★ ✔ Comedic live show demonstrates make-up effects. *Hollywood.*

Universal's Cinematic Spectacular. ★★★★ A celebration of movies; fireworks, fountains, water screens. *Central lagoon.*

Universal's Superstar Parade. ★★★ Despicable Me, Dora the Explorer, Hop and SpongeBob stars, floats, performers. *New York, Production Central, Hollywood.*

Woody Woodpecker's Nuthouse Coaster. ★★★ Kiddie coaster with silly signs. *Woody Woodpecker's KidZone.*

Street performers. Many musicians and acrobats perform at the park. They're all good; most are out from about 11 a.m. to 5 p.m.

Beat Builders. ✔ Construction workers create driving beats using boards, buckets, pipes, springs… there's even a xylophone made of wrenches. *New York, in front of Louie's Italian Restaurant. 20-minute show.*

Flying Fish Market. ✔ Wearing fish-market aprons, acrobats fling fake fish, bounce, juggle, swing. *San Francisco. 15-minute show.*

Sing It! ✔ A cappella vocalists compete for audience love. *New York, near Revenge of the Mummy. 20-minute show.*

Straight Outta Food Truck. ✔ Cooks break out into hip-hop; DJ Macaroni (he's cheesy) spins. Signs plug condiments Lil' Dijon, Dr. Dréssing. *San Francisco. 20-minute show.*

Street Breakz. ✔ Dancers compete; viewers join them. *San Francisco. 15-minute show.*

Mel's Drive-In recalls the 1973 movie "American Graffiti," complete with its vintage vehicles.

Studio Brass Band. ✔ Live combo plays songs that relate to park attractions, characters. *Production Central. 20-minute show.*

Restaurants. A summary of the park's full-service and counter-service restaurants (book full-service tables at opentable.com):

Ben & Jerry's. ✔ Small hideaway offers quality hand-scooped ice cream with little if any wait. *5th Avenue, New York. Opens 11 a.m. $4–$17. Seats 36 inside, 12 outside.*

Beverly Hills Boulangerie. ✔ Sandwiches, pastries, desserts, coffee. Convenient; right at the park entrance. Quality food sits in display cases; the cheesecake is always good. Cultured marble tables, metal chairs, tile floor. The Studio Brass Band plays out front; Lucy Ricardo may stop by. *Beverly Hills, Hollywood. Park hours. $3–$11 (children $7). Seats 46 inside, 40 outside at umbrella tables.*

Bumblebee Man's Taco Truck. ✔ Fresh tacos: carne asada, chicken, fish, Korean beef. Some of the best fast food in the park. *Springfield. Opens 11 a.m. $7–$9. Shares 200 outdoor seats with other nearby spots.*

Cafe La Bamba. A Superstar Character Breakfast has stars from "Hop," "Despicable Me," "SpongeBob SquarePants," "Dora the Explorer," "Go Diego Go." The cafe sometimes serves a Southwestern lunch of burritos, tacos, ribs and skirt steak. Its building resembles the 1902 Hollywood Hotel, a famed society venue. *Hollywood. Breakfast 9–11 a.m. Thursday–Saturday, some Mondays, $26 (children $13). Lunch, dinner starting at 11 a.m., $8–$16 (children $7). Seats 256.*

Chez Alcatraz. Overlooked waterside bar has flatbread, Cajun shrimp cocktails, specialty drinks; usually a nice breeze. *San Francisco. Opens at noon. $5–$13. Seats 10 at the bar with five shady picnic tables nearby.*

Duff Brewery. Shaded outdoor bar serves Duff beer (unique local brews), hot dogs, turkey wraps. *Springfield. Opens 11 a.m. $8–$11. Seats 24 at the bar, shares 200 outdoor seats with other nearby spots.*

Fast Food Boulevard. ✔ You'll be happy with the chicken dinner (battered chicken with corn on the cob and mashed potatoes) or the fish and chips (with thick chunks of cod); wacky folks like the chicken waffle sandwich. Often referred to as Krustyburger (perhaps because of the big sign above it that reads "Krustyburger"), this indoor food court has separate ordering lines for each of its cuisines; if your group wants more than one you wait in more than one line. A loop of food-related clips from "The Simpsons" plays on video screens. *Springfield. Opens 11 a.m. $8–$15 (children $7). Seats 256 inside, 14 at the bar in Moe's Tavern, 132 outside. Staffers seat parties during busy periods.*

You'll earn $50 or so if you preview a program at the NBC Media Center. Park guests are chosen to match particular demos; shows are tested sporadically. Reps look for participants in front of the building, which sits on the walkway between Hollywood and World Expo.

Finnegan's Bar & Grill. ✓ The park's best table-service restaurant, this casual Irish-American eatery feels like a neighborhood pub and in a way is; many Universal staffers are regulars; some bartenders have been here for decades. Reasonable prices tempt you to try everything on its varied menu; best bets include Guinness stew and seafood pie. Complimentary soda bread comes with apple butter. A singer performs near the bar daily after 3 p.m. *New York. Opens 11 a.m. $10–$23 (children $7). Seats 298 inside, 32 at the bar.*

Florean Fortescue's Ice-Cream Parlour. ✓ Hand-scooped and soft-serve ice cream from the world of Harry Potter. Flavors include Butterbeer and Sticky Toffee Pudding. *Diagon Alley. Opens 11 a.m. $5–$7. No seats.*

KidZone Pizza Co. Walk-up counter offers pizza, chicken fingers, funnel cakes. *Woody Woodpecker's KidZone. Hours vary. $8–$13 (children $7). Seats 72 outside, 20 covered.*

Lard Lad Donuts. ✓ Big enough to share with at least two people, this stand's giant Big Pink donut is perfect with a Diet Coke when you need a pick-me-up. It's sold throughout Springfield. *Springfield. Park hours. $2–$7. Shares 200 outdoor seats with nearby spots.*

Leaky Cauldron. ✓ The park's best fast-food spot serves quality English-inspired plates in an outstanding setting. Top choices include bangers and mash and an American chicken sandwich. For dessert you can't beat the sticky toffee pudding. And then of course there's the butterbeer. Best is the warm one; a whole different brew. *Diagon Alley. Opens 9 a.m. $12–$15 (children $8). Seats 280.*

Lombard's Seafood Grille. Table-service restaurant offers seafood, hamburgers, sandwiches. Sourdough bread service. Two-story building; arched windows overlook the lagoon. The former home of fictional marine biologist Louis Lombard; the downstairs was his lab; the upstairs his living room, library, dining room. *San Francisco. Opens 11 a.m. $11–$20 (children $7). Seats 148 inside, 88 on second floor (peak periods only), 80 outside.*

Louie's Italian Restaurant. Fast-food pasta, pizza by the slice or pie, salads. Relaxing and comfortable, with Italian ambient music. Eat before noon to avoid long lines and get made-to-order pasta. Pizza slices sit under heat lamps; whole pies are made to order and a decent deal for a group. The best pasta is the chicken parmigiana, especially after sprinkling it with parmesan packets. *New York. Opens 10:30 a.m.; a separate gelato counter is rarely open. $8–$14 (children $7), whole pizzas $32–$36. Seats 208 inside, 56 outside.*

Mel's Drive-In. Burgers, chicken sandwiches, shakes. Resembles the Mels (yes, no apostrophe) of 1973's "American Graffiti." Vehicles out front match the film's; include a yellow 1932 Ford hot rod (with THX 138 plate), black 1955 Chevy and white 1956 Thunderbird. *Hollywood. Opens 10 a.m. $9–$15 (children $7). Seats 272 inside, 76 outside.*

Moe's Tavern. Duff Beer, Flaming Moes (non-alcoholic citrus drinks on dry ice). "The Simpsons" references include a Love Tester machine, a pink TV and a bottle of Alkie's Choice Whiskey above the bar. Connects to Fast Food Boulevard; its patrons can sit here if it's not crowded. *Springfield. Opens 11 a.m. Drinks $4–$8. Seats 40 inside, 14 at the bar.*

Richter's Burger Co. Burgers, veggie burgers, chicken. The best place to sit is a small, quiet balcony that overlooks the order counter. *San Francisco. Opens 11 a.m. $9–$15 (children $7). Seats 180 inside, 72 outside.*

San Francisco Candy Co. Fudge, caramel apples. Fresh, packaged, loose treats. *San Francisco. Seats 44 inside, 52 outside.*

San Francisco Pastry Co. Croissant and panini sandwiches, pastries. *Opens 9 a.m. $9–$12 (children $7). Seats 32 outside.*

Starbucks. Coffee, pastries. *New York. Park hours. $3–$7. Seats 14 inside, 16 outside.*

Schwab's Pharmacy. ✔ Hand-scooped ice cream treats. *Hollywood Boulevard. Opens at noon, closes at either 5 or 6 p.m. $4–$7. Seats 28 inside, including 7 at bar, 16 outside.*

Universal Studios' Classic Monsters Cafe. Hamburgers, hot dogs and the like. Themed rooms display some vintage artifacts; video screens play kitschy trailers. *Production Central. $8–$16 (children $7). Opens 10:30 a.m. Seats 256 inside, 40 outside.*

Shops. There are many, including a few unique ones that are worth seeking out:

The Barney Store. Everything Barney. *Woody Woodpecker's KidZone.*

NEW! Betty Boop store. ✔ Everything Betty. Totally redone in 2016. *Hollywood.*

Borgin and Burkes. ✔ Dim, high-ceilinged Knockturn Alley shop offers dark-magic items themed to Death Eaters, Deathly Hallows, skulls, Voldemort. *Diagon Alley.*

Brown Derby Hat Shop. Visors, novelty hats, wigs, Universal logo caps. *Hollywood.*

Carkitt Cart. Gryffindor keychains with names. Collectible pins. *Diagon Alley.*

Cyber Image. Superhero collectibles, "Big Bang Theory" items, Terminator gear. *Hollywood, at the exit to Terminator 2 3-D.*

Doc's Candy Store. Impossibly small corner shop sells candy, ice cream bars, Blues Brothers items. *New York.*

E.T.'s Toy Closet & Photo Spot. E.T. items, Reese's Pieces. Two photo ops; in one E.T. hides in Gertie's closet. *Woody Woodpecker's KidZone, at the exit to E.T. Adventure.*

The Film Vault. Movies and TV-show merchandise related to the park. *New York.*

Gringotts Money Exchange. ✔ A talking goblin oversees the conversion of your muggle money into Gringotts notes. *Diagon Alley.*

NEW! Hello Kitty Store. Everything Hello Kitty, including Kitty herself. *Hollywood.*

It's a Wrap. Apparel, toys, novelty hats. *Production Central, park exit.*

Kwik-E-Mart. Simpsons stuff. *Springfield, World Expo.*

Madam Malkin's. Hogwarts robes, house apparel. *Diagon Alley.*

Magical Menagerie. ✔ Plush Wizarding World animals, creatures. Unusual, delightful items; fascinating shop. *Diagon Alley.*

MIB Gear. Men In Black gear. *World Expo, at the exit to Men In Black Alien Attack.*

Ollivanders. ✔ Wands, including ones that trigger magical effects throughout the Wizarding World. *Diagon Alley.*

On Location. Camera supplies. The park's photo pick-up location. *Production Central.*

Park Plaza Holiday Shop. Christmas-themed merchandise, including hand-painted Universal ornaments. *New York.*

Quality Quidditch Supplies. ✔ Quidditch, Hogwarts apparel, decor, toys. *Diagon Alley.*

Rosie's Irish Shop. Emerald Isle apparel and other items. *New York.*

Sahara Traders. Mummy merch, toys, jewelry. *New York, Revenge of the Mummy exit.*

Scribbulus Writing Instruments. Ink, notebooks, quills, stationery. *Diagon Alley.*

Shrek's Ye Olde Souvenir Shoppe. Ogre goods. *Production Central, at Shrek 4-D exit.*

Shutterbutton's Photography Studio. ✔ You film yourself or you and your group for a DVD of 12 different moving pictures on Harry Potter-themed backgrounds. *Diagon Alley.*

SpongeBob StorePants. ✔ Everything SpongeBob in a totally SpongeBob store; a sign promises "Free receipt with every purchase!" Mr. SquarePants and his friends pose for photos with fans here, too. *Woody Woodpecker's KidZone.*

Studio Styles. Oakley, designer sunglasses, watches, some apparel. *Hollywood.*

Studio Sweets. Candies, fudge, caramel apples. *Production Central.*

Sing It! A cappella vocalists challenge each other in live shows in the park's New York area.

NEW! Sugarplum's Sweet Shop. ✔ Candy, other Wizarding World sweets. *Diagon Alley.*

Super Silly Stuff. ✔ Despicable Me and Minions merchandise. *Production Central, at the exit to Despicable Me Minion Mayhem.*

Supply Vault. Transformers action figures, car decals, model EVACs. *Production Central at the exit to Transformers The Ride 3-D.*

Universal Studios Store. The best stock of general park souvenirs. *Production Central.*

Wands by Gregorovitch. Tiny shop has wands from Ollivanders. *Diagon Alley.*

Weasley's Wizard Wheezes. ✔ Candy, jokes, novelty items, toys. *Diagon Alley.*

NEW! Williams of Hollywood. ✔ This little oddity might have something you'd love. Some items are old props from the Universal Orlando parks (recently the flying cow from the "Twister" attraction went for $2,500, as did its understudies), others are vintage movie props from California's Universal City warehouse, which unfortunately kept no records of what movie or television show any of this stuff was in. Which makes it... unique. New items arrive often. *Hollywood.*

Wiseacre's Wizarding Equipment. ✔ House apparel, housewares; Hogwarts Express apparel, toys. *Diagon Alley.*

If it rains. With its many indoor attractions, the park is easy to enjoy during a shower.

Hollywood's Rip Ride Rockit, Kang & Kodos' Twirl 'n' Hurl and the outdoor playgrounds in Woody Woodpecker's KidZone stay open during a light rain but close when there's lightning in the area. Rain and lightning can cancel The Blues Brothers show, Universal's Superstar Parade and Universal's Cinematic Spectacular. Good spots to duck into when it's raining include the Barney playground (enter it through The Barney Store) and the shops of Diagon Alley. Most stores sell umbrellas and ponchos; many stands have ponchos.

Family matters. Most of the major park's rides have height minimums. *Despicable Me Minion Mayhem:* 40 inches (though people less than that height can view its 3-D movie from a stationary seat in its front row). *E.T. Adventure:* 34 inches. *Harry Potter and the Escape from Gringotts:* 42 inches. *Hollywood Rip Ride Rockit:* 51 inches, with a height maximum of 79 inches. *Men in Black Alien Attack:* 42 inches. *Revenge of the Mummy:* 48 inches. *The Simpsons Ride:* 40 inches. *Transformers The Ride 3D:* 40 inches. *Woody Woodpecker's Nuthouse Coaster:* 36 inches.

Two shows may be too much for toddlers. Universal Orlando's Horror Make-Up Show has realistic effects, scary film clips and some adult humor. Universal's Cinematic Spectacular has some scary film clips.

Universal's Superstar Parade is all about children; all of its superstars are animated characters. Every park restaurant offers a children's menu; "Despicable Me" and other characters appear at Cafe La Bamba for breakfast every Thursday through Saturday.

"Where can I find..." You want it. You need it. You know it exists. But just where is...

...the American Express Lounge? It's at the back of the building that holds the Classic Monster's Cafe. Open to visitors who bought tickets, annual passes, a vacation package or a VIP Tour with an American Express card.

...a baby care spot? Two Health Services centers (indicated by First Aid icons on the upcoming map) have changing rooms, a microwave and chairs for nursing moms. They sell diapers, formula and baby supplies.

...a bar? Try Finnegan's Bar and Grill (New York) or Chez Alcatraz (San Francisco).

...a battery? At the Universal Studios Store and On Location (Production Central), Cyber Image (Hollywood), Sahara Traders and the Central Park kiosk (New York), E.T.'s Toy Closet (Woody Woodpecker's KidZone), Kwik-E-Mart (Springfield), MIB Gear (World Expo).

...breakfast? At Beverly Hills Boulangerie (Hollywood), Starbucks (New York), San Francisco Pastry Co. (San Francisco), Leaky Cauldron (Diagon Alley).

...camera gear? Just inside the gate at On Location (Production Central).

...a Coca-Cola Freestyle machine? Near the Classic Monsters Café (Production Central), Louie's Italian Restaurant (New York), Mel's Drive-In (Hollywood), Richter's Burger Co. and the San Francisco Pastry Co. (San Francisco), the London restrooms (in front of Diagon Alley), and Men in Black Alien Attack (World Expo). Special cups allow unlimited refills every 10 minutes. Each spot sells the cups too (about $15 per day).

...coffee? At Beverly Hills Boulangerie (Hollywood), Starbucks (New York), Leaky Cauldron (Diagon Alley) and San Francisco Pastry Co. (San Francisco).

...fresh fruit? Louie's Fruit Stand (New York); Café La Bamba Slush Cart (Hollywood).

...a funnel cake? At KidZone Pizza (Woody Woodpecker's KidZone).

...a hot dog? At the Classic Monsters Cafe and RockIt Cart (Production Central), Animal Actors Hot Dog Cart (Woody Woodpecker's KidZone), Simpsons Hot Dog Cart and Fast Food Boulevard (World Expo) and the London Cart (outside Diagon Alley).

...hand-scooped ice cream? At Ben & Jerry's (New York), Schwab's Pharmacy (Hollywood) and Florean Fortescue's Ice-Cream Parlour (Diagon Alley).

...a locker? Just inside the main entrance at the far right; expect to pay $8–$10 per day. Large lockers are just outside the park.

...Lost and Found? Near the lockers, under a sign that reads "Studio Audience Center."

...a mailbox? By the restrooms at the exit.

...medicine? Health Services has complimentary pain medications and bandages; basic meds are sold at the Universal Studios Store (Production Central), San Francisco Candy Co. (San Francisco), SpongeBob StorePants (Woody Woodpecker's KidZone) and MIB Gear (World Expo).

...package pickup? It's a Wrap (park exit).

...a postage stamp? At the Universal Studios Store (Production Central).

...a prepaid phone card? At the Universal Studios Store and On Location (Production Central) as well as MIB Gear (World Expo).

...a stroller, scooter or wheelchair? Just inside the gate on the far left are single, double strollers and kiddie cars with steering wheels (about $15–$30 per day); wheelchairs ($12) and mobility scooters with optional canopies ($50–$70). All require a $50 deposit.

...a turkey leg? At the Turkey Wagon (5th Avenue, New York), T-2 Beer and Café La Bamba Veranda Bar (Hollywood), the Animal Actors Hot Dog Cart (Woody Woodpecker's KidZone) and Expo Eats, the Simpsons Hot Dog Cart, Fast Food Boulevard and Fear Factor Turkey Cart (World Expo).

Fun finds. Most people walk right past them—the building facades, statues and other items that line most of the park's walkways. But you shouldn't. They're fascinating.

Hollywood. On Hollywood Boulevard, many facades honor signature buildings from the real Hollywood's golden age. Among them: ❶ The Brown Derby shop recalls the Brown Derby restaurant, a star hangout with a foyer shaped like a big hat. ❷ Schwab's Pharmacy is topped with the neon signs of the real Schwab's on Sunset Blvd., where in 1937 16-year-old Lana Turner was said to be discovered sipping an ice-cream soda. ❸ The Darkroom replicates a Wilshire Blvd. shop known for the huge SLR in its window. ❹ The Pantages Theater recalls the Hollywood Pantages, an Art Deco movie palace that hosted the Academy Awards for a decade, including the first televised ceremony.

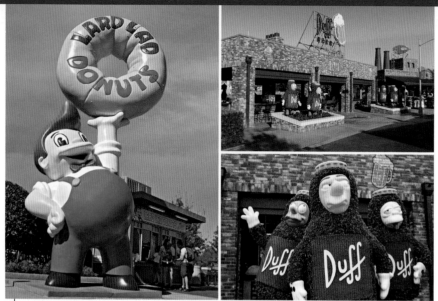

The Lard Lad's a Big Boy; the Duff Brewery; topiaries of Duffs Tipsy, Surly and Queasy.

New York. ❺ A window in the building that the Hollywood Rip Ride Rockit coaster zooms through identifies it as the office of the Paranormal Travel Agency from the 1984 movie "Ghostbusters"; the facade was once the entrance to the Ghostbusters Spooktacular, a special effects show that opened with the park in 1990. ❻ Nearby on 5th Avenue is The Priscilla Hotel for Single Young Ladies, a key residence in the 1967 film "Thoroughly Modern Millie." ❼ Farther down 5th, the Ben & Jerry's ice cream shop is, upon close inspection, The Hudson Street Home for Girls, the orphanage of Little Orphan Annie; ❽ the nearby Empire Hotel is where Kim Novak stayed in the 1958 Alfred Hitchcock thriller "Vertigo." ❾ Across the street, Louie's Italian Restaurant is the Bronx eatery where, in 1972's "The Godfather," Michael Corleone excuses himself from a table, retrieves a revolver from a bathroom toilet and returns to shoot his rival in the forehead. ❿ At the corner of Delancey and 7th Avenue the Kitty Kat Club recalls the Kit Kat Klub of the 1972 musical "Cabaret." ⓫ On 7th, O'Rourke's Bar & Grill is run by Kelly O'Rourke, somehow still alive after passing away during childbirth in "The Godfather." ⓬ Gritty Sting Alley meanders nearby, a nod to the Chicago alleys seen in 1973's "The Sting." ⓭ And finally, between the Empire and Louie's stands a statue of Lew Wasserman, the longtime head of MCA Universal who greenlighted the construction of Universal Studios Florida in the 1980s. He holds his trademark glasses behind his back.

San Francisco. ⓮ Just inside Richter's Burger Co. is a replicated relic from the city's devastating 1906 earthquake: a statue of geologist Louis Agassiz that flipped upside down and embedded its head in the ground. A photo of the real buried statue hangs on a wall in the nearby dining room.

Springfield. ⓯ As you enter the Simpson's hometown from Hollywood you pass two key props from the Back to the Future film series, its Delorean and steam locomotive time machines. They serve as a tribute to Back to the Future The Ride, the attraction that The Simpsons Ride replaced. ⓰ Holding a giant donut that reads "Lard Lad Donuts," a statue of the Lard Lad is a shout-out to both the plump mascot of the 1960s Big Boy restaurant chain and Randy's Donuts, a 1950s Los Angeles stand that's still today topped by a giant donut that reads "Randy's Donuts." ⓱ Last but absolutely not least, in front of the Duff Brewery in an obvious parody of Disney's Seven Dwarfs, are Duff mascots the Seven Duffs. Appearing as Disneyesque topiaries are Dizzy, Edgy, Queasy, Remorseful, Sleazy, Surly and Tipsy.

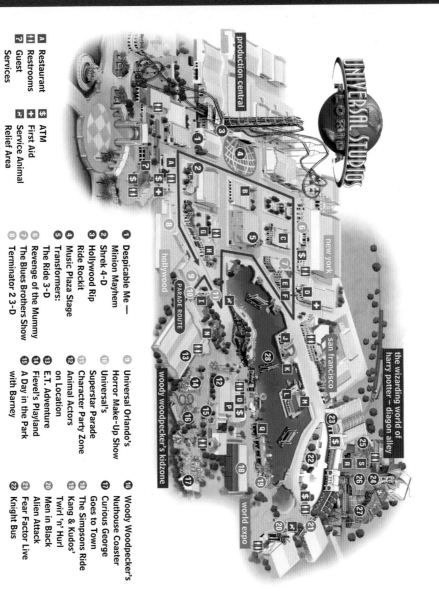

UNIVERSAL STUDIOS
UNIVERSAL ORLANDO

production central

new york

hollywood

PARADE ROUTE

san francisco

woody woodpecker's kidzone

world expo

the wizarding world of harry potter · diagon alley

A Restaurant
H Restrooms
? Guest Services

$ ATM
+ First Aid
A Service Animal Relief Area

1 Despicable Me — Minion Mayhem
2 Shrek 4-D
3 Hollywood Rip Ride Rockit
4 Music Plaza Stage
5 Transformers: The Ride 3-D
6 Revenge of the Mummy
7 The Blues Brothers Show
8 Terminator 2 3-D

9 Universal Orlando's Horror Make-Up Show
10 Universal's Superstar Parade
11 Character Party Zone
12 Animal Actors on Location
13 E.T. Adventure
14 Fievel's Playland
15 A Day in the Park with Barney

16 Woody Woodpecker's Nuthouse Coaster
17 Curious George Goes to Town
18 The Simpsons Ride
19 Kang & Kudos' Twirl 'n' Hurl
20 Men in Black Alien Attack
21 Fear Factor Live
22 Knight Bus

23 Hogwarts Express — King's Cross Station
24 Harry Potter and the Escape from Gringotts
25 Knockturn Alley
26 Ollivanders
27 Diagon Alley
28 Universal's Cinematic Spectacular

A Beverly Hills Boulangerie
B Universal's Classic Monsters Cafe
C Finnegan's Bar & Grill
D Louie's Italian Restaurant
E Ben & Jerry's Ice Cream
F Starbucks
G Schwab's Pharmacy
H Mel's Drive-In
I Cafe La Bamba
J Richter's Burger Co.
K Chez Alcatraz
L Lombard's Seafood Grille
M San Francisco Pastry Co.
N KidZone Pizza Co.
O Mel's Tavern
P Fast Food Boulevard
Q Duff Brewery
R Leaky Cauldron
S Florean Fortescue's Ice-Cream Parlour

© Universal Orlando Resort

Gru's adopted daughters lead you through a challenging Minion training ground.

Despicable Me Minion Mayhem
Hilarious 3-D movie appeals to all ages, is filled with detail

★★★★★ ✔ *EXPRESS* You can't help but giggle at this funny (and truly state-of-the-art) 3-D attraction. From Gru's living room in the queue where you watch Minions being blasted during goggle testing, to the holding room where a video Gru points out actual people in the crowd who haven't showered in a week ("Go back to your hotel now… and don't stop at the pool first!"), to the movie itself in which masses of chortling Minions are being bounced, sprayed and tempted by bananas, you'll constantly be tempted to burst out laughing. Yet Minion Mayhem also plucks at your heartstrings—when littlest daughter Agnes gives Gru his adoption-day gift, it's hard to keep tears from welling as the two embrace. Ditto for Gru's over-the-top celebration present to the girls at the end of the film. The first attraction you see as you walk into the park, Despicable Me Minion

Mayhem is a rarity at Universal—a big-time ride that almost anyone of nearly any age can enjoy. Razor-sharp for a 3-D film, its 4K visuals appear on a huge screen and match the swooping movements of your seat perfectly.

You're a Minion… *Warning; spoilers ahead.* The queue starts outside, where video screens clue you in to the story, explain why Gru needs more Minions (he's too busy to handle all his evil-villain responsibilities since he's now a devoted dad) and quiz you to determine if you're suited to become one. Then you head inside Gru's house and into his living room, which is decorated in his laughably villainous style. Soon he appears on a video screen to announce his plans—he's not only turning you into a Minion, but training you to become a great one. His daughters pop up to interrupt his speech; the youngest, Agnes, wants to give

Average wait times

9am	10am	11am	Noon	1pm	2pm	3pm	4pm	5pm	6pm	7pm	8pm	9pm
30m	35m	50m	45m	35m	35m	30m	40m	45m	40m	35m	35m	30m

him a gift to commemorate the anniversary of their adoption. Gru says he's too busy at the moment. At the last minute, however, he lets his daughters handle your training, and you head into the theater.

...you're at a training ground... As the movie begins, you and the rest of the audience are zapped by a "Minionizer" and head down to a huge training ground under Gru's home. Flying in a hovercraft in front of you, the girls test your strength, speed and "ability to not die" as they lead you and your fellow yellow orbs down a conveyor belt to dodge water cannons, fly swatters, laser beams and giant boxing gloves. Next you test your teamwork skills, as your Minion group joins together to form a bridge across an abyss. And that's when things go wrong. As one of the girls dangles a banana from a fishing pole to test how well the Minions in front of you resist temptation, they... well... don't.

Chaos ensues as the bridge of Minions falls, and you and the girls crash into Gru's Anti-Gravity Recycling Room, full of pounding crushers. After several close calls, the Minions save the day, by forming a hand that stays together and catches everyone.

...you boogie down. The show concludes as Gru opens his gift—a handmade stuffed doll of him—and announces that he has a present for the girls: he's turned a huge underground auditorium into an amusement park. Balloons and fireworks fill the air; dozens of Minions dance to the Silvers' 1976 disco hit "Boogie Fever." Then the Minionizer accidentally tips over and zaps you and the rest of the audience. "Ah man! They're human again!" Gru grumbles. "Bring in the next group!"

Tips. *Where to sit:* In the middle of a back row; the screen is huge; your seat is determined as you are sorted into rows in the living room. *How to catch all the action:* Look around the screen; the edges hide lots of silliness such as Minions working out on treadmills and squabbling with each other.

Fun finds. The living room has many references to "Despicable Me": ❶ the cardboard-box moon helmet Gru wears as a little boy; ❷ the macaroni moon rocket he made as a child; ❸ the movie's subtle Disney joke: a trophy head of a lion that holds in its jaws a stuffed dog, which holds in its jaws a stuffed cat eating a rat—a Circle of Death; ❹ Gru's family tree, which reveals that his great-great grandfather Marcel was a werewolf, and his relatives Helmut and Jane produced a Frankenstein-like offspring; ❺ the crayon doodles of the girls on his walls, including one of him with a pointy nose; underneath it reads "Gru = Daddy"; ❻ Gru's SR6 shrink-ray gun; ❼ the Bank of Evil portrait of Mr. Perkins that depicts him as Julius Caesar; ❽ above the fireplace, a stuffed piranha from Vector's piranha gun; hanging from its needle-sharp teeth are Gru's smiley-face-covered boxer shorts; ❾ just beneath that fish, a portrait of Gru's parents and the baby picture of him, showing his bare bottom; ❿ the cannon Gru uses as an elevator to his lair; ⓫ the portrait of Dr. Nefario at the beach, which Gru set as his cellphone's contact image of the old man; ⓬ Gru's iron maiden, standing open but with its spikes covered with tennis balls—some thoughtful child-proofing on his part; ⓭ decorated urns that portray Minions as Romans; ⓮ Gru's huge stuffed rhinoceros chair; ⓯ a portrait of Gru with the girls, the family's monstrous pet Kyle hanging from his leg. ⓰ In the 3-D movie, when the Minion bridge collapses you hear the Wilhelm scream, an iconic Hollywood sound effect that's been used in more than 300 pictures. Voiced by singer Sheb Wooley (best known for his 1958 novelty hit "The Purple People Eater"), the sound is named after Private Wilhelm, who shouted it in the 1953 Western "The Charge at Feather River" after being shot with an arrow. ⓱ The first blast of fireworks forms a unicorn, Agnes' favorite animal. ⓲ Nearby is a pink kitty balloon, a nod to Gru's "Despicable Me" bedtime story, "Three Sleepy Kittens." ⓳ In the exitway's dance party, Minion eyes make up the reflections of the disco ball.

Key facts. *Duration:* 4 minutes. *Capacity:* 112, 96 in 12 motion-simulated "transformation pods" (each with 2 4-seat benches) and 16 in stationary bench seats. *Height minimum:* 40 inches to sit in a motion-simulator seat; no minimum to sit in a stationary seat. *Access:* Rider Swap available; assistive listening, closed captioning, open captioning available; service animals allowed. *Restraint:* Lap bar. *Queue:* Indoor, overflows into shaded outdoor area. *Debuted:* 2012. *Fear factor:* The story isn't scary, but the film is accented with strobes and loud noises; seat movements include sudden jarring and tilting. *Location:* Production Central.

Health advisory. Universal recommends you avoid the attraction if you are pregnant or have heart conditions; abnormal blood pressure; back or neck conditions; issues with dizziness, heights, motion sickness or strobe effects; or recently had surgery.

© Universal Orlando Resort

Dragon helps out Shrek and Donkey as they fight to save Fiona in Shrek 4-D.

Shrek 4-D

Sick of fairy tales? Love Disney digs? Here's the show for you.

★★★ *EXPRESS* The world of fairytales is turned upside down in this 3-D movie. Its hero is no Prince Charming, but rather a green ogre, who showers in mud and uses his earwax for a candle. The heroine is no slim airhead but an ogress herself, a stout, proud kickboxer. And a fire-breathing dragon—a creature that's usually a villain in fairytales—saves the day.

Also turned upside down: the wonderful world of Disney. In the preshow trussed captive Pinocchio is the target of incessant jokes. In the movie a frog nearly gobbles up Tinker Bell for lunch; at the end she flies off the screen and crashes into a wall, her little legs sticking out just like Donald Duck's do when he crashes through a wall at the end of the Disney World 3-D film Mickey's PhilharMagic.

Living up to its 4-D title, the show is laden with special effects—spritzing water, blowing wind, "spiders" at your ankles.

A damsel in distress. *Warning; spoilers ahead.* The story picks up at the end of the first "Shrek" theatrical movie, just as the newly wedded ogre and his love Fiona are headed off on their honeymoon. Immediately, though, she's kidnapped by Thelonius, a henchman of the ghost of the evil Lord Farquaad, who plans to kill her and marry her spirit. To save Fiona, Shrek and Donkey gallop off in pursuit, along the way passing through a haunted cemetery, hitching a ride on the back of Donkey's wife Dragon and plunging down a waterfall. Eventually, all ends well, and the honeymoon begins.

Fun finds. ❶ In front of the building, a sign for stroller parking mimics those in Disney lots: "You are parked in Lancelot 17." **❷** Along the outdoor queue, a page from the guestbook of Shrek and Fiona's wedding notes that Snow White gave the couple "a questionable

Average wait times

9am	10am	11am	Noon	1pm	2pm	3pm	4pm	5pm	6pm	7pm	8pm	9pm
10m	15m	25m	30m	15m	15m	10m	10m	10m	10m	10m	10m	10m

Housed in Soundstage 4-D, Shrek 4-D sits across from Despicable Me Minion Mayhem.

apple"; ❸ Sleeping Beauty's gift was "the gravy boat Cinderella gave her for her wedding." ❹ Movie posters promote attractions at the Disney-like Dulocland theme park: Lord Farquaad's Enchanted Tick Room and ❺ ("you'll hurl in your tea cups when you ride…") Donkbo the Flying Talking Donkey. ❻ Rapunzel ("Single shut-in princess seeks anyone with a romantic spirit and a ladder. Must like big hair") and ❼ Snow White ("Single princess seeks prince or better. Seven little men can't be wrong! You've had the rest, now try the fairest of them all.") are among those who have posted personal ads on a nearby bulletin board. The film alludes to many popular movies, including ❽ 1980's "The Blues Brothers" (Donkey's line "We got a donkey driving a carriage made from an onion, it's dark and our horses are wearing sunglasses. Hit it boys!" recalls Elwood and Jake's "It's 106 miles to Chicago, we got a full tank of gas, half a pack of cigarettes, it's dark and we're wearing sunglasses"; "Hit it."), ❾ 1999's "The Matrix" (Fiona freezes in mid-air when faced with a villain), ❿ 1999's "The Sixth Sense" (Donkey in the graveyard: "I feel dead people") and ⓫ 1977's "Star Wars Episode IV: A New Hope" (Donkey says "This is Red Dragon, we're going in!" before he, Shrek and Fiona swoop into a Death Star-like rock trench).

Missed the movie? Once upon a time (during 2001's "Shrek") there lived in a swamp an ugly green ogre. Then came a day when it suddenly filled with fairytale characters including Cinderella, Pinocchio, Sleeping Beauty and her godmothers, Snow White and her dwarfs… all of them so annoying they'd been banished there by Lord Farquaad, an evil man who needed a princess to become king. To clear his swamp Shrek agreed to free the fair Fiona for Farquaad, fighting off a Dragon with the help of a wise-ass Donkey. But at the wedding Shrek declared it was he who loved Fiona, she revealed her true ogress self and said she loved him, Dragon ate the livid Lord… and Fiona married Shrek instead.

Key facts. *Duration:* 12 minutes. *Capacity:* 324 in each of two theaters. The last 8 seats in the front row are stationary. *Access:* Rider Swap available. Assistive listening and closed captioning available; service animals allowed. *Queue:* Outdoor, covered. *Debuted:* 2003. *Fear factor:* The story itself is too cartoonish to be scary, but the preshow dungeon looks realistic and the film has many loud noises. *Location:* Production Central.

Health advisory. Universal recommends you avoid the show if you are pregnant or have heart conditions; abnormal blood pressure; back or neck conditions; issues with dizziness, motion sickness or strobe effects.

Hands in the air, minds in their music. Riders on Hollywood Rip Ride Rockit.

Hollywood Rip Ride Rockit

Harness-free coaster rocks, rolls to your choice of tunes

★★★★★ ✓ *EXPRESS* Many roller coasters are thrilling, but few are as fun as this one. Some of the reasons for this are obvious: Thanks to its 17-story vertical launch tower, you start off flat on your back, with your face pointed at the sky. Thanks to its open vehicles, air rushes over your entire body, blowing through your hair, buffeting your knees, tingling your toes. Thanks to the brakes at the top of each big hill, you get time to anticipate each major fall. And, of course, it's fun to pick out a song and listen to it as you swerve, curve, dip and drop.

But there's another reason this coaster is fun, one you'd never guess ahead of time. Thanks to its requirement that all riders must stow all of their loose items—including cellphones—before getting in line, you spend your time in the queue as part of a very social crowd. A group of happy, smiling strangers who chat to each other, get to know each other, even play Rock Paper Scissors and Patty Cake with each other. And how often in today's world do you get to do that?

Winding around, over and through the left side of the theme park, the coaster is thrilling but not terrifying. Though it starts with a hair-raising dive that reaches 65 mph, it averages less than 30 mph, and though its track banks more than 90 degrees (more than sideways), you never go upside down. The result is a ride that's exciting, yet still gives you time to appreciate its height and take in its views.

The ride's name refers to its most distinctive feature—the fact that you "Rip" (select a song for) your "Ride" and then can "Rockit" (dance in your seat to it). "Rockit" is also a pun, a play on the ride's rocket-like qualities.

A late addition to the theme park, the coaster is shoehorned into a sliver of space,

Average wait times

9am	10am	11am	Noon	1pm	2pm	3pm	4pm	5pm	6pm	7pm	8pm	9pm
15m	30m	35m	40m	25m	20m	20m	20m	20m	20m	20m	20m	15m

Flashing lights on the side of a coaster train blur as it accelerates off the launch tower.

between Universal's commercial sound-stages and the park's southern edge—its music stage and attractions Despicable Me Minion Mayhem and Race Through New York Starring Jimmy Fallon. The ride's red steel rails can be seen throughout the park.

Ground control to Major Tom. To reach the loading platform you climb two flights of stairs. Unlike most coasters this one doesn't stop for boarding; instead it slows to a crawl to match the speed of a moving walkway. Once you're on it you have about 45 seconds to take your seat, lower your lap bar and tap through a touch-screen to choose your song. If you don't pick one you'll get the coaster's default tune, "Busy Child" by the Crystal Method, which fits it pretty well.

Then your ride begins, your train reaching the launch tower and turning straight up to climb it. You aim for the heavens, positioned just like an astronaut at nearby Cape Canaveral. Your song starts to play through speakers in your headrest. It takes 16 seconds to climb the tower, which seems like forever. What doesn't is how fast you come back down—2.7 seconds.

Twist and shout. From there you're off on a series of maneuvers most coasters simply can't do, all of which have musical monikers. The first is the Double Take—a 103-foot loop behind the park's concert stage. From the side it looks like a circle, one that most certainly will turn you upside down. But on the ride, just as you brace for that flip, the track itself turns over, shifting you from the inside of the loop to the outside, keeping you upright.

Then you're off to the back of the park, to its New York area, rocketing through a building facade, flying out over spectators 33 feet below as you wrap around the Guggenheim Museum. This upward helix forms the first turn of the Treble Clef, a section of track that resembles the shape of that musical signature when viewed from above. A subsequent Hi-Hat stall (a pause high above the ground, named for hi-hat cymbals that stand high above a drum kit) and a twisting vertical dive forms the rest of the shape.

Next it's the Jump Cut, a spiraling cork-screw that throws off some negative Gs and seems to spin you forward in time—much like how a jump cut in a music video (a cut from one camera to another that's closer to its subject) seems to jump forward in time.

After that, a Crowd Surfer section of track turns you on your side as you zip over the waiting line. Then there's some Drop Tuning (a step-like drop, named for a type of guitar tuning in which a string is dropped down a step) alongside the Blue Man Group theater, and finally a Chorus of maneuvers that include a spiraling 540-degree turn.

Mystery train. What makes all this possible isn't the track, it's the train, or rather the trains. They're short. Each has only two cars, and each car has a wheelbase of only 4 feet—about that of a go-kart. The result is a coaster that can turn tighter and twist quicker than maybe any you've ever ridden before.

The trains are unusual in other ways, too. From a distance, the most obvious oddity is that they light up—lights line their front and sides and flash in patterns—pulsing, racing, strobing, twinkling, rainbow streaking. From onboard what you'll notice most is your seat. It's a large wraparound shell that holds you in place solely by a thick lap bar—there's no over-the-shoulder restraint. Each seat also has a private sound system: two stereo speakers that pump out 90 decibels of music pointed straight at its occupant. The speakers don't bleed over each other; while you're rockin' out to "Le Disko" you'll have no idea that your friend who you thought was so cool is kickin' back to "The Devil Went Down to Georgia."

As you ride, a video system records your experience with your song as its soundtrack; you can buy the result as a souvenir.

A modern Mouse. Hollywood Rip Ride Rockit was built by Maurer AG (Maurer Söhne), a German firm founded in 1876 as a metal factory. It began building roller coasters in the 1960s, specializing in a style known as the Wild Mouse, in which tiny short-wheelbase trains picked up speed as they switchbacked through a series of hairpin turns punctuated with drops. Today the company builds coasters, Ferris wheels, bridges and seismic control dissipaters—devices that protect buildings from earthquake damage.

Tips. *How to save time:* Use the Single Rider Line; it cuts way back on your wait. To do so, tell the ride attendant just beyond the metal detector that you're by yourself when he asks how many are in your group. Your party will be split up into singles, however. Note: The Single Rider Line temporarily closes when it gets too long to make much difference. *Where to sit:* In the front row; you'll have a great view with no one in front of you. To get it, just ask the boarding attendant, even from the Single Rider Line; you may have to wait an extra minute or so for the next train. *How to get the most legroom:* There's more of it in the

The ride's track twists around its tall loop, keeping riders from turning upside down.

Hollywood Rip Ride Rockit song options

CLASSIC ROCK AND METAL
"Born to Be Wild," Hinder
"Bring Me to Life," Evanescence
"Gimme All Your Lovin'," ZZ Top
"Kickstart My Heart," Motley Crue
"Paralyzer," Finger Eleven
"Rollin'," Limp Bizkit

CLUB AND ELECTRONICA
"Busy Child," The Crystal Method
"Harder Better Faster Stronger," Daft Punk
"Intergalactic," Beastie Boys
"Keep Hope Alive," The Crystal Method
"Le Disko," Shiny Toy Guns
"Pump Up the Volume," MARRS

COUNTRY
"All Night Long," Montgomery Gentry
"The Devil Went Down to Georgia,"
    The Charlie Daniels Band
"Guitars, Cadillacs," Dwight Yoakam
"I Can Sleep When I'm Dead,"
    Jason Michael Carroll
"Living in Fast Forward," Kenny Chesney
"Midnight Rider," The Allman Brothers Band

POP AND DISCO
"Bad Girls," Donna Summer
"Glamorous," Fergie
"Hella Good," No Doubt
"I Will Survive," Gloria Gaynor
"That's the Way (I Like It),"
    KC & The Sunshine Band
"U Can't Touch This," MC Hammer

RAP AND HIP-HOP
"Don't Phunk With My Heart," Black Eyed Peas
"Insane in the Brain," Cypress Hill
"Pump It," Black Eyed Peas
"Rock Star," N.E.R.D.
"Sabotage," Beastie Boys
"Stronger," Kanye West

SECRET SONGS (3-Digit Code: Name, Artist)
101: "The Temples of Syrinx," Rush
102: "Blues Before and After," Smithereens
103: "Break on Through," The Doors
104: "Crocodile Rock," Elton John
105: "Do it Again," Steely Dan
106: "Don't You," Candlebox
107: "Drivin' Rain," Government Mule
108: "8 Miles High," The Byrds
109: "Fantasy," Aldo Nova
110: "Fool," Rollins Band
112: "Freebird," Lynyrd Skynyrd
113: "Immigrant Song," Led Zeppelin
114: "Just Because," Jane's Addiction
115: "Live," Lenny Kravitz

116: "Mexicola," Queens of Stone Age
121: "Runnin Down a Dream," Tom Petty
122: "Start Me Up," The Rolling Stones
123: "Stockholm Syndrome," Muse
124: "Diary of Jane," Breaking Benjamin
127: "Urgent," Foreigner
128: "Vertigo," U2
129: "Wheel in the Sky," Journey
130: "Won't Get Fooled Again," The Who
131: "K. Mandelbrot Mix," Blue Man Group
132: "Drumbone," Blue Man Group
301: "Float On," Modest Mouse
302: "I Want You Back," Jackson Five
303: "In My Pocket," The Cat Empire
304: "It's Still Rock And Roll To Me," Billy Joel
305: "Brothers Gonna Work it Out,"
    Public Enemy
306: "Lose Yourself," Eminem
307: "Ride Like The Wind," Christopher Cross
308: "Run to You," Bryan Adams
309: "Save Room," John Legend
310: "Vogue," Madonna
311: "You Make Loving Fun," Fleetwood Mac
312: "My Everything," Barry White
504: "Smokin' Gun," Robert Cray
506: "The Thrill is Gone," BB King
507: "Who Did You Think I Was," John Mayer Trio
508: "Pivot," Dry
701: "Cyanide," Metallica
702: "Endangered Species," Flaw
703: "For Whom The Bell Tolls," Metallica
704: "Forever Down," Black Label Society
705: "How Heavy This Axe," The Sword
706: "Just One Fix," Ministry
707: "Know Your Enemy,"
    Rage Against the Machine
708: "Let's Go," Ministry
709: "Mouth for War," Pantera
710: "Painkiller," Judas Priest
711: "Paranoid," Black Sabbath
712: "Temptation's Wings," Down
713: "The Wicker Man," Iron Maiden
714: "Unreal," Ill Nino
715: "Wake Up Dead," Megadeth
716: "We Call This Mutha Revenge,"
    Suicidal Tendencies
718: "You've Got Another Thing Comin',"
    Judas Priest
901: "Movin' Right Along,"
    Kermit The Frog, Fozzy Bear
902: "Rainbow Connection," The Muppets
903: "Your Attitude Towards Cuttlefish,"
    Paper Moon
904: "Night on Bald Mountain," Mussorgsky
    (from Disney's 1939 movie "Fantasia")

Popping out of a building facade, a coaster train circles over a New York street.

front rows of each car (rows 1 and 4). *How to avoid getting a sore neck:* Lean back; your seat provides little support for your head or neck.

Secret songs. Besides the song choices you're given, dozens more are available; everything from the Byrd's perfectly themed "Eight Miles High" and Black Sabbath's perfectly paced "Paranoid" to insane options like "The Rainbow Connection" by The Muppets. A full list appears on the page on the left.

Choosing one of these songs is easy; once your lap bar is lowered, just follow these three steps: (1) Press the Hollywood Rip Ride Rockit logo on your screen and hold it for at least 10 seconds. (2) Release your finger to bring up a numeric keypad. (3) Tap in the 3-digit code of the song and then touch "Enter." You'll need to memorize the code of your tune ahead of time; the keypad screen doesn't show them. Note: If you choose a hidden song you won't be able to buy an on-ride video. If you enter a 3-digit number that doesn't link to a song (or fail to select a tune in time) you'll get the default "Busy Child" by the Crystal Method.

Key facts. *Duration:* 1 minute, 39 seconds. *Closed by:* Rain or the presence of lightning. *Capacity:* 84; 7 trains, each with 2 cars that have 3 2-seat rows. *Height minimum:* 51 inches. *Height maximum* 79 *inches. Access:* Single Rider Line, Rider Swap available;

closed captioning, test seats available. *Restraint:* A seat shell wraps around your back and thighs, a divider splits your legs, a thick lap bar curves around your waist. *Restricted items:* No personal belongings in hands or pockets, including cameras, car keys, loose change and phones, wallets; locker use provided; as you enter the attraction you pass through an electronic security system much like that at an airport. *Fear factor:* The scariest moment comes right away as you climb the vertical lift tower and feel almost like you're tipping over backward; then comes the other big panic point when you dive nearly straight down; there's one open loop and the track tilts slideways more than once beyond 90 degrees but you never turn upside down. *Queue:* Outdoor, partially covered. *Top speed:* 65 mph. *Track length:* 3,800 feet. *Track type:* Steel tubes filled with gravel and sand. *Manufacturer:* German firm Maurer AG. *Coaster type:* Custom X-Coaster. *Designer:* Universal Creative. *Music volume:* 90 dB. *Debuted:* 2009. *Optional:* Souvenir photos and videos $20–$45. *Location:* Production Central.

Health advisory. Universal recommends you avoid the coaster if you are pregnant or have heart conditions; abnormal blood pressure; back or neck conditions; issues with dizziness, heights, motion sickness or strobe effects; or recently had surgery.

Autobots leader Optimus Prime towers over the entrance of Transformers The Ride 3D.

Transformers the Ride 3-D

Love these guys? Do it. Never heard of 'em? Do it anyway.

★★★★★ ✔ *EXPRESS* Walking down the ride's exitway, a dad wearing a backward baseball cap looks at his 6-year-old son. "Remember when Bumblebee grabbed us? That was awesome!" His son beams at him. "Yeah!" Others around them are smiling too, some of them rolling their eyes. Because that's what this is. An awesomely cheesy, thrilling adventure that's perfect for a dad and his young son yet still a blast for just about anyone else. If you're a fan of the "Transformers" movie franchise, if you played with them when you were little, if your kids do today or if you just love thrills you'll get a kick out of it.

A high-tech indoor dark ride, it immerses you in a retelling of the climactic battle of the first Transformers movie—the one from 2007 titled simply "Transformers" that was actually pretty good. As good-guy Optimus Prime takes on bad-guy Megatron, you feel like you're right in the middle of the action, the ride's crystal-clear 3-D action all around and above you as your vehicle speeds down city streets and hurls high in the sky. Startling 3-D effects bring bombs, broken glass and other flying shrapnel right up to your face. Technically similar to The Amazing Adventures of Spider-Man ride at Islands of Adventure, it uses the same type of ride vehicle, its action takes place on huge screens, and between you and those screens are elaborate real environments with their own scenery and props. It's a lot to take in.

The fate of the world. *Warning; spoilers ahead.* The story starts as you enter the top-secret headquarters of the Nonbiological Extraterrestrial Species Treaty (NEST), an alliance between the U.S. government and the Autobots (good Transformers). Its purpose is to protect Earth from Decepticons

Average wait times

9am	10am	11am	Noon	1pm	2pm	3pm	4pm	5pm	6pm	7pm	8pm	9pm
5m	20m	40m	40m	35m	25m	15m	15m	10m	20m	15m	15m	5m

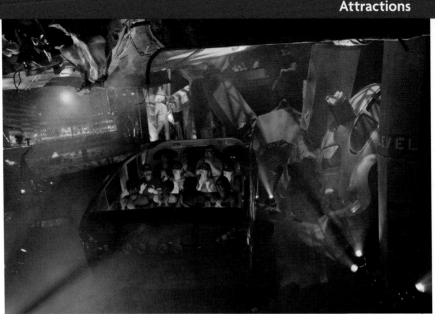

© Universal Orlando Resort

Safe and sound. The ride's final scene takes you through wreckage beneath a city street.

(evil Transformers) and keep them from getting the last remaining shard of AllSpark, a mystical substance that's the source of all Transformer life. You're there because you're a NEST recruit, ready for your orientation.

But suddenly... bad news! The Decepticons have invaded Earth and are headed straight for the building you're in! They've learned the AllSpark is there, and will stop at nothing to get it. So ready or not, you're assigned your first mission—to get the stuff out of there. There's a Transformer in the building who can help, Evac, who morphs into an armed troop carrier. But like you, he's a rookie.

You grab the AllSpark and board Evac, but before you can get underway the Decepticons show up, including the dumb-as-donuts Devastator, who sucks you up into his massive body before spitting you out. Soon you're in the core of a battle that will decide the fate of the world. The good guys struggle but emerge victorious. But then yet something else goes wrong, and only at the very last moment—thanks to Transformer fan fave Bumblebee—are you safe and sound.

Tip. The ride's extreme 3-D effects and motions can make some riders queasy and create long-lasting headaches. If you're prone to these troubles stare straight ahead during your ride. This will take some effort, as there's always a lot going on around you.

Fun finds. ❶ A real 1970s yellow-and-black Volkswagen Beetle, the car Bumblebee transformed into in the original 1980s series of Transformer toys. Part of the wreckage under a street you crash through after Bumblebee saves you, the car is slammed into a wall on your left (see photo above) just as your attention is drawn to the right to an appearance of Optimus Prime. ❷ As he thanks you for saving the world you're so close to him you can feel his breath. ❸ The remains of Megatron are above you during that same moment.

Key facts. *Duration:* 4 minutes. *Capacity:* 72; six vehicles, each with three 4-seat rows. *Height minimum:* 40 inches. *Access:* Single Rider Line, Rider Swap available; assistive listening, closed captioning available; service animals allowed. *Restraint:* Lap bar on a bench seat. *Fear factor:* The story's not scary, even for a child; the ride itself however is intense, as your vehicle will often suddenly accelerate, climb, drop, spin, stop or tilt. *Perceived top speed:* 60 mph. *Actual top speed:* 10 mph. *Track length:* 2,000 feet. *Queue:* Indoor, overflows into shaded outdoor area. *Debuted:* 2013. *Location:* Production Central.

Health advisory. Universal recommends you avoid the ride if you are pregnant or have heart, back, blood pressure, dizziness, fog, height, motion sickness or strobe-effect issues or have recently had surgery.

A museum exhibit. Revenge of the Mummy takes place inside the "Museum of Antiquities."

Revenge of the Mummy

Melodramatic indoor coaster has fun story, scenes, effects

★★★★★ ✔ *EXPRESS* An over-the-top bad guy and some surprising special effects make this indoor roller coaster an exhilarating experience. The villain—a mummy named Imhotep—keeps popping up during the ride, threatening to steal your soul. He hams up his performance like a bad but enthusiastic actor, eliciting giggles instead of shivers. Sudden visual effects create swarms of scarab beetles that crawl over walls, flames that envelop a ceiling and a fiery descent into a demonic pit. Throughout it all are the physical joys of riding a twisting coaster in the dark, which dips and turns on smooth tracks through detailed scenes and environments. At one point it stops, reverses directions then shoots uphill.

You're making a movie. *Warning; spoilers ahead.* The experience is based on Universal's 1999 remake of its classic 1932 movie "The Mummy" and the first sequel to that retelling, 2001's "The Mummy Returns." As you enter the queue you're part of a 1940s film crew that's shooting a new "Mummy" movie on location. Concept drawings, molds and props litter the space, an archeological dig in a creepy Egyptian tomb—the sacred burial chamber of an ancient high priest named Imhotep. Portions of the tomb were recently excavated by the filmmakers and since then the set seems cursed. To stay safe, the cast and crew display symbols of the Medjai—a secret society of ancient Egyptian warriors who protect pharaonic interests—on its clothes. That is, every cast and crew member but the assistant production assistant, a guy named Reggie who has gone missing.

You board a small mining train to head deeper into the tomb. You find Reggie. Barely able to move, he's partially mummified, and

Average wait times

9am	10am	11am	Noon	1pm	2pm	3pm	4pm	5pm	6pm	7pm	8pm	9pm
5m	20m	20m	15m	15m	15m	10m	10m	15m	10m	10m	10m	5m

The Treasure Room begins to burn as the mummy Imhotep demands their souls.

warns you that the curse is real. Suddenly Imhotep bursts out of a sarcophagus, silences Reggie and commands that you hand over your soul. You escape just before he catches you—not once, not twice, but three times.

Tips. *Where to sit:* In the front row for the best view and clearest audio. *If you need legroom:* There's slightly more in the front row.

Fun facts. ❶ The animatronic Imhotep weighs 680 pounds. **❷** Unlike most coasters, Revenge of the Mummy doesn't start off with a lift hill and doesn't rely on gravity for its power. Instead it starts flat, powered by a linear induction system embedded in its track. Its mine cars move by being quickly pushed away from, and pulled to, a sequential series of magnets. **❸** As your car takes off you feel up to 1.5 Gs of pressure for about a second and a half. **❹** After your car reverses direction it reaches a speed of 45 mph in 2.5 seconds. **❺** Its tightest turns have 80-degree banks. **❻** Its final fall is a 50-degree drop of 25 feet. **❼** The heat you feel at the first unload station is 107 degrees; at the ceiling it's 3,200 degrees. **❽** The ride was the first indoor coaster that switched tracks to change direction.

Fun finds. ❶ Covered in hieroglyphics, a statue in the queue has a sign that translates them: "Evil by one hand, protection by two." If one person places a hand on the statue, a button lets him or her spray a blast of air toward

unsuspecting others in line. If two people do it, the symbol of the Medjai appears on the ceiling. **❷** Other hieroglyphics translate to ominous warnings such as "Abandon all hope forever" and "The cursed! The cursed!" **❸** In the ride's treasure room, a golden statue King Kong on your left is a nod to the attraction that first occupied this space, Kongfrontation (1990–2002). **❹** Reggie appears on a missing-person poster at the ride exit.

Key facts. *Duration:* 3 minutes. *Capacity:* 176; 11 16-seat vehicles each with four 4-seat rows. *Height minimum:* 48 inches. *Access:* Single Rider Line, Rider Swap available; closed captioning, test seats available; service animals allowed. *Restraint:* Lap bar. *Restricted items:* All personal belongings in hands and pockets, including cameras, car keys, loose change and phones, wallets; locker use provided. *Fear factor:* Sudden acceleration, climbing, tilting, dropping in the dark; flames; threatening villain. *Queue:* Indoor, overflows into shaded outdoor area. *Top speed:* 45 mph. *Track length:* 2,220 feet. *Track type:* Sand-filled tubular steel. *Launches:* 3. *Debuted:* 2004. *Location:* New York.

Health advisory. Universal recommends you avoid the ride if you are pregnant or have heart, back, blood pressure, dizziness, fog, motion sickness or strobe-effect issues or have recently had surgery.

Jake (right) and Elwood belt out a number during a Blues Brothers show.

The Blues Brothers Show

All ages shake their tail feathers to this soulful tribute act

★★★★ ✔ Catchy Chicago blues fills the air thanks to these two performers, who channel Jake and Elwood Blues and are backed up by a female singer and live sax player. And they do a good job. They look like their namesakes, with the same thin and stocky builds of the young Dan Aykroyd and John Belushi; wear the same dark sunglasses, suits and porkpie hats; kick out the same frantic dance moves. And though many of the people in the audience are way too young to remember the Blues Brothers, most totally get into the groove and willingly shake their tail feathers.

Only two things keep the act from being all it could be: it performs on a tiny stage, and most of its backup music is prerecorded.

King Bees. The act that became the Blues Brothers got its start in 1976, during the first season of the television series "Saturday Night Live." Costumed as two of the show's recurring Killer Bee characters, their heads topped with springy antennae, their bodies wrapped in yellow-and-black striped tunics, comedians John Belushi (singing lead) and Dan Aykroyd (harmonica) played it straight as they performed "I'm a King Bee," a 1957 Slim Harpo swamp-blues tune. The buzz from that skit led the comedians to create an actual duo, with a backup band of top studio musicians. Naming themselves "Joliet" Jake and Elwood Blues, Belushi and Aykroyd borrowed the look of blues legend John Lee Hooker: black suits and Wayfarer sunglasses. Soon they had a top-selling album ("Briefcase Full of Blues") and two hit singles, "Rubber Biscuit" and "Soul Man." Wayfarer sales shot up 500 percent, saving the forgotten Ray-Ban style from extinction.

The park act's entrance re-creates how they came onstage. Aykroyd would arrive with a small case handcuffed to his wrist. Belushi produced a key and unlocked the cuff, then Aykroyd drew his harmonica from the already unlocked case. Universal produced two Blues Brothers movies, an acclaimed 1980 original and a panned 1998 sequel.

Key facts. *Duration:* 15–20 minutes. *Showtimes:* Scheduled; typically 5 starting late morning. *Viewing area:* Unshaded street. *Access:* An area near the stage is reserved for viewers with disabilities; service animals allowed. *Debuted:* 1991. *Location:* New York.

© Universal Orlando Resort

"A future beyond your imagination." Robots turn against mankind in Terminator 2 3-D.

Terminator 2 3-D

Ambitious theatrical adventure syncs live action with film

★★★★ ✔ *EXPRESS* He said he'd be back. Reprising his famous role, Arnold Schwarzenegger reunites with waitress-turned-warrior Sarah Connor and her son John to go back in time from the wasteland of the mid-21st century to the 1990s, to stop the destruction of the world by robot-controlled defense system Skynet by stopping clueless corporation Cyberdyne Systems from ever creating it.

Live performers, stunts and lots of in-your-face 3-D action portray the resulting battle between man and machine. Towering robots fire bullets over your head. Arnold's Terminator rides his signature Harley Fat Boy right into the theater. A liquid-metal villain shatters into globs that drip on your head.

'Our most exciting technology.' The show begins as you arrive at Cyberdyne headquarters in 1999, just as the company is expanding its reach. You're there, as chipper Director of Community Relations and Media Control Kimberly Duncan explains, "to see a classified presentation of our latest, most exciting technology." To kick things off she plays a slick video (updated in 2015) that exhorts the benefits of a fully automated world.

"Imagine a world," the voice of a confident female urges, as a montage of schoolrooms shows scrubbed attentive kids, "where an entire semester of coursework is downloaded directly into a student's brain. In the blink of an eye. Every lesson... every subject... every student... total recall."

A montage of computer screens leads to a shot of robot-guided lasers in an operating room. "Imagine a high-tech medical center, where a neurosurgeon can remove a brain tumor... with absolute technological precision...without missing the sunset." You see the doctor controlling the operation from a tablet, sipping a drink on a tropical beach.

"A world where a mother can tuck in her child and say good night... from halfway around the planet." Smiling into her computer, a woman in a hotel room waves to her little girl, then tucks her into bed using giant remote-controlled claws.

"It's happening. Today. At Cyberdyne Systems... We're ready to lead the world into a future beyond your imagination..."

Suddenly the video cuts out, replaced by a fuzzy live feed from Sarah and John, who tell

Top gun. Arnold Schwarzenegger uses a shotgun to fight off robots in Terminator 2 3-D.

you they're about to blow up the building and urge you to get out of it. You don't, of course, and the resulting chaos blends live action, video and special effects so seamlessly you'll have trouble distinguishing one from the other. On-stage actors seem to be the actual stars from the films; thanks to an ingenious use of video close-ups of the stars that sync with the actions of the actors, who are often in silhouette. It really makes you feel like you're spending time with characters you care about.

Tips. *When to go:* In the late afternoon, when the crowds thin out. *Where to sit:* In the center of the theater, halfway back.

Fun facts. ❶ Though it's not obvious today, the Cyberdyne video is a parody of a series of AT&T "You Will" commercials that ran in the early 1990s. Narrated by Tom Selleck, each presented a futuristic service or system that AT&T would soon make possible. The innovations included electronic toll collection ("Have you ever paid a toll without slowing down?"), GPS navigation ("Have you ever crossed the country without stopping to ask directions?") and video on demand ("Have you ever watched the movie you wanted to, when you wanted to?"). Each commercial ended the same way. "You will. And the company that will bring it to you is AT&T." ❷ Despite all the gunfire only one person dies during the show: chipper Cyberdyner Kimberly Duncan.

Fun finds. ❶ The opening presentation is held in the Miles Bennett Dyson Memorial Auditorium. In the movies Dyson invented the Neural Net CPU, which allows robots to reason through problems. ❷ During the film, an unskinned T-800 fixes its infrared red-dot sighting mechanism on John's forehead just before Schwarzenegger destroys it… just like in the 1984 movie the evil Arnold fixes his red dot on Sarah's forehead just before a resistance fighter attacks him. ❸ "Stop whining!" he orders a spinning weapon as it hunts him down, repeating a command he gave a classroom of kids in 1990's "Kindergarten Cop."

Key facts. *Duration:* 25 minutes. *Showtimes:* Scheduled; usually every 45 minutes starting mid-morning. *Capacity:* 700. *Access:* Rider Swap available; assistive listening, closed captioning, reflective captioning, stationary seating available; service animals allowed. *Queue:* Indoor. *Debuted:* 1996. *Fear factor:* Children may be frightened by menacing onscreen 3-D robots, loud noises, faux shotgun blasts, strobe and fog effects and sudden seat movements; Universal urges parental discretion. *Location:* Hollywood.

Health advisory. Universal recommends you avoid the show if you are pregnant or have heart, back, blood pressure, dizziness, fog, motion sickness or strobe-effect issues or have recently had surgery.

"And then you start getting these super awesome spurts..." "Cutting" a hapless volunteer.

Universal Orlando's Horror Make-Up Show

"Hey kid, this isn't Disney. I don't have to be nice."

★★★★ ✔ *EXPRESS* You don't see much of this at a theme park anymore: a live show in a small theater, with professional actors focused on something that's not tied into the latest princess product or adventure franchise. This fact alone makes it worthwhile; that it's also interesting and has a snarky attitude about itself make it almost a must. Blending stage presentations with video clips, nearly every minute is entertaining, as you learn some classic tricks and see demonstrations of a vintage prop or two. Footage from Universal horror movies such as 1931's "Frankenstein" and 1932's "The Mummy" include signature moments as well as behind-the-scenes prep. Still, the heart of the show is in its jokes and skits, which its actors pull off with aplomb.

Meet the Makers exhibit. Small display cases line the lobby, most of them focused on Universal make-up legends such as Lon Chaney, Lon Chaney Jr., Jack Pierce and his successor Bud Westmore. Authentic items include masks, molds and prosthetic devices used in the production of 1954's "The Creature from the Black Lagoon," 1982's "The Thing" and the long-running "Halloween" franchise.

Tips. *When to go:* Pick a show, any show. *How early to arrive:* 15 minutes before showtime, 30 minutes to take in all the lobby exhibits. *Where to sit:* In the center of the second or third rows. *How to be in the show:* Performers select one female to join them onstage; to increase the odds they choose you, wear something sleeveless, sit in the front row and look lively. *For families:* Don't just wander into this one; the arm-cutting moment often seems real, and a few jokes are too risqué for young children.

Key facts. *Duration:* 25 minutes. *Show-times:* Scheduled; typically 7 afternoon shows. *Capacity:* 310 in 10 rows; theater seating with no armrests. *Access:* Service animals allowed. *Fear factor:* It appears a woman gets her arm cut and bleeds from it. *Queue:* Indoor lobby. *Debuted:* 1990. *Location:* Hollywood.

Health advisory. Universal recommends you avoid the show if you have issues with strobe effects, though there aren't many.

She's got the Boogie Fever. A park visitor dances with human Minions-in-training.

Character Party Zone

A parade float stops in front of you and totally comes to life

★★★★★ ✔ All parade floats will eventually do one thing: pass you by. Except here. During each of these shows, one of the floats from Universal's Superstar Parade (for Despicable Me, SpongeBob SquarePants, Dora the Explorer and Hop) pulls up in front of you and stops. For 15 minutes. It's better than the parade, as the performers do more and you can pick which show you want to see.

The first five minutes is a song-and-dance routine that you watch from the sidewalk.

And then come the other 10 minutes, which are—and this is kind of the best part—absolutely nothing. Ten minutes of the float just sitting there, its characters and performers just standing there. With you free to do whatever you want—walk around the float and check out its details, wander up to a dancer or a drummer or stiltwalker and just chat, go up to as many characters as you want to take photos with them and get autographs.

The floats and their performers—"parade units" in theme-park speak—come out one at a time, a different one every half hour, and set up in front of Mel's Drive-In. There's rarely a crowd, which makes it all even better.

Dance routines. The best shows are those by the Despicable Me unit, in which human "Minions-in-training" groove to the 1975 Silvers hit "Boogie Fever" and invite park visitors to come out on the street and dance with them. Complete with young women dressed in candy costumes and a top-hatted drum line of young men, the Hop unit puts on quite a show to the song "I Want Candy," still best known (despite its appearance in "Hop") as a 1982 hit for the group Bow Wow Wow.

Characters. The Despicable Me dancers include Gru, his daughters Margo, Edith and Agnes; also Vector. SpongeBob, Patrick and Squidward highlight the SpongeBob unit; Dora, Diego and Boots the Dora the Explorer unit. Hop dancers include the Easter Bunny, his teenage son E.B. and his Pink Berets body guards and Easter chicks Carlos and Phil. All of them can be met easily after their shows; the longest lines are usually less than a dozen people deep. Also eager to pose and chat are the supporting players—the human Minions, the Hop girls and drummers (those guys *love* getting their picture taken), a school of roller-skating fish in the SpongeBob unit and in the

"I call him Lollipop, Lollipop..." Dancers from the Hop unit sway to the tune in front of Mel's Drive-In. Meanwhile, Hop drummers let children in the crowd play along with them. Universal's follow-up to "Despicable Me," the 2011 animated movie "Hop" bombed at the box office; oddly this theme-park take on it is a real crowd-pleaser.

Dora unit a jungle of towering plants (stilt-walkers), one of which has tulips for hands.

Late shows. As the day wears on the performers ditch their floats and change up their routines. The human Minions do a tight line dance to the 1977 Bee Gees hit "You Should Be Dancing." The Hop girls form a swaying chorus line to kick out the 1958 Chordettes novelty song "Lollipop" *("Call my baby lollipop. Tell you why. His kiss is sweeter than an apple pie…").* Sometimes when SpongeBob and friends act out the B-52s' campy 1979 tune "Rock Lobster" *("It wasn't a rock… Was a rock lobster!!!"),* Patrick breaks out in the frug.

Key facts. *Duration:* 5-minute show followed by 10 minutes of open-street performer interaction with visitors. *Showtimes:* Vary; up to 12 shows daily (3 per parade unit), on the half hour from late morning to late afternoon; park maps and Party Zone team members have daily schedules. *Cancelled by:* Rain or the presence of lightning. *Access:* Mobility scooter and wheelchair accessible; special viewing area available; service animals allowed. *Location:* Hollywood, in front of Mel's Drive-In. *Other performances:* The Despicable Me characters often dance with park visitors in the morning (usually at 9:30 a.m.) in front of the Despicable Me Minion Mayhem attraction, as well as occasionally on Hollywood Blvd. near Terminator 2 3-D.

See also **Characters.**

'Go ahead... give her a great big kiss.' A Saint Bernard prepares a slobbery smooch.

Animals Actors on Location

No matter when you see it, everything always goes wrong.

★★ *EXPRESS* Go down and pet the dogs afterward when they line up on the edge of the stage. That's how you get the most out of this lightweight stage show, in which dogs, cats and birds perform silly tricks. Pet owners will enjoy it; it's the only chance in either park to see animals.

Three volunteers—an adult and two children—interact with the creatures. The adult holds out a dollar bill for a bird to fly out and fetch. The first child volunteer directs a large dog's actions and gets a slobbery kiss in reward. The second child—always a boy—instructs a dog as to which clothing item to gather from a basket; hilarity ensues when the dog brings back a... well, let's just say the French poodle doesn't need it, as she's wearing a corset.

Cynics will note that the jokes aren't all that funny and that the show skimps on plot and execution. But it does make its point, which is nothing more than when you work with animals, everything always goes wrong.

Animal Actors. And these people should know. Since the 1970s, Animal Actors of Hollywood has been one of the top trainers of mammals, birds and reptiles for movies and television shows. Famous alumni include Cinnamon from "The Big Bang Theory," Frank the pug from "Men in Black" and Precious from "Silence of the Lambs."

Tips. *When to go:* In the afternoon when lines are long elsewhere; crowds are rare. *Where to sit:* For the best view sit in the center, halfway up. *How to be in the show:* To be picked to have the bird fly to you have a dollar bill at the ready and sit high in the stands.

Fun finds. Eclectic music playing before the show begins includes the 1982 Stray Cats hit "Stray Cat Strut," "Talk to the Animals" from the 1967 movie "Dr. Doolittle" and the classic 1958 Bobby Day ditty, "Rockin' Robin."

Key facts. *Duration:* About 25 minutes. *Showtimes:* Scheduled; typically 5 afternoon performances. *Capacity:* 1,400. *Access:* Assistive listening available; service animals allowed; a viewing area near the stage is reserved for people with disabilities; an American sign-language interpreter sometimes stands near the performers. *Queue:* Outdoor, covered. *Debuted:* 2006. *Location:* Woody Woodpecker's KidZone.

Home sweet home. E.T. makes it back to his home planet on the classic E.T. Adventure.

E.T. Adventure

It's been here since opening day. And probably always will be.

★★★ *EXPRESS* "Goodbye, Julie," croaks E.T. at the end of this ride, in an oddly robotic cadence; where else can you get such a strange experience? From the evocative whiff of pine needles in the queue to ride vehicles that are bicycles to the sensation of riding one off into space, this proud Universal original is memorable. Yes its tech is creaky and yes it's inspired by Peter Pan's Flight, but that's all charming here. For many adults it brings back fond memories of their first Universal visit; kids enjoy it at face value.

There's no place like home. *Warning; spoilers ahead.* The ride's story is simple. E.T.'s home—the Green Planet—is dying; he must get back to it and save it with his healing touch. Your job is to help him, by dodging cops and NASA types on your bicycle as he hides safely in its basket, then flying over the city into space and onto the Green Planet.

Instantly revived by E.T.'s mere presence, its Cloud Bearers, Water Sprites, Jumpums and Tickley Moot Moots celebrate his return by dancing, playing and singing. Fountains spurt, lights flash, E.T. bids you farewell.

Tips. *When to go:* Anytime is good. *Where to sit:* Front row, on the left for a good view of the lit-up cityscape underneath you.

Key facts. *Duration:* 4 minutes, 30 seconds. *Capacity:* 168 (3 rows of 4 in 14 groups). *Height minimum:* 34 inches. *Access:* Rider Swap, closed captioning; service animals allowed. *Restraint:* Lap bar. *Queue:* Covered outdoor area, then indoor. *Debuted:* 1990. *Location:* Woody Woodpecker's KidZone.

Health advisory. Universal recommends you avoid the ride if you are pregnant or have heart, back, blood pressure, dizziness, fog, height, motion sickness or strobe-effect issues or have recently had surgery.

Average wait times

9am	10am	11am	Noon	1pm	2pm	3pm	4pm	5pm	6pm	7pm	8pm	9pm
5m	10m	20m	15m	15m	10m	10m	15m	10m	10m	10m	10m	5m

© Universal Orlando Resort

Put your hands up... put your hands up... It's easy on this coaster, which tops out at 21 mph.

Woody Woodpecker's Nuthouse Coaster

Preschoolers may love the silly humor at this kiddie coaster

★★★ *EXPRESS* Good for toddlers, this coaster thrills just enough to tantalize but not terrify. Its gentle drops and swoops are exhilarating but not scary; with only 25 seconds of ride time past its chain lift tots don't have much time to be scared. Silly nut-themed signs help keep the tone light; many are rebus puzzles that use letters and drawings to represent words or parts of words. For example, the letters "RUA" followed by a drawing of a walnut, a plus sign, a suitcase and a question mark. Get it? "Are you a nutcase?"

Tips. *When to go:* Early in the day for the slowest track (before its grease melts), late for the fastest one. *Where to sit:* In the front seat for the best view, in back for the most thrilling ride. *For your stuff:* There's a "baggage claim" shelf at the boarding area.

Key facts. *Opens:* 10 a.m. *Duration:* 1 minute. *Closed by:* Rain or the presence of lightning. *Capacity:* 16 ; 8 2-seat coaster cars form one train. *Height minimum:* 36 inches. *Access:* Rider Swap available. *Restraint:* Lap bar on small bench seat. *Restricted items:* No handheld phones or loose hats. *Fear factor:* Sudden acceleration, mild dives. *Queue:* Outdoor, partially covered. *Specs:* Top speed 21 mph, length 679 feet, sand-filled tubular steel track. *Debuted:* 1999. *Location:* Woody Woodpecker's KidZone.

Health advisory. Universal recommends you avoid the coaster if you are pregnant or have heart conditions; abnormal blood pressure; back or neck conditions; issues with dizziness, heights or motion sickness; or recently had surgery.

Average wait times

9am	10am	11am	Noon	1pm	2pm	3pm	4pm	5pm	6pm	7pm	8pm	9pm
n/a	5m	5m	10m	10m	15m	10m	5m	5m	5m	5m	5m	5m

Still smiling after all these years, Barney seems blissfully unaware his crowds have thinned.

A Day in the Park with Barney

A super-dee-dooper show for fans; a fun playground for all

★★★★★ *EXPRESS* Obey the dinosaur. Stand when he says stand. Clap when he says clap. Sing when he says sing. And when he says go to the playground, make *sure* you do that. That's the best way to experience this gentle sing-a-long show, which speaks directly to preschoolers present and past who have fond memories of the happy purple T-Rex and his friends Baby Bop and BJ. All three sing and dance in an indoor theater that does a good job re-creating a city park; leaves, rain and snow fall from its sky, stars come out when it gets dark. Other characters are on hand too—a farmer, his wife, an odd guy named Mr. Peekaboo, a bunch of inflatable animals.

Barney's Backyard. Afterward kids meet Barney, then head to an indoor toddler playground that's even more elaborate. Six play areas offer Fun With Music (with multiple ways to make lovely noise, including log bongos, an echo chamber, and buttons that create singing rainbows), Climbing (slides and hanging padded weights), Exploration (an open maze with balls to spin, wheels to steer and mirrors to gaze into), Pretend Play (anchored by a brightly colored train,

BJ's Express), Sand Play (a huge sandcastle, with sand) and Water Play (troughs of gently running water).

Tips. *When to go:* Anytime; the theater is rarely crowded. *Where to sit:* In the front row for the most legroom and the best view. You'll be close to the characters on their in-the-round slightly elevated stage. *If you're not a huge fan of Barney:* You can visit the playground without seeing the show. It's an excellent way to get out of the weather, and many of its play spots are very well done.

Fun fact. Either BJ or Baby Bop are adopted; the siblings are different species.

Key facts. *Duration:* 15 minutes (preshow 5 minutes). *Showtimes:* Scheduled; typically 5 performances between 11 a.m. and 4 p.m. *Capacity:* 600 on wooden benches. *Access:* Assistive listening available; service animals allowed. *Fear factor:* None. *Queue:* Outdoor, covered. *Debuted:* 1995. *Location:* Woody Woodpecker's KidZone.

Health advisory. Universal recommends you avoid A Day in the Park with Barney show if you have issues with strobe effects.

See also **Characters.**

You're a mouse. That's the idea behind the oversized props at Fievel's Playland.

Fievel's Playland

Looks can be deceiving: mild playground hides super slide

★★★ Be patient. Let your children pick what they do at this sprawling playground. But make sure they know about the water slide. Hidden in the back of the area, it is by far the playground's best thing; the thing many kids insist they go on over and over and over again. The 200-foot-long slide twists and turns through a dark tunnel and spirals through two open areas. Perhaps best of all, each of its rafts seats two, so a parent and child can ride on one together and zoom down the slide really fast. Expect to get splashed but not soaked (there's barely any water on the slide); on a hot day the cool water feels especially good.

The rest of Fievel's Playland holds more traditional play spots, most worn but still worthwhile, each decorated with oversized props inspired by the 1986 movie "An American Tail" and its sequel, 1991's "Fievel Goes West." A giant cattle skull holds a small slide and a drum to bang; a giant gramophone has hanging weights to bang. The Mouse Climb is a multi-story maze with slides, steps, netting and a suspension bridge. A small bounce house sits inside a 1,000-gallon cowboy hat; a water-play area resembles a hand pump; a ball pit looks like a pot of beans.

Tip. *When to go:* Early in the morning. Though the playground as a whole is rarely crowded, on summer days the wait for its waterslide can reach 30 minutes.

Fun finds. In the water play area, water will spray on your head if you pull on the big blue rope that leads to the hand pump. Near the ball pit, a small slide looks like a harmonica and makes the sound of one when someone goes down it.

Key facts. *Opens:* 10 a.m. *Allow:* 45 minutes to check out the whole area. *Closed by:* Rain or the presence of lightning. *Service animals:* Allowed in all areas but not on water slide. *Water slide specs:* 20 seconds; combined weight maximum 300 pounds, outdoor covered queue. *Debuted:* 1992. *Fear factor:* None. *Location:* Woody Woodpecker's KidZone.

Health advisory. Universal recommends you avoid the activities of Fievel's Playland if you are pregnant or have heart conditions; abnormal blood pressure; back or neck conditions; issues with dizziness, motion sickness; or recently had surgery.

Put away that phone! Water pours onto a plaza at Curious George Goes to Town.

Curious George Goes to Town

Supersoak your friends at this "children's" playground

★★★ It's a kick to ambush other people at this unique spot, which is supposedly a playground for children. You have your choice: shoot them with water cannons, dump troughs of water on their heads or pelt them with lightweight balls. It's all in fun of course; the wet zone feels especially good on a hot day. Based in spirit on the "Curious George" children's books about the mischievous brown monkey, the area hides at the very back of Woody Woodpecker's KidZone. It's rarely crowded.

And talk about deceiving! From the front this area looks indeed like a toddler spot—a little splash pad, a play spot under a circus tent, buttons that when pushed make animal sounds. But venture past those quarters and you'll enter a mischievous town that seems designed for older kids and playful adults. Ways to get someone wet are everywhere—water cannons to shoot, buckets of water to spill, overhead bathtubs to drain. Spray guns—ten of them on balconies—let you get people below. Meanwhile up on top of the buildings, two 500-gallon troughs automatically dump their loads every five minutes.

In the very back is something else completely different, the screened Man in the Big Yellow Hat's Ball Factory, where kids of all ages can blast foam balls at each other from stationary guns on two levels. Thousands of balls are scattered everywhere.

Tips. *When to go:* Anytime it's hot; the area is rarely crowded. *To stay dry:* Beware of children! For many of these impish creatures, soaking strangers is apparently quite a thrill. *To avoid a major expense:* Keep your phone in your pocket or someplace even safer; the downpours here are enough to ruin it.

Fun finds. Inside the post office, open the mailbox for Le Phant and you'll be sprayed with water, presumably from an elephant. To get someone else wet, find the sign that reads "Look Thru For Service" and have them look through the nearby hole—while you're standing on the other side, pulling on a blue rope that drenches them with water.

Key facts. *Opens:* 10 a.m. *Allow:* 30 minutes. *Closed by:* Strong rains or the presence of lightning. *Service animals:* Allowed. *Fear factor:* None. *Debuted:* 1998. *Location:* Woody Woodpecker's KidZone.

Visitors get the red-tongue treatment at Krustyland, home of The Simpsons Ride.

© Universal Orlando Resort

See Sideshow Bob? His wrecking ball? Your coaster ride has just started, but it's about to end.

The Simpsons Ride

The best ride in the park? If you judge by jokes, absolutely.

★★★★★ ✔ EXPRESS If you're a fan of "The Simpsons," this is the Universal ride you'll remember, and the one you'll most want to go on again. Based, of course, on the characters and settings in the long-running television show, it's an open motion simulator, a topless stationary vehicle that syncs its movements with a video that fills your field of vision. Hidden sprayers mist you with water, wind and scents. Yes, the park has plenty of those, but this one's funny. Really funny; packed with so many jokes and gags you can't possibly take them all in. Some riders are disappointed by the video's sleek CGI animation—*we want our Bart crude, dude!*—but other than that it seems everyone who goes on the ride loves it. It was developed with the help of Simpsons creators James L. Brooks and Matt Groening.

Upsy Downsy Spins-Aroundsy. *Warning; spoilers ahead.* Its premise is that you and

the Simpson family are the first riders of a brand-new roller coaster—Krusty's All-New Thrilltacular Upsy-Downsy Spins-Aroundsy Teen-Operated Thrill Ride—at Krustyland, a theme park operated by Krusty the Clown. But as soon as you take off, everything goes wrong. Pursued by the murderous Sideshow Bob, you and the Simpsons are tossed off the coaster's rickety tracks, and career madly through all of Krustyland as well as the city of Springfield. You even go to hell. All ends well, of course, until you pull back into the station and Krusty discovers a big red button on the ride's control panel. "Hey?" he wonders. "What does this do?"

Tips. *To fully understand the ride:* Tell the preshow attendant you'd like to watch the entire pre-boarding video, from the beginning; it sets up the ride's story, some things won't make sense without seeing it; it's also

Average wait times

9am	10am	11am	Noon	1pm	2pm	3pm	4pm	5pm	6pm	7pm	8pm	9pm
10m	20m	35m	45m	45m	50m	40m	35m	30m	25m	25m	20m	15m

Not the Haunted Mansion, just an Itchy & Scratchy game in front of The Simpsons Ride.

hilarious. *Where to sit:* In the front row of your two-row vehicle; the view is better and there's more headroom. *Where to look:* Not just straight ahead, but also above you and to the sides; there's a lot going on.

Fun finds. ❶ As soon as you enter the queue, a map of the Krustyland theme park on your right (on your left if you're using Universal Express) shows that it has many attractions that are similar to those at Walt Disney World—Krustyland Main Street ("The America of 1895 at Today's Prices!"); It's a Long Long Line; Krusty's Futuristic Rootin' Tootin' BBQ Review 3000; and Krusty's Haunted Condo ("Visit our 999 Unhappy Teen Employees!"). ❷ Signs in the outdoor queue and video slides in the holding room promote other Krustyland attractions such as Captain Dinosaur's Pirate Rip-Off, a jab at Disney's Pirates of the Caribbean and Dinosaur rides. ❸ One slide is a Krustyland Warning: "When riding Krusty's Stagecoach Stampede, please avoid the Groping Undertaker." ❹ In the preboarding video, Homer is so thrilled that his family will be the coaster's first riders that he proclaims "We're like that space guy who did that moon thing." "Neil Armstrong?" Lisa asks. "No. Chewbacca!" ❺ As the coaster goes up its lift hill Lisa confides "I'm scared, Dad." Homer replies "Don't worry honey. They won't kill you in an amusement park if you

have a dime left in your pocket." ❻ Later you crash through a sign that reads "Send Money to Universal Studios." ❼ Toward the end of the ride, as a giant Maggie sucks on your vehicle like a pacifier, you smell baby powder.

Fun facts. ❶ Your vehicle's inverted gull-wing doors hint at the beloved attraction that this one replaced: Back to the Future: The Ride (1991-2007). ❷ More than two dozen Simpsons characters appear in the attraction, all of whom are voiced by their original actors. Characters voiced by Harry Shearer do not have speaking roles, however, as he refused the deal the others accepted.

Key facts. *Duration:* 4 minutes, 30 seconds. *Capacity:* 192, 24 8-seat simulators. *Height minimum:* 40 inches. *Access:* Single Rider Line, Rider Swap available, closed captioning available in special-access vehicles. *Restraint:* Lap bar. *Fear factor:* Multiple cartoonish decapitations and killings; riders briefly fall into hell and see the devil; intense simulated motion with many dives and drops. *Queue:* Indoor. *Debuted:* 2008. *Location:* Springfield, World Expo.

Health advisory. Universal recommends you avoid the ride if you are pregnant or have heart conditions; abnormal blood pressure; back or neck conditions; issues with dizziness, enclosed spaces, fog, motion sickness or strobe effects; or recently had surgery.

"Next time, let your dog try." Slimy one-eyed Kang is disgusted by your saucer skills.

Kang & Kodos' Twirl 'n' Hurl

Cool hub-and-spoker has flying saucers, Simpsons humor

★★★★ ✔ *EXPRESS* A green alien drools from the center of this hub-and-spoke ride, which is funny from start to finish. As you ride—in a purple and green flying saucer that lights up at night—Kang (the slimy alien star of many Simpsons "Treehouse of Horror" Halloween specials) bullies you into "betraying the human race," which in this case means flying close enough to the face of Bart Simpson and other Springfield residents to make them spin. Aside from coasters, Kang & Kodos' Twirl 'n' Hurl is the only outdoor ride in the park.

Tips. *When to go:* At night, when white lights edge the ride's tentacles and spokes, the flying saucers blink with lights and Kang's head glows green. *For families:* Aim at the character faces to make them spin. *For couples:* You share a seat belt on this cozy ride.

Fun finds. Signs along the queue read: ❶ "Please! Do not be frightened! We do not like the way frightened tastes!" ❷ "Clearly humans like waiting in line. You will be happy to know there is much more line to come." ❸ "Warning. Texts sent from line must not have spelling mistakes." ❹ As you board a soothing female safety announcer asks you to "Please relax and enjoy the sincerity of everything I'm saying... Welcome trusting tourists to this non-threatening time waster." ❺ Saucer names include Space Oddity, Ronald Ray Gun and Citizen Kang.

Key facts. *Duration:* 2 minutes. *Closed by:* Rain or the presence of lightning. *Capacity:* 24; 12 2-seat saucers. *Access:* Rider Swap available. *Restraint:* Seat belt on bench seat. *Queue:* Outdoor, partially covered. *Debuted:* 2013. *Location:* Springfield, World Expo.

Health advisory. Universal recommends you avoid the ride if you suffer from dizziness or motion sickness or recently had surgery.

Average wait times

9am	10am	11am	Noon	1pm	2pm	3pm	4pm	5pm	6pm	7pm	8pm	9pm
5m	5m	10m	5m	5m	5m	10m	15m	10m	5m	5m	5m	5m

Flying saucers. As fans of the movie know, that's what those yellow platforms really are.

Men in Black Alien Attack

Have a blast scoring big at this ride-through shooting gallery

★★★★★ ✔ *EXPRESS* You play cops and crooks on this ride-through shooting gallery, with you as the cop and a bunch of silly space aliens the crooks. They're all around you—some easy to see, some hidden—and they react when you hit them. You blast away through the dark streets of New York, your ride vehicle occasionally spinning like a top. No matter your score, your memory is wiped with a flash from a neuralizer to make sure you don't remember any of this alien hokem. Although the ride isn't as state-of-the-art as it used to be, it's still a blast. Its building channels those of the 1964 New York World's Fair, complete with the tower platforms of its New York pavilion.

Galaxy defender. *Warning; spoilers ahead.* The story adds to the fun. In the waiting line, posters promote a 1964 New York "World Expo" exhibit called The Universe and You, which explores whether there is

intelligent life on other worlds. Once inside you learn the truth: you're really entering the Men in Black headquarters, where you're about to be tested to see if you have the right stuff to be an MIB agent; as the ride starts you're in a training ground, shooting fake-alien targets. But then there's a surprise—an MIB prison transport ship has crash-landed in Manhattan, letting loose a swarm of dangerous aliens. Your training session suddenly turns real, as you head off on an emergency mission to stop them. As you shoot your way through the night streets of the Big Apple, you get ambushed, move through a Bio-Scanner and reach Times Square. In the end, you face the worst alien of them all: a bug. And he's hungry.

Tips. *When to go:* During the first two hours the park is open, or use the Single Rider Line. Go at least once in the regular queue, though;

Average wait times

9am	10am	11am	Noon	1pm	2pm	3pm	4pm	5pm	6pm	7pm	8pm	9pm
5m	20m	25m	20m	15m	20m	30m	30m	20m	15m	15m	10m	5m

you'll want about 20 minutes in line to see all the detail there. For the full experience go after 10:45 a.m., when the right-hand track opens. *Where to sit:* In the back row for more legroom and a more comfortable backrest. Shooting is easiest from a side seat; you have room to maneuver your shots carefully, and can turn around to aim backward. *Which track to choose:* The one on the right, to have a better shot at Frank the pug and the Fusion Exhaust Port of your companion car. *How to see more:* Ask a ride attendant for a tour of the queue's Immigration/Control room, which is on the floor below the standby line. You'll fill out an alien citizenship form; the bottom of which reads "As a reminder, while visiting Earth visitors MUST be able to assume Earth 'normal' appearance when in public areas."

General scoring tips. ❶ Learn how to aim at targets by watching for the red tracer dot that flashes from your gun barrel. ❷ Choose a target and stick to it, hitting it over and over again to rack up points. Avoid flailing around trying to shoot as many things as possible. ❸ Steady your aim by holding your gun with both hands and resting your elbows against your lap bar. ❹ Hold your finger down on the trigger for the fastest fire rate. Keep shooting the whole time; you get 1,000 points for every 10 shots even if you don't hit anything. ❺ Indicator lights on the back of your gun flash green for a successful hit and red for a missed hit. Your accuracy ratio doesn't affect your score. ❻ Successful hits cause your gun to make a noise; it makes a different louder noise when hitting certain high-value targets. ❼ Most aliens have glowing green eyes when active; when shot their eyes flash red. ❽ "The red button" is below your gun's holster; it can be easy to miss if you don't know where it is. ❾ Aim for targets that are high up, small, moving or partially obscured; these are typically worth 10,000-20,000 per hit. ❿ Don't bother shooting the big aliens at ground level; they're only worth 1,000 points or less per hit. Instead aim at their guns; a shot into a barrel is typically 10,000-20,000 points.

Specific scoring tips. As you travel through the ride what you can shoot at depends in part on which side of the track you're on, the left or the right. ❶ At the training grounds on both sides of the track, swaying targets behind windows are worth 10,000 points. ❷ On the right side of the crash site under an "Auto Keys" sign, the head and collar of Frank the pug are each worth 15,000 points. ❸ Just past the crash site on the left, the rattle-like antennae

of an alien in a baby carriage is worth 10,000 points. ❹ On a bench to the right, an alien disguised as Steven Spielberg is worth 15,000 points. Aim for the fake Spielberg's head as it waves back and forth. ❺ Rack up points by repeatedly hitting cutout targets in second-story windows on the right. Each is worth 15,000 points. ❻ In a second-story apartment on the right, a one-eyed tentacled alien waves two guns. Each barrel is 15,000 points. ❼ At the ambush site on either side of the lead green alien, smaller aliens pop out holding guns. Again, each barrel is 15,000 points. ❽ After the ambush, rack up points by hitting the glowing green eyes of aliens hiding in the trees. Yet again, 15,000 points each. ❾ After moving through the Bio-Scanner, aim for the other car's Fusion Exhaust Port, above and behind the second row of riders. Its red center is worth 20,000 points; the blue ring around it 10,000 points. When the center is flashing hits make the car spin. To really boost your score, steady your aim and hit the car over and over again. ❿ It's actually possible to shoot your own car, though it can be tricky to maneuver you gun around to aim behind you. If your port's center is flashing, successful shots make you spin. ⓫ On the right wall, monster movie posters have glowing eyes worth 10,000 points. ⓬ On the right, a parking meter with glowing eyes is worth 10,000 points. ⓭ When faced with the giant bug, the first person in your car to hit their red button gets a 100,000 point bonus. When Zed says "Only one thing left to do: Push the red button," press it right as he says the word "push"; hold it down until your score indicator says "bonus." Everyone in your car will earn the bonus if they hit their buttons at the same time. ⓮ After facing the giant bug return your gun to its holster so the ride can calculate your car's average score.

Key facts. *Duration:* 4 minutes, 20 seconds. *Capacity:* 264. 44 6-seat vehicles, each with two 3-seat rows. *Height minimum:* 42 inches. *Access:* Single Rider Line, Rider Swap available. Assistive listening and closed captioning available. *Restraint:* Lap bar. *Restricted items:* All personal belongings must be in pockets or in a provided complimentary locker. *Queue:* Indoor, overflows into shaded outdoor area. *Debuted:* 2000. *Location:* World Expo.

Health advisory. Universal recommends you avoid the ride if you are pregnant or have heart conditions; abnormal blood pressure; back or neck conditions; issues with dizziness, fog effects, motion sickness or strobe effects; or recently had surgery.

See the Expo from the air
Sky Lounge

Re-Opening Soon!

...ch for the stars
and enjoy spectacular
360-degree bird's-eye
panoramas at Expo Center's
only sky-high lounge,
at "The Universe and You!"

At Expo Center!

Are We Alone? Find out at

the **UNIVERSE** and **You**

an informative, entertaining ride
through tomorrow's dreams today
and the truth about what lies
beyond our solar system!

At Expo Center!

Artwork © Universal Orlando Resort

Posters outside the building promote its Sky Lounge and the show The Universe and You...

Fun finds in Men in Black Alien Attack

Mickey Mouse? The Marx Brothers? The designers of this attraction must have had a lot of fun when they created it, as it's packed with in-jokes, sly references and secret treats.

Outside. ❶ At the far right, the entrances to the attraction's gift shop and restrooms form the letters "M" and "I." If not for budget constraints, the full "MIB" would have been spelled out with the addition of a "B"-shaped entrance to a restaurant. **❷** Posters along an expansive outdoor queue promote The Universe and You, the World's Fair-like show that supposedly fills the building.

In the queue. ❸ In the foyer, the audio introduction to The Universe and You says it was relocated from "the 1964 New York World Expo," just like Disney's Carousel of Progress attraction was relocated from the 1964 New York World's Fair. **❹** As you descend in the elevator, Zed (actor Rip Torn) apologizes for the "phony theme-park nonsense." **❺** In the hallway, a female announcer speaks over the PA system. "Attention: Agents E and I, Agent O will now meet you in Mission Debriefing. Once again, to Mission Debriefing; that's Agents E, I; E, I, O." **❻** The building's office directory lists "Covert Media Ops," "Roswell Conference Room," "Urban Legend Archive," "Human Resources," "Alien Resources" and

"Child & Spore Daycare." Each has an alien translation below it. **❼** A door marked "Oxygen Free Zone" is down the hall on the right. **❽** Inside a break room, two gangly animatronic aliens watch as you and other visitors pass by. "Oh hey... It's Zed's new MIB recruits!" one says. "Eh... Look's like someone's scraping the bottom of the human research pool." **❾** "Take me to your leader!" they tease. "Yeah! Live long and, uh... eat your vegetables!" **❿** They claim the initials "MIB" stand for "More Insect Bait" or "Mentally-Impaired Bug food." **⓫** A bulletin board has clippings from the Weekly World News. In the films, this real tabloid's ridiculous stories report actual alien activity. **⓬** "Fingerprint Removal" reads a door past the room. **⓭** "All-You-Can-Eat BBQ Lubotha" and "Sloppy Xyoes" are among meals on a cafeteria menu on a hallway bulletin board. Several items are "not for human consumption."

Immigration/Control room. ⓮ Desk paper trays hold issues of the Weekly World News; headlines shout "Baby parts Lake Michigan!" and "Bat Child Found In Cave!" **⓯** A blaring alarm warns that a "Korillian Death Ray" is aimed at Earth and is about to fire. With five seconds to spare, the alarm clicks off with the *"cheep-cheep"* of a car lock.

Artwork © Universal Orlando Resort

COULD THERE BE **FLYING SAUCERS?** *and what could they be looking for?*

Find out the truth about man's place in the cosmos at *the UNIVERSE and YOU!*

Do They Exist *What do They Eat* *When will They Get Here* *What do They Want*

find out the answers to these *and* other questions at *the UNIVERSE and YOU!*

...neither of which actually exist. The show promises to reveal the truth about aliens...

⑯ An announcement about alien lifeforms reassures you that "perceived resemblance to close relatives is a common neuropsychological phenomenon." ⑰ "Would the pilot of the titanium 37 Galaxicon Solar Craft please report to the landing platform?" a page asks. "Your lights are on."

Video screens. ⑱ On a control room monitor Zed welcomes your party. "Nice tourist disguises, by the way. We don't see about a million of those coming through here every day." ⑲ Explaining that you'll become an MIB agent if you score enough points during training, he adds "But, if by some chance you choke... Let's just say that our friendly, experienced counselors will help you get over the memories of your failure." With a flash from his neuralyzer, the scene cuts to him shaking hands with a confused tourist. "Thank you for flying with us. You'll find your baggage on carousel B. Enjoy your stay in Orlando!" ⑳ A black-and-white training video ("Aliens and You") shows how aliens disguise themselves among the populace. "Rover appears to be this farmer's best friend," explains its narrator, "but each time he barks, he's transmitting information back to the home planet. 'Bow-wow' lets his friends from space know, 'It's all right. He's preoccupied. Take the cattle!'" ㉑ "Where's the alien here?" the narrator asks as you see a crate of oranges.

"Why, it's right in front of your eyes!" As some oranges become blinking eye stalks. he explains that "This isn't a pile of fruit, it's the meeting of a gang of Space-Nepupods, taking over our planet one supermarket at a time." ㉒ "One of the alien prisoners won't get on the shuttle," Zed grumbles, pulling up a prisoner's portrait. "Remind this nitwit that he's being banished to a prison colony." You'll see him later; he ambushes you as the ride photo is taken. ㉓ The video provides background information on alien criminals that appear on the ride near the transport ship's crash site. Their punny descriptions hint at where they show up. Greenthorp is a plant-like alien recognizable by its "Fresh Spring Scent." On the ride, it pops up out of a flowerbox. ㉔ Saramiss of Poincy is a green alien with a Barbie-like body and fruit piled on its head. Its home planet "Aipotuirf" is an anagram of "Fruitopia." On the ride it pops out of a barrel near fruit crates. ㉕ "Implicated in a string of newsstand robberies," Ocihc, Oparh and Ohcourg are the names of a three-headed alien that hides behind a newspaper and the fake head of Steven Spielberg, the executive producer of the MIB films. ㉖ Its three heads are a reference to David Geffen, Jeffrey Katzenberg and Spielberg, the three media moguls who founded the Dreamworks production label. ㉗ "Ocihc," "Oparh" and

...by teasing you that they actually do. The show is a cover for Men In Black operations.

"Ohcourg" are anagrams of "Chico," "Harpo" and "Groucho"... the Marx brothers.

Weapons room. ㉘ A glass case along the left wall is filled with MIB weapons and technology, including specially-tinted sunglasses, the Noisy Cricket, some neuralyzers and training guns used on the ride. ㉙ Green slime oozes from the rightmost locker.

On the ride. ㉚ The ride's first room, a training ground with cutout alien targets, recalls the scene in the first MIB film in which Agent J (actor Will Smith) trains to be an agent. ㉛ Just past the crash site, Frank the pug rests on the counter on the right, under an "Auto Keys" sign. He wears his "NYC" hoodie and collar from the film. ㉜ On the left, a baby rattle waves around inside a carriage; shooting it reveals that it's actually the antennae of a small, toothy alien that rises up and screeches. ㉝ Farther down, one hiding inside a car slams its doors and peeks out from its hood. ㉞ On the right a green alien disguises itself as a crate of fruit. ㉟ At the foot of a building on the right, green glowing eyes peer from a mailbox. ㊱ On the left, two elderly aliens look up at you from their chess game.

Times Square. ㊲ Glowing-eyed creatures camouflage themselves among B-movie monster posters on the right wall. ㊳ Another alien has disguised itself as a parking meter. ㊴ On the left, a crouching alien is playing a shell game; tiny aliens hide under each shell. ㊵ On the right, more aliens hide under three hats on a table. The first hat is the starry wizard's cap worn by Mickey Mouse in "The Sorcerer's Apprentice," an animated short featured in Disney's 1940 movie "Fantasia"; ㊶ the second is the tall red and white cap of the Cat in the Hat; ㊷ the third is the green topper of the Mad Hatter from Disney's 1953 film "Alice in Wonderland." ㊸ "Extra! Extra! Read all about it!" calls a burly green alien at a newsstand. ㊹ Advertising its Old World Antiquities, an antique shop is named I. M. Hotep. That's a none-so-subtle reference to Imhotep, the name of the villain in the Revenge of the Mummy ride. ㊺ On a video screen, Agent J warns that a huge alien bug is loose in Times Square. "It's muy grande!" he says. "That's Spanish for 'very grande.'" ㊻ Just past that screen is a billboard advertising Zap 'Em, an extermination company seen in the Men in Black films. ㊼ When your car stops spinning, the big bug lets out a loud belch.

Exit area. ㊽ Disney fans will recognize that "The Universe and You" tune that plays in the unloading area is a shameless parody of "It's a Great Big Beautiful Tomorrow," the theme song of Disney's Carousel of Progress. ㊾ The shadow of an alien worm appears in a window of a door at the exit. You can hear him grumbling about his job.

"Hey! If you hold your nose you can't taste the eyeballs!" A contestant outsmarts a host.

Fear Factor Live

We understand. You don't want to watch this. Of course not.

★★★★ *EXPRESS* This live show may bring out the rubber-necker in you—the person who, driving by, can't help but look at the fender bender on the side of the road. It can be compelling but cringe-worthy to watch volunteers hang in midair, or have scorpions placed on their head, or gulp down a cup of chunky milk and insects. You may look through your fingers, but you'll look. For the best time pick a favorite contestant and cheer for him or her, or even better, sit down front and volunteer to pelt them with foam balls or splash them with water cannons.

Based on the now-cancelled NBC television series "Fear Factor," this attraction uses park volunteers as contestants in a variety of stunts inspired by the show, both difficult physical feats and ick-inducing "food challenges." The winner of a "Guess What's Crawling to Dinner" contest gets a cheap plastic mug that reads "I Ate a Bug."

Tips. *When to go:* Go to any of the shows; the auditorium does not fill up. *Where to sit:* Near the front row to see the stunts close up, or if you want to be picked to pelt people. *For families:* Consider not bringing children under age 10 or so; it could disturb them seeing scorpions crawl on a volunteer's head, or watch another volunteer drink a disgusting brew; the show is surely too intense for toddlers. *If you're female:* Think twice about volunteering; the first challenge requires a great deal of upper-body strength which eliminates most women; nearly the only time one makes it to the second round is when there are more than two female contestants.

To be in the show. Contestant casting takes place 70 minutes before each show at a kiosk in front of the stadium. Volunteers must weigh at least 110 pounds and be at least 18 years old (a photo ID is required), or at least 16 to compete in the Food Challenge with a supervising adult's consent.

Key facts. *Duration:* 25 minutes. *Showtimes:* Scheduled; typically 4 afternoon performances. *Capacity:* 1,400. *Access:* Assistive listening available; service animals allowed. *Fear factor:* The show includes loud noises, sudden sound effects and intense and atypical ingestion that some may find discomforting. *Queue:* Outdoor, partially covered. *Debuted:* 2005. *Location:* World Expo.

The conductor and shrunken head of London's Knight Bus greet visitors outside Diagon Alley.

London's King's Cross Station sits outside Diagon Alley.

The Hogwarts Express — King's Cross Station

Filled with detail, a magical train takes you to Hogsmeade

★★★★★ ✓ *EXPRESS* It's dreamlike riding the Hogwarts Express—it's as if you are transported directly into the Harry Potter series. The train itself looks absolutely right, from the clouds of steam pouring from its smokestack to the scuffed, worn-looking red color, to the coal stored in the car behind the engine. It sounds right, too, with its "Toot! Toot!" before departing. Inside, the cozy 8-person compartments have just the right slightly old-fashioned look; the cabin walls decorated with drawings of foreign wizarding schools.

King's Cross Station. You get to the train by entering a replica of King's Cross, a famed train depot in London. It sits to the left of the hidden gateway to Diagon Alley itself, next to the park's San Francisco area. After showing your ticket (either a two-park ticket or annual pass), you enter what seems to be the real station itself—everything from its musicians to its posters to its little snack stand is spot on. As every Harry Potter fan knows, students board the Hogwarts Express from Platform 9 3/4, a secret passageway that appears to muggles as a solid brick wall. It's here too; thanks to a convincing optical illusion you'll see the people in front of you walking straight through it. Once you're through and in the magical world, you pass a pile of luggage that includes a cage holding a hooting Hedwig, Harry's snowy owl—and then wait a few minutes to board the train.

On the train. *Warning; spoilers ahead.* Once onboard you'll sit in a cabin with a handful of other riders; little touches like clouds of steam rising outside its window

Average wait times

9am	10am	11am	Noon	1pm	2pm	3pm	4pm	5pm	6pm	7pm	8pm	9pm
10m	15m	15m	20m	20m	20m	25m	25m	35m	25m	15m	15m	5m

© Universal Orlando Resort

Ready for boarding, the Hogwarts Express sits at hidden platform 9 3/4.

make it seem totally real. Once underway you'll see and hear things on both sides of you—through the window on one side as well as a frosted glass door on the other; though you can't tell it at first both are really video screens.

Outside the train. The window shows you what the train is passing on its journey, first the streets of London, alongside a small brown owl carrying a Hogwarts letter, then the magical sights and notable landmarks from the series. Stormy skies surround foreboding Malfoy Manor. Hagrid pulls alongside the train in his flying motorcycle; fire spurts from its exhaust. As you travel through the Forbidden Forest, a flying Ford Anglia makes a bit of a crash landing. Since the train is actually moving all the illusions are especially convincing. As you approach Hogwarts castle, silvery merpeople swim just under the surface of the Black Lake. As the train begins to slow, Hagrid waves you into Hogsmeade station, Fang at his side.

Inside the train. Periodically during your journey, you also see things through the frosted glass doors. In silhouette appear Harry, Hermione, and Ron. They chat. A spooky dementor threatens to enter your cabin, its handprint leaving a chilled impression on the glass; it's chased off by Harry's glowing Patronus. Spiders crawling over the

door freak out Ron before he realizes they're licorice and eats one.

Tips. *When to go:* Lines are shortest in the morning and late afternoon. *Where to sit:* In the middle of a seat, so you can clearly see the window and the frosted glass door.

Fun finds. ❶ Dark trails of apparating Death Eaters soar over the rooftops of London after the post owl flies past. **❷** When passing through the thunderstorm at Malfoy Manor, you can hear rain pattering on the train's roof. **❸** Just past Malfoy Manor, a flock of birds forms the shape of a skull during a flash of lightning. **❹** During the dementor attack, the cabin's lights flicker out and the air becomes chilly. **❺** As the train comes to a stop, Hagrid calls out to Hogwarts first years. **❻** An invisible thestral is tethered to a Hogwarts carriage parked along the exit walkway. The carriage rocks and shifts with the movements of the winged horse.

Key facts. *Duration:* 7 minutes. *Capacity:* 168; 3 train cars each with 7 compartments which hold 8 people. *Access:* Service animals allowed. *Fear factor:* Loud noises, threatening villain. *Queue:* Indoor. *Debuted:* 2014. *Location:* Diagon Alley; travels one-way to Hogsmeade at Islands of Adventure.

Health advisory. Universal recommends you avoid the train if you have issues with enclosed spaces or fog effects.

Breathing fire, an escaped dragon from Gringotts Bank perches on its roof.

© Universal Orlando Resort

The lobby of Gringotts Bank, ready for you to open an account.

Harry Potter and the Escape from Gringotts

Break-though tech and storytelling raise the theme-park bar

★★★★★ ✔ This full-throttle adventure ride thrusts you in the middle of Harry Potter's dangerous world. You're surrounded by menace—from thuggish security trolls to an escaped fire-breathing dragon to Voldemort himself, who's backed up by his second-in-command, Death Eater Bellatrix Lestrange. The centerpiece of Diagon Alley, the ride blends the thrill of a modern dark coaster with a particular event in the Potter story, using motion-based ride carts with detailed environments, immersive 3-D screens and additional special effects. Fun and exhilarating without being terrifying, it sharply turns and twists but has no steep drops and never goes upside down. Less intense than Harry Potter and the Forbidden Journey at Islands of Adventure, it's more family-friendly.

The ride takes place in the middle of the seventh book, "Harry Potter and the Deathly Hallows," when Harry, Ron and Hermione infiltrate Gringotts to steal a Horcrux from Lestrange's bank vault, which will help them destroy Lord Voldemort. In the book and movie, you experience these events from the point-of-view of Harry and his gang. But here you witness them as an outsider, one who happens to be opening an account at Gringotts at precisely the same time.

Gringotts Bank. The 60-foot-tall bank towers over Diagon Alley and is topped with a massive fire-breathing dragon who has already escaped the vault. On the inside, the main hall looks just like a major bank should, resplendent with tall ceilings, marble columns and crystal chandeliers. Over a dozen

Average wait times

9am	10am	11am	Noon	1pm	2pm	3pm	4pm	5pm	6pm	7pm	8pm	9pm
10m	25m	25m	20m	35m	35m	20m	20m	45m	35m	25m	25m	10m

Animatronic goblin tellers look up at you occasionally and make eye contact.

animatronic goblins work on paperwork with feather quills, occasionally glancing up and making eye contact with you.

You continue past some vaults and enter a security area. Here you get your photo taken for your "Gringotts ID," a souvenir you can buy after the ride either as a traditional photo or as an actual plasticized ID you wear around your neck.

How 'bout a tour? You then step into Bill Weasley's office. After a bit of clowning around, he offers to take you on a tour of the vaults with Blordak the goblin. You board a lift that takes you miles underground, to the tour's boarding area. Between the compartment's creaking and rattling and the views of the cavern through overhead windows, the illusion is believable. Grabbing your 3-D glasses, you climb a curved staircase to the cave-like boarding area, surrounded by stalagmites and stalactites. Clambering into a rickety cart, you're ready for your tour.

A leery Lestrange. *Warning; spoilers ahead.* Once the ride begins, Bill and Blordak offer to show you to your new vault. But then Bellatrix Lestrange shows up and accuses you of trying to rob her. She thinks you're in cahoots with Harry and his friends, who are trying to do exactly that. A blast from her wand sends you off on a chaotic trip through the depths of the Gringotts vaults. Though

Bill scrambles to keep you safe, during your careening cart ride you encounter one danger after another, including You-Know-Who himself. All the while, Harry, Ron and Hermione fight to get into Lestrange's vault and retrieve the Horcrux. In the end, they flee from the bank on the back of an escaped dragon, pausing to rescue you from Bellatrix and Voldemort just in the nick of time.

The special effects are striking. From the black plumes of smoke that Voldemort and Bellatrix apparate on to the balls of fire from the dragon, it all seems real. You feel heat of the dragon's breath and a mist of water when Bill stops the flames with a watery shield.

How best to experience it. Go through the regular line at least once; it sets up the plot of the ride and includes the lift that takes you down into the bowels of Gringotts where the tour begins. If you want to go again, take the Single Rider Line; while it's usually significantly quicker, it also skips nearly all of the queue, including the little preshow and the lift. Be warned that there can be a line even there, and the lack of things to look at can make the wait tedious.

Tips. *When to go:* First thing in the morning or after dark; the detailed Standby queue won't be too crowded. *Where to sit:* In the front row for the best view of Voldemort, Bellatrix and the murderous security trolls;

Supposedly nine miles under the bank, carts await to take visitors on a tour of its vaults.

© Universal Orlando Resort

in the back of the second car to experience a bigger drop at the beginning and more stimulating 3-D effects; the seats are positioned higher the farther back they are, so the view problem is mitigated somewhat; if you sit on the far left or right, try not to turn your head too far to the side; the face-level walls of the cart can easily smack your nose or forehead against the metal. *If you're scared of snakes:* Don't sit in the front; Voldemort's huge pet snake Nagini strikes directly at that row.

Fun finds. ❶ In the outdoor queue, a Gringotts cart in need of repairs sits behind a fence; one of its wheels is missing. On top is a goblin-sized seat and levers that control its mechanisms. ❷ Just inside the bank on the left wall, a poem serves as a threat to thieves: "Enter, stranger, but take heed of what awaits the sin of greed. For those who take, but do not earn must pay most dearly in their turn. So if you seek beneath our floors a treasure that was never yours, thief you have been warned, beware of finding more than treasure there." ❸ Banners proclaim

Gringotts the safest place in the wizarding world. ❹ In the main lobby, small carts hold sacks of coins and gold bars. ❺ A goblin at the end of the hall asks people in line if they've come there to open an account. ❻ A talking portrait of Gringott himself speaks to people at the end of the hall. ❼ At the bank's security offices, low-security vaults are behind a gate on the right. ❽ Elaborate mechanics cover the back of an open vault door. ❾ A wagon filled with gold bars sits in front of the vaults. ❿ Issues of the Daily Prophet with moving photos lay on wooden tables; headlines call for the capture of "Undesirable Number 1" (Harry), claim that Dumbledore's posthumous secrets have been revealed, announce Snape's new position as Hogwarts headmaster and warn of a mass breakout from Azkaban prison. ⓫ Scattered among the newspapers are Umbridge's Naziesque "Mudbloods and the Dangers They Pose to a Peaceful Pure-Blood Society" pamphlets. ⓬ Shadows of Harry, Ron, Hermione, and the goblins Griphook and Bogrod stop in

See Harry, Ron and Hermione? They're on the dragon's back. Bill Weasley protects you.

front of one window and discuss their plans to break into Bellatrix's vault. ⓭ Hermione has taken Polyjuice Potion to pass as Bellatrix Lestrange; Ron has had his face features altered to disguise his identity; Harry and Griphook hide under the Invisibility Cloak. ⓮ Bogrod tags along blearily; Harry is controlling him using the Imperius Curse so that they can access the vaults. ⓯ Names of goblins who work at the bank are printed on the office doors you pass; they include Griphook, Bogrod and Blordak. ⓰ Three sets of goblin armor stand at the end of the hall. ⓱ In Bill's office, a framed photo on a table shows the Weasley family on their summer trip to Egypt. ⓲ Another photo from the same trip shows Bill admiring an owl-faced urn. ⓳ Towers of messy filing cabinets form the walls. ⓴ An Anubis-faced sarcophagus tucks into the back right corner. ㉑ In the lift waiting area, people in its safety video wear appropriate wizarding clothing. ㉒ A portrait of a goblin recites the ride's safety information. When he gets to its height minimum he says "You must be 42 inches to ride... unless you are a goblin." ㉓ A marker above the lift doors has ticks labeled "Deep," "Deeper," "Extraordinarily Deep," "Even Deeper Again" and "Bottom"; the lowest marker is 9 miles down. ㉔ A transom at the top of the lift has a view of the stone cavern and the adjacent elevator shafts. ㉕ A dragon roars in the distance just before the exit doors open. ㉖ On the ride itself, when they first appear Harry and the gang are soaking wet, having passed through the Thieves' Downfall. ㉗ As you rush out of the magma-filled cavern Harry shouts "Hermione, let them go!" She yells "Relashio!" to disconnect your vehicle from the dragon's chain. ㉘ At the attraction's exit, souvenir ride photos are topped with text that reads "Gringotts Bank. Registered with the Consortium of Goblinary Finance & Red-Nosed Wizard Inventors."

Key facts. *Duration:* 5 minutes. *Capacity:* 96; 8 12-seat ride vehicles, each with 3 4-seat rows. *Height minimum:* 42 inches. *Access:* Single Rider Line, Rider Swap, test seats available. *Restraint:* Lap bar. *Restricted items:* All personal belongings must be kept in pockets including cameras and phones; no bags; locker use provided. *Fear factor:* Threatening villains, some frightening segments but no jump scares. *Queue:* Indoor, overflows into a shaded outdoor area. *Debuted:* 2014. *Location:* Diagon Alley.

Health advisory. Universal recommends you avoid the ride if you are pregnant or have heart conditions; abnormal blood pressure; back or neck conditions; issues with dizziness, enclosed spaces, motion sickness or strobe effects; or recently had surgery.

© Universal Orlando Resort

A puppet of Death gestures to the audience in "The Tale of Three Brothers."

Diagon Alley live shows

One dynamite singing group, two moving puppet shows

★★★★★ ✓ Two terrific but very different live shows take place on an outdoor stage in Diagon Alley's Carkitt Market. Taking turns on the stage are Celestina Warbeck and the Banshees, a musical group that belts out upbeat, jazzy songs, and members of The Wizarding Academy of Dramatic Arts, which use sophisticated puppetry to re-enact classic wizarding fables from the book "The Tales of Beedle the Bard."

Celestina Warbeck and the Banshees. Barely mentioned in the Harry Potter books, Celestina Warbeck is Mrs. Weasley's favorite singer, the popular Singing Sorceress of "The Witching Hour," a radio program on the Wizarding Wireless Network. Author J.K. Rowling based her on Shirley Bassey, a Welsh jazz singer best known in the United States for the 1964 hit "Goldfinger," the title tune of a James Bond movie. When Universal wanted to bring the diva to life, it chose Broadway composers Alan Zachary and Michael Weiner to write her songs.

So the "witch who's always on pitch" was born, along with tunes such as "You Stole My Cauldron But You Can't Steal My Heart,"

"A Cauldron Full of Hot Strong Love" and "You Charmed the Heart Right Out of Me." Another number supports the Puddlemere United Quidditch team: "Beat Back Those Bludgers, Boys, and Chuck That Quaffle Here." The sparkly star commands the stage as she knocks out the tunes; her saucy backup singers add choreographed routines and spend some time up on a balcony. They also enter the audience. A man from the crowd often ends up on stage with the group, dancing with them in a chorus line, a feather boa draped around his neck.

The Tales of Beedle the Bard. The second show features a quartet of puppeteers from the Wizarding Academy of Dramatic Arts, which act out stories from the wizarding world akin to Aesop's fables. The troupe engages in some comedic foreplay before performing either "The Fountain of Fair Fortune" or "The Tale of Three Brothers." The actors use evocative hand-held puppets and masks to create a serious tone.

"The Tale of Three Brothers" explains the mysterious origins of the Deathly Hallows, three powerful objects created by Death and

'Oh come and stir my cauldron... and if you do it right... I'll boil you up some hot, strong love... to keep you warm tonight!' Sultry stuff from Celestina Warbeck and the Banshees.

given to three brothers. "The Fountain of Fair Fortune" tells of the quest of three witches to acquire something they each desire most. Its moral: Magic is not the path to happiness, it comes from resources inside you.

Key facts. *Duration:* Both shows are 12–15 minutes. *Showtimes:* Celestina Warbeck and the Banshees typically 1:30 p.m., 2:30 p.m., 3:30 p.m., 5 p.m., 6 p.m., 7 p.m.; The Tales of Beedle the Bard typically 10:30 a.m., 11:30 a.m., 12:30 p.m., 2 p.m., 3 p.m., 4 p.m. *Access:* Service animals allowed. *Fear factor:* The Death puppet has an ominous appearance. *Debuted:* 2014. *Location:* Diagon Alley.

Who lives in a pineapple under the sea? As if you don't know.

Universal's Superstar Parade

Four-float procession is geared to children

★★★ This sweet little parade is proudly child-centric, with each of its four segments focused on an animated movie or television show. It's not the most elaborate procession you'll ever see, but a couple of its segments have a lot to them. Often it's led by park mascot Woody Woodpecker and his girlfriend Winnie.

The first float unit celebrates the 2010 film "Despicable Me." It includes the wildly oversized industrial-steel vehicle of Gru and the sleek orange-and-white one of his arch-enemy Vector, as well as the tiny one of two Minions who, just like in the movie, have disguised themselves as husband-wife-and-baby humans. Gru's daughters Margo, Edith and Agnes ride with him.

Roller-skating fish lead the next float, the pineapple home of SpongeBob SquarePants. Silly starfish Patrick and stern octopus Squidward ride with the ever-smiling sponge.

Rolling in third is an elaborate shout-out to the 2011 Easter-themed movie "Hop." Teenage rabbit E.B. plays drums atop the float, surrounded by his dad the Easter Bunny, baby chicks Carlos and Phil and a squad of bunny bodyguards called the Pink Berets.

The final segment is a jungle treehouse for Dora the Explorer and her cousin Diego. Monkey friend Boots is along for the ride, as is Dora's talking purple backpack. On the float swinging monkeys hang from vines; Diego's friend Jaguar brings up the rear.

Tip. The parade stops twice for its entertainers to perform choreographed routines, once centered on 5th Avenue in front of Revenge of the Mummy, once stretched out on Hollywood Boulevard. Most lively are the "Despicable Me" and "Hop" segments, the former has human-Minion dancers, the latter an enthusiastic drum line, dancing candy girls and acrobats on pogo sticks. To nab a good viewing spot in these areas show up at least 20 minutes early.

Key facts. *Duration:* 10 minutes. *Step-off:* Typically 5 p.m. *Cancelled by:* Rain or the presence of lightning. *Access:* Service animals allowed; reserved viewing areas for people with disabilities and character-breakfast diners. *Debuted:* 2012. *Route:* Enters at Mel's Drive-In, circles New York and Production Central; returns on Hollywood Boulevard.

See also **Characters.**

Fountains, fireworks, water screens, and so many film clips you'll read our history chapter.

Universal's Cinematic Spectacular: 100 Years of Movie Memories

The country's oldest film studio celebrates itself

★★★★ It's not the fireworks. Not the colorful fountains that sync with them, nor the colorful laser beams that sync with the fountains. It's not even the giant waterfall screens, although the little preshow they do is pretty cool. No, the undisputed stars of this nighttime spectacular are its dozens upon dozens of film clips, a video scrapbook of Universal Pictures' century of movie-making that's projected onto those waterfalls. Film buffs will be delighted, even though some of the clips get a little too watery to see.

The clips are grouped into five categories—Heroes (including "Erin Brockovich" and "Spartacus"); Horror ("Dracula," "Jaws"), Laughter ("American Pie," "Harvey"), Good vs. Evil ("Gladiator," "Snow White and the Huntsman") and Triumph ("A Beautiful Mind," "To Kill a Mockingbird.") Each is short; there are many, many more than the ones mentioned here.

Fireworks launch from several locations; screens of mist emerge periodically. A narration by Morgan Freeman ties it all together.

Dinner package. Lombard's Seafood Grille offers a meal-and-viewing-spot combo, which incudes access to a dessert buffet on its waterfront deck. Expect to pay about $45 for adults, $13 for children. Reservations are required; call 407-224-3663 for information.

Tips. *When to go:* Show up 15 to 30 minutes before the show for a good spot. *Where to watch:* From Central Park, in a semi-circular area that arcs out in the water.

Fun finds. ❶ The fountains and lasers turn red when the stabbing scene begins in the "Psycho" clip. ❷ In the "Blues Brothers" clip, fireworks immediately shoot off after Jake says "Hit it!"

Key facts. *Duration:* 18 minutes. *Cancelled by:* Rain or the presence of lightning. *Showtimes:* Scheduled; time varies; typically one show at closing time. *Access:* Service animals allowed. *Fear factor:* The experience includes threatening villains in movie clips from movies such as "Halloween," "Psycho," "The Birds," "The Silence of the Lambs." *Debuted:* 2012. *Location:* Universal Studios lagoon.

Islands of Adventure

FANS OF THRILL RIDES love this doughnut-shaped park, which holds a collection of mostly outdoor attractions designed to take your breath away. Two intense high-speed roller coasters hurl you upside down; a smaller coaster provides a more moderate but still exhilarating experience. You get splashed—and sometimes soaked—on three rollicking water rides. A drop tower attraction launches you 150 feet in the air in less than 3 seconds. Spider-Man rescues you from his arch-enemies in an award-winning 3-D adventure. A groundbreaking combination ride and simulator whips you through and above Hogwarts castle.

The park, which circles a large central lagoon, immerses you in the worlds of comic books, vintage cartoon strips, Jurassic Park, Harry Potter and wacky Dr. Seuss. Two table-service restaurants, five cafeteria-style eateries, and more than a dozen fast-food spots hold nearly 3,500 seats; more than 20 snack carts line the park's walkways.

Best of the park. Although known for its thrill rides, Islands of Adventure outdoes itself in its experiences for children. Nine varied attractions cater to kids, including three playgrounds and a flying ride that adults can't experience on their own.

Rides, rides, rides. They make up 17 of the 25 attractions at the park. That compares with sister park Universal Studios, which has 24 attractions but only 10 rides. These mostly outdoor attractions run the gamut from roller coasters and log flumes to drop towers and 3-D adventures.

Marvel Super Hero Island. This area immerses you in the colorful, in-your-face world of comic book villains and heroes. Oversized melodramatic 2-D graphics of Marvel characters decorate its storefronts and restaurants; live versions of the same stars hold meet-and-greets in the street. Dozens of references to the Marvel universe hide in plain sight. Some of the best attractions in the park live here, including The

Amazing Adventures of Spider-Man and the Incredible Hulk Coaster.

Best rides and shows. *Best outdoor rides:* The Incredible Hulk and Flight of the Hippogriff coasters. *Best indoor rides:* The Amazing Adventures of Spider-Man and Harry Potter and the Forbidden Journey. *Best show:* The Frog Choir.

Hidden gems. The Marvel Super Hero Island Easter-egg-type references. The unpredictable Raptor Encounter. For kids, the spitting dilophosaur water cannons and Pteranodon Flyers ride at Camp Jurassic, and naming a baby (animatronic) velociraptor at the Jurassic Park Discovery Center.

Compared to Universal Studios Florida. Islands of Adventure has more water rides and outdoor attractions, including two roller coasters that go upside down, and has better attractions for toddlers. However it has a smaller Harry Potter area, few live performers, and no parade or fireworks.

Attractions at a glance. Here's a summary of the park's rides and shows, rated from one to five stars (★) based on how well they live up to their promise (not how they compare to each other). The authors' top choices have a checkmark (✔).

The Amazing Adventures of Spider-Man. ★★★★★ ✔ Motion simulator travels through scenes; screens portray battle with Spidey's enemies. *Marvel Super Hero Island.*

Camp Jurassic and Pteranodon Flyers. ★★★★★ ✔ Expansive playground with soaring treetop-level ride for kids. *Jurassic Park.*

Caro-Seuss-el. ★★★★ Merry-go-round with Seuss-inspired creatures instead of horses. *Seuss Landing.*

The Cat in the Hat. ★★★★ ✔ Indoor dark ride through a re-creation of Dr. Seuss's book. *Seuss Landing.*

Doctor Doom's Fearfall. ★★★★ Drop-tower ride hurls riders 150 feet high. *Marvel Super Hero Island.*

Dragon Challenge. ★★★ High-speed roller coaster has two tracks with different experiences. *Hogsmeade.*

Dudley Do-Right's Ripsaw Falls. ★★★ Log-flume ride through cartoon landscape. *Toon Lagoon.*

The Eighth Voyage of Sindbad Stunt Show. ★★★ Performers duke it out in this live show. *The Lost Continent.*

Flight of the Hippogriff. ★★★★★ ✔ Fun but short roller coaster twists past Hagrid's hut. *Hogsmeade.*

Harry Potter and the Forbidden Journey. ★★★★★ ✔ High-tech, intense ride through Hogwarts castle and grounds. *Hogsmeade.*

The High in the Sky Seuss Trolley Train. ★★★ Tour above Seuss Landing, set to Seussian narration. *Seuss Landing.*

Hogsmeade Stage. ★★★★ Hosts two live shows, including an a cappella quartet and a dancing and acrobatic display. *Hogsmeade.*

Hogwarts Express—Hogsmeade. ★★★★ Train ride to Diagon Alley in the Universal Studios Florida theme park (requires two-park ticket). *Hogsmeade.*

If I Ran the Zoo. ★★★ Small play area has water-play zone, interactive elements. *Seuss Landing.*

The Incredible Hulk Coaster. ★★★★★ ✔ High-speed roller coaster re-creates Hulk's transformation. *Marvel Super Hero Island.*

Jurassic Park Discovery Center. ★★★ Indoor hands-on dinosaur education area. *Jurassic Park.*

Jurassic Park River Adventure. ★★★★ Thrilling raft ride past menacing dinosaurs and down an 85-foot drop. *Jurassic Park.*

Me Ship, The Olive. ★★★ Three-level playground is on Popeye's boat. *Toon Lagoon.*

Oh! The Stories You'll Hear. ★★★ Dr. Seuss characters star in an upbeat song-and-dance routine then a short, sweet reading of a Seuss story. *Seuss Landing.*

One Fish, Two Fish, Red Fish, Blue Fish. ★★★★ Hub-and-spoke ride squirts water at riders in colorful fish. *Seuss Landing.*

Popeye & Bluto's Bilge-Rat Barges. ★★★★ Churning white-water raft ride as Popeye rescues Olive Oyl. *Toon Lagoon.*

Poseidon's Fury. ★★★ Walk-through effects show in a temple. *The Lost Continent.*

NEW! Skull Island: Reign of Kong. ★★★★★ ✔ King Kong saves you from prehistoric predators in this high-tech 3-D truck ride. *Between Toon Lagoon and Jurassic Park.*

Storm Force Accelatron. ★★★ Round spinning seats help Storm defeat Magneto. *Marvel Super Hero Island.*

Street performers. There aren't many, but they're easy to meet.

Port of Entry stiltwalkers. ✔ An exotic guy and girl wander. *20-min. appearances.*

Hogwarts Express conductor. ✔ He happily answers questions and poses for photos in front of a full-size replica of the Hogwarts Express scarlet engine, which rumbles clouds of steam just inside the Hogsmeade gate. *Hogsmeade. Continual appearances.*

See all the forks? The egg-cup lamps? Whimsical Seuss Landing is filled with fun touches.

Restaurants. A summary of the park's full-service and counter-service restaurants (book full-service tables at opentable.com):

Backwater Bar. Full bar has Seagram's whiskey, other Seagram's products. Connects to Confisco Grille. *Port of Entry. Opens 11:30 a.m. Seats 46.*

Ben & Jerry's. ✓ Small window offers quality hand-scooped ice-cream. *Marvel Super Hero Island. Opens 11 a.m. $4–$6. No seats.*

Blondie's. Sub sandwiches. *Toon Lagoon. 11 a.m.–3 p.m. $6–$9. Seats 40.*

The Burger Digs. Burgers, chicken sandwiches, Gardenburgers. *Jurassic Park. Opens 11 a.m. $9–$17 (children $7). Seats 168, 124 outside on a covered patio.*

Café 4. Jumbo pizza slices, subs, salads. In the Baxter Building, headquarters and lab of the Fantastic Four. *Marvel Super Hero Island. Opens 11 a.m. $8–$13, $30–$33 for whole pies. Seats 140, 60 outside on a covered patio.*

Captain America Diner. Cheeseburgers, chicken, chicken salads. *Marvel Super Hero Island. 11 a.m.–3 p.m. $7–$11. Seats 140, 16 outside. Open seasonally.*

Cathy's Ice Cream. ✓ Outdoor counter has Ben & Jerry's shakes, sundaes, waffle cones. *Toon Lagoon. Opens 11 a.m. $4–$6. No seats.*

Cinnabon. Cinnamon rolls. *Port of Entry. Park open to a half hour after park close. $4–$6. Seats 40 outside.*

Circus McGurkus Café Stoo-pendous. Fried chicken, spaghetti, pizza. Resembles a circus tent. Booths surround the circular dining room. *Seuss Landing. 11 a.m.–4 p.m. $8–$15 (children $7). Seats 260, 64 outside.*

Comic Strip Café. Fried chicken, fish & chips, hot dogs, pizza. *Toon Lagoon. Opens 11 a.m. $8–$13. Seats 168, 176 outside.*

Confisco Grille. ✓ Why "Confisco"? Because it has confiscated dishes from all around the world, with Asian, Italian, Mexican, Greek as well as American dishes. The huge variety makes it a good choice for groups with a broad range of tastes. Try the house specialty pad thai; it's creamy and generous. Complimentary flatbread comes with a sun-dried tomato spread. A Moroccan-inspired decor has arches, tile floors and big wooden beams. Ask for a booth along the back wall. *Port of Entry. Opens 11 a.m. $9–$20 (children $7). Seats 198, 58 outside.*

Croissant Moon Bakery. ✓ Deli sandwiches, paninis, pastries. Serves Lavazza, an Italian coffee. *Port of Entry. Opens 8:30 a.m. $3–$12 (children $7). Seats 20.*

Doc Sugrue's Desert Kebab House. ✓ Outdoor stand. Fresh, tasty sticks of tender grilled meat and tomatoes rest in pita bread with lettuce, gyro sauce. Also Greek salads, hummus. *The Lost Continent. Opens 9 a.m. $4–$12. Seats 36 outside on a covered patio.*

Fire Eater's Grill. ✔ Outdoor stand. Gyros, chicken, hot dogs, salads. *The Lost Continent. 10 a.m.–5 p.m. $5–$12. Seats 48 outside.*

Green Eggs and Ham Café. ✔ Outdoor stand. Green eggs and ham sandwiches, burgers. *Seuss Landing. Hours vary. $5–$11. Seats 44 outside. Open seasonally.*

The Hog's Head. ✔ This full-service bar is tucked in a dark corner of The Three Broomsticks, with a separate entrance of its own. It serves Hog's Head Brew (a light, malty Scottish ale brewed exclusively for the pub hand-picked by J.K. Rowling) and seven British beers, including Boddingtons and London Pride. Stronger is cinnamon-flavored firewhiskey, a drink unique to Universal parks. Butterbeer is here, too, served cold, frozen or hot. During busy lunchtimes most of the pub's seats are used by the restaurant. *Hogsmeade. Opens 10 a.m. $7–$14. Seats 36.*

Hop On Pop Ice Cream Shop. Outdoor counter. Ice cream bars, waffle cones. *Seuss Landing. Hours vary. $4–$6. No seats.*

Lost Continent hot dog stand. Foot-long dogs, daiquiris, draft beer. *The Lost Continent. Hours vary. $3–$12. Seats 24 outside.*

Moose Juice, Goose Juice. Juice, frozen juice, hot dogs and cookies. *Seuss Landing. Opens 10 a.m. $2–$10. No seats, but room for 16 on outdoor benches.*

Mythos Restaurant. The park's most formal table-service restaurant. Steaks, seafood, sandwiches, pasta. Complimentary Pugliese bread, which is heavy-bodied with a crispy crust; served with molded butter. Plaster ceiling and walls combine with a concrete floor to amplify sounds, making the dining area noisy. *The Lost Continent. Opens 11 a.m. $12–$20 (children $7). Seats 100, 36 outside overlooking a lagoon.*

Pizza Predattoria. Outdoor stand. Pizza, subs, salads. *Jurassic Park. Opens 11 a.m. $8–$13. Seats 152 at umbrella-covered tables.*

Starbucks. Coffees, pastries. *Port of Entry. Park open to a half hour after park close. $4–$7. Seats 7, 40 outside.*

The Three Broomsticks. ✔ Tall, sharply angled ceilings and winding wooden staircases powerfully recall the world of Harry Potter at this rustic restaurant, the only one in Hogsmeade. Best for breakfast are pancakes or the English platter with baked beans and black pudding (an acquired taste). Luscious desserts include a whipped butterscotch pudding, a pot-pie-like apple pie and a rich chocolate trifle. This popular eatery serves as many as 30,000 people a day; avoid it between noon and 3 p.m. when the wait creates a long switchback line of up to 40 minutes or so. For most of the day diners can't hold tables. If it is crowded consider the outdoor patio, which has a stone floor and wood tables; at night it's lit by lanterns. Look into the shaded water for 200 big purple-gilled tilapia ("Harry Potter piranha") that everyone feeds. If Jack greets you in front of the restaurant, tell him you saw his name in this book and watch him smile. *Hogsmeade. Opens 8:45 a.m.; lunch starts at 10:30 a.m. Breakfast $16 (children $12), lunch and dinner $9–$16 (children $7). Seats 350, 150 outside on the back deck under umbrellas.*

Thunder Falls Terrace. ✔ Try the tasty, not-too-wet rotisserie chicken at this classy food court which also offers smoked turkey legs, barbecue ribs, soups and salads. Side dishes include corn on the cob and potatoes seasoned with rosemary. Two circular seating areas have tall ceilings lined with logs. Windows overlook the splashdown of the Jurassic Park River Adventure next door. *Jurassic Park. 11 a.m.–4 p.m. $10–$16 (children $7). Seats 280, 32 outside with umbrellas.*

The Watering Hole. Outdoor stand. Full bar, hot dogs, nachos, wings. *Jurassic Park. Opens 11 a.m. $3–$10. Seats 24, covered tables.*

Wimpy's. Double cheeseburgers, chicken, chili dogs. Three shady tables overlook floating riders on Popeye & Bluto's Bilge-Rat Barges. *Toon Lagoon. Hours vary. $7–$12. Seats 56 outside. Open seasonally.*

Shops. Psychic readings? That's just one of the unusual things you can buy at Islands of Adventure, which has many unique shops:

All the Books You Can Read. ✔ Dr. Seuss books, apparel, toys and DVDs. Kids coloring table. *Seuss Landing.*

Amazing Pictures. Magazine covers that can have your portrait incorporated. Open-air shop. *Marvel Super Hero Island.*

Betty Boop Store. ✔ Betty Boop-inspired apparel, collectibles, toys. *Toon Lagoon.*

Cats, Hats & Things. Cat in the Hat themed merchandise, child and baby apparel. At the exit to The Cat in the Hat ride. *Seuss Landing.*

The Coin Mint. Metal coins, medallions forged and struck on-site using your chosen design. The coin-master bangs a gong after each cast. Open-air shop. *The Lost Continent.*

Comic Book Shop. ✔ Comic books, graphic novels, collectibles. *Marvel Super Hero Island.*

DeFoto's Expedition Photography. Film, camera needs. The park's photo pick-up location. *Port of Entry.*

Toon Lagoon shops stock items based on vintage cartoons and Sunday comics.

Dervish and Banges. ✔ This all-purpose Harry Potter store sells a variety of apparel, books, robes, the Quibbler complete with Spectrespecs, toys and wands. It's connected to Ollivanders and the Owl Post. *Hogsmeade.*

Dinostore. ✔ Dinosaur-themed apparel, books, toys, fossil replicas; amber jewelry. Jurassic Park items. *Jurassic Park.*

Filch's Emporium of Confiscated Goods. Accessories, apparel, toys. All of the items are supposedly various goods taken from students over the years by grumpy Mr. Filch, the Hogwarts caretaker. At the exit of Harry Potter and the Forbidden Journey, inside Hogwarts castle. *Hogsmeade.*

Gasoline Alley. Beach bags, towels, collectible license plates. *Toon Lagoon.*

Historic Families Heraldry. Family coat of arms keepsakes, collectibles. Open-air shop. *The Lost Continent.*

Hogsmeade cart. Personalized Wizarding World keychains, pins, lanyards. *Hogsmeade.*

Honeydukes. ✔ This candy shop next to The Three Broomsticks sells sweets from the Harry Potter world, such as Bertie Bott's Every Flavour Beans, Chocolate Frogs, Lemon Drops (Dumbledore's favorite), Pepper Imps and Sugar Quills. A bakery counter offers caramel apples, fudge and other treats. What looks like Zonko's is actually the exit to Honeydukes. *Hogsmeade.*

Islands of Adventure Trading Company. ✔ The park's largest general merchandise store. Comfortable, often calm. *Port of Entry.*

Island Market and Export. Backpacks, handbags, pajamas, UPixel station, candy counter. *Port of Entry.*

Jurassic Outfitters. Jurassic Park merchandise. The Jurassic Park River Adventure exits here. *Jurassic Park.*

Kingpin's Arcade. Arcade and video games. *Marvel Super Hero Island.*

Local Articles Boutique. ✔ Three dozen local artists display and sell handmade art, vintage jewelry; "rescued vintage" clothing. Worth a look. *The Lost Continent.*

Lucky Eye Jewelry Stand. Items with the "lucky eye" glass bead, a symbol of circles that resemble an eye. *The Lost Continent.*

Marvel Alterniverse Store. Marvel character apparel, costumes, toys. Spider-Man poses for photos. *Marvel Super Hero Island.*

Mulberry Street Store. Adult, child and baby apparel. Seussian artwork, some for thousands of dollars. *Seuss Landing.*

Oakley. Oakley sunglasses, watches, sandals. *Marvel Super Hero Island.*

Ocean Traders. Exotic apparel, accessories, artwork. Open-air shop. *Port of Entry.*

Ollivanders. Many wand replicas from Harry Potter characters, 13 wands based on the Celtic calendar. Some cast spells (trigger special effects) throughout both Hogsmeade and Diagon Alley. *Hogsmeade.*

The Owl Post. ✔ Small shop sells writing quills, stationery and owl-related toys as well as exclusive postage stamps showing either Hogwarts castle or the Hogwarts Express. If you mail a postcard or letter from here it will have a Hogsmeade postmark; the witch or wizard posting your mail hands it off to Errol, Pigwidgeon or whichever owl is up next for delivery. *Hogsmeade.*

The Pearl Factory. Select an oyster to be opened; you keep the pearl. Settings. At Treasures of Poseidon. *The Lost Continent.*

Port of Entry Christmas Shoppe. ✔ Character ornaments, decor. *Port of Entry.*

Port Provisions. T-shirts, hats, some toys. *Port of Entry.*

Snookers & Snookers Sweet Candy Cookers. Candies, fudge, treats. At the exit to The High in the Sky Seuss Trolley Train Ride. *Seuss Landing.*

Spider-Man Shop. Action figures, apparel, toys. *Marvel Super Hero Island.*

Star Souls Psychic Reading. Open-air readings, henna body art. *The Lost Continent.*

Toon Extra. Toys, DVDs, create and costume your own plush animals. *Toon Lagoon.*

Treasures of Poseidon. Fashion apparel, handbags, jewelry. *The Lost Continent.*

Wossamotta U. Beach towels, shorts, sundresses. *Toon Lagoon.*

If it rains. With its many outdoor attractions, the park is significantly affected by weather. Many attractions—Camp Jurassic, Doctor Doom's Fearfall, Dragon Challenge, Dudley Do-Right's Ripsaw Falls, Flight of the Hippogriff, Me Ship The Olive, Popeye & Bluto's Bilge-Rat Barges, Pteranodon Flyers and the outdoor attractions in Seuss Landing—stay open during a light rain but close if there's lightning in the area. Good spots to duck into when it's raining: the two Lost Continent shows and the Jurassic Park Discovery Center. Most stores sell umbrellas and ponchos; many stands have ponchos.

Family matters. Most of the park's rides have height minimums, including a couple in the Seuss Landing kiddie zone. *The Amazing Adventures of Spider-Man:* 40 inches. *The Cat in the Hat:* 36 inches. *Doctor Doom's Fearfall:* 52 inches. *Dragon Challenge:* 54 inches. *Dudley Do-Right's Ripsaw Falls:* 44 inches. *Flight of the Hippogriff:* 36 inches. *Harry Potter and the Forbidden Journey:* 48 inches. *The High in the Sky Seuss Trolley Train Ride:* 40 inches. *The Incredible Hulk:* 54 inches. *Jurassic Park River Adventure:* 42 inches. *Popeye & Bluto's Bilge-Rat Barges:* 42 inches. *Pteranodon Flyers:* 36 inches; those over 56 inches must be accompanied by a child. *Skull Island: Reign of Kong:* 34 inches.

Two shows may be too much for toddlers. The Eighth Voyage of Sindbad Stunt Show has loud explosions and fire effects. Poseidon's Fury has loud noises, fire effects, scary video and threatening villains.

The park has three wildly different playgrounds. Me Ship, The Olive offers water play on Popeye's three-level boat. The tiny mazelike If I Ran the Zoo also has a waterplay zone, as well as games, puzzles and interactive elements. The sprawling Camp Jurassic (the best playground in either Universal park) contains a little of everything, including an amber mine to explore and extensive netting to climb.

Every restaurant offers a children's menu.

"Where can I find..." You want it. You need it. You know it exists. But just where is…

…a baby care spot? Two Health Services centers (indicated by the First Aid icons on the upcoming map; the main one is in the Lost Continent area) have changing rooms, a microwave and chairs for nursing moms. They sell diapers, formula and baby supplies.

…a bar? Try Backwater Bar (Port of Entry), The Watering Hole (outside, Jurassic Park) or The Hog's Head Pub (Hogsmeade).

Port of Entry is an exotic wonderland; "Casablanca" with a touch of Swiss Family Treehouse.

...a battery? At Island Market Exports, carts and The Trading Co. (Port of Entry), Marvel Alterniverse and the Spider-Man Store (Super Hero Island), the Comic Book Store, Gasoline Alley, Ripsaw cart and Toon Extra (Toon Lagoon), Dinostore, Jurassic Park Outfitters and Triceratops cart (Jurassic Park), Dervish and Banges, Filch's Emporium and Honeydukes (Hogsmeade), Treasures of Poseidon (Lost Continent), Cats, Hats & Things and Mulberry Street Store (Seuss Landing).

...breakfast? At Cinnabon, Croissant Moon and Starbucks (Port of Entry), the Magic Neep cart until 10 a.m. and The Three Broomsticks (Hogsmeade).

...camera gear? Just inside the park entrance at DeFotos (Port of Entry).

...a Coca-Cola Freestyle machine? At Oasis Coolers (Port of Entry), Captain America Diner (Super Hero Island), Comic Strip Café (Toon Lagoon), Burger Digs (Jurassic Park) and Circus McGurkus (Seuss Landing). Special cups (about $15 per day) allow unlimited refills every 10 minutes.

...coffee? At the Cinnabon, Croissant Moon Bakery and Starbucks (Port of Entry), Café 4 (Super Hero Island), Blondie's and Comic Strip Café (Toon Lagoon), Burger Digs and Thunder Falls (Jurassic Park), The Three Broomsticks (Hogsmeade) and Circus McGurkus (Seuss Landing).

...fresh fruit? At Fruit Stand (Port of Entry) and Natural Selections (Jurassic Park).

...a funnel cake? At Croissant Moon Bakery (Port of Entry).

...a hot dog? At the Marvel Chomp Cart (Super Hero Island), Ale to the Chief and Blondie's (Toon Lagoon), Fire-Eater's Grill and Lost Continent Beer (Lost Continent) and Jurassic Turkey Cart (Jurassic Park).

...hand-scooped ice cream? At the Ben & Jerry's (Super Hero Island) and Cathy's (Toon Lagoon) walk-up windows and at The Three Broomsticks (Hogsmeade).

...a locker? Just inside the main entrance on the far right; expect to pay $8–$10 per day. Large lockers are just outside the park.

...Lost and Found? Just inside the park gate on the far right, inside Guest Services.

...a mailbox? By the restroom and lockers near the park exit (Port of Entry) and The Owlery (Hogsmeade, items sent from it have a Wizarding World of Harry Potter postmark).

...medicine? Health Services has complimentary pain meds and bandages. Basic meds are sold at The Trading Co. (Port of Entry), Marvel Alterniverse (Super Hero Island), Toon Extra (Toon Lagoon), Jurassic Park Outfitters (Jurassic Park), Filch's Emporium of Confiscated Goods (Hogsmeade), Treasures of Poseidon (Lost Continent) and Mulberry Street (Seuss Landing).

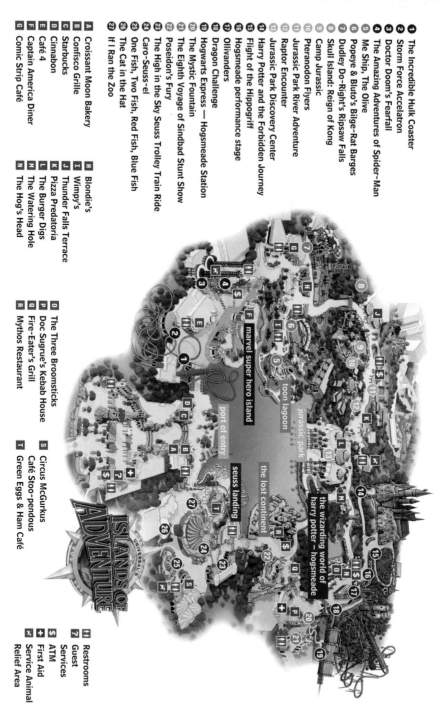

ISLANDS OF ADVENTURE — UNIVERSAL'S

marvel super hero island

port of entry

toon lagoon

jurassic park

the lost continent

seuss landing

the wizarding world of harry potter – hogsmeade

🚻 Restrooms
❓ Guest Services
$ ATM
➕ First Aid
🐾 Service Animal Relief Area

Held prisoner in the Lost Continent, Princess Amoura is a damsel in distress.

...package pickup? At the park exit at the Ocean Traders gift shop.

...a postage stamp? At The Trading Company (Port of Entry) and the Owl Post (Hogsmeade).

...a prepaid phone card? At Island Market and Export and The Trading Company (Port of Entry), Wossamotta U (Toon Lagoon), Jurassic Park Outfitters (Jurassic Park) and Treasures of Poseidon (Lost Continent).

...a stroller, scooter or wheelchair? Just inside the gate on the far left are single, double strollers and kiddie cars with steering wheels (about $15–$30 per day); wheelchairs ($12) and mobility scooters with optional canopies ($50–$70). All require a $50 deposit.

...a turkey leg? A theme-park staple, it's sold at the Fruit Stand (Port of Entry), Hero Turkey Cart (Super Hero Island), Toon Popcorn (Toon Lagoon), Jurassic Turkey Cart and Thunder Falls (Jurassic Park) and The Three Broomsticks (Hogsmeade).

Fun finds. There's a ton in the front half of the park (for Hogsmeade see the Wizarding World of Harry Potter Field Guide):

Port of Entry. ❶ A time machine "stuck in the 6th century," a dirigible and a submersible are among the items listed on a "Reliable Rentals" sign outside the stroller and wheelchair rental window. ❷ An homage to the former executive vice president of Universal Creative David Codiga, a second-floor window for "Codiga Adventures" is next to the stroller and wheelchair rental area. ❸ Two cuddling white love birds spoon to the right of the window; hidden speakers play soft coos. ❹ A prisoner has flown the coop at the Hoosegow jailhouse, tucked between the Island Market and Export store. The jailbird scrawled "Cabined, cribbed and confined" on the wall; then later, "See ya!" ❺ "Fire Brigade Moving Closer to Water" reads a sign over what was the fire department, next to the Islands of Adventure Trading Co. A fire bell and fire hoses hang at eye level. ❻ "From Merlin's mambo to the stegosaurs stomp" reads a sign next to Cinnabon on the Sumatra Hari World of Dance studio, a nod to the park's Lost Continent and Jurassic Park areas.

Marvel Super Hero Island. ❼ A sign over Café 4 reads "Baxter Annex," a reference to the Baxter Building, the New York home of the Fantastic Four. ❽ "Stark Industries" reads the sign on the back of the Marvel Alterniverse Store. Tony Stark is Iron Man. ❾ A sign near The Amazing Adventures of Spider-Man reads "Stark Enterprises." ❿ A sign for Osborn Industries, a nod to Spider-Man's arch-enemy Norman Osborn, is left of the entrance for Doctor Doom's Fearfall, flanked by busts of the symbiote Venom. ⓫ Succinct

Carefully trimmed so it doesn't catch fire, a green jungle frames the Jurassic Park arch.

signs for food and merchandise locations such as "Fruit," "Cotton Candy" and "Comics" mimic the generic store monikers in classic comic books. ⑫ A meteor which crashed onto the small plaza between the "Fruit" stand and the Marvel Alterniverse Store represents the supernatural event that gave once-normal humans super powers. The crash site, with spires around the crater, holds murals of the characters found throughout the area. ⑬ The head of Thor's hammer, Miu Miu, has crashed into a window on the second story of the Captain America Diner. Inside, Thor throws Miu Miu across the room. ⑭ Phones and blue call boxes scattered on the walkways throughout Marvel Super Hero Island contain secret messages. You may hear Daredevil talking to Electra, Captain America calling the rest of the Avengers to join him in fighting Carnage, Professor Xavier asking Wolverine to settle down, or Iron Man leaving a message saying his powers are nearly depleted. A villain may say that the Avengers are in space, so now is the right time to rob a jewelry store, or that Iron Man has been spotted so don't forget to bring your can opener. ⑮ Yancy Street is the name of the walkway that leads to Doctor Doom's Fearfall. The Yancy Street Gang harasses the Thing in Marvel comic books; New York's Delancey Street inspired its name. ⑯ The Marvel Alterniverse Store contains

a sign for "Nelson & Murdoch: Attorneys at Law," which references Marvel's Matt Murdock—Daredevil—and his best friend, Foggy Nelson. ⑰ Doc Ock's huge tentacle has knocked over the "O" in a Frozen Ice sign, next to The Amazing Adventures of Spider-Man attraction. ⑱ Longtime Marvel artist Adam Kubert created the larger-than-life 2-D graphics of heroes and villains throughout Marvel Super Hero Island. In each one he hid the letters "ADAM." For example, they're in the clenched fist of Doctor Octopus and between the thumb and index finger of the Incredible Hulk.

Toon Lagoon. ⑲ Carrying a note from his dad telling him to "make sure to mark trail," son Billy has walked off the Family Circus panel on the Betty Boop store. A wandering dashed line leads to where he's gone: a panel for the strip Mark Trail. ⑳ The land's ambient music is one carefully constructed musical round, blending lyrics from Betty Boop, Hagar the Horrible and Dagwood and Blondie.

Seuss Landing. ㉑ Three dignitaries appear behind a police motorcycle and sidecar next to the Mulberry Street Store. The white-bearded one on the left represents Dr. Seuss himself, Theodor Seuss Geisel.

The Lost Continent. ㉒ At the entrance to the Sindbad show, the Mystic Fountain will chat with you for days on end.

A crowd pleaser. Nearly everyone loves the Hulk experience (2015 ride shown).

The Incredible Hulk Coaster

Rebuilt from head to toe, the new Hulk is a smooth operator

★★★★★ ✓ *EXPRESS* After a rocket-fast launch through a tube (0 to 40 mph in 2 seconds), this signature Universal coaster is always twisting, turning or flipping you upside down (7 times!) Halfway through you zoom into a foggy underground tunnel. The coaster is an abstract replication of the experiment that exposed Dr. Bruce Banner's body to gamma rays and changed him into the Hulk. That's why you go through a "gamma ray tube" at launch—you're experiencing the Hulk's transformation for yourself. The ride was closed in 2015 for a near-total refurbishment; the update's new queue, track and vehicles offer a more elaborate, smoother experience.

Tip. *Where to sit:* Front row for the scariest ride (you'll wait in a slower queue, but it's worth it), on an end of a row for the best view.

Key facts. *Duration:* 4 minutes. *Closed by:* Rain or the presence of lightning. *Capacity:* 32 (8 4-seat rows). *Height minimum:* 54 inches. *Access:* Single Rider Line, Rider Swap available. *Restraint:* Shoulder harness. *Restricted items:* All personal belongings, including cameras, car keys, glasses, hats, loose change, phones and wallets; locker use provided; as you enter the attraction you pass through an electronic security system much like that at an airport. *Fear factor:* Intense. *Queue:* Indoor, overflowing into partially covered outdoor area. *Top speed:* 67 mph. *Track length:* 3,700 feet. *Track type:* Steel tubes filled with gravel and sand. *Manufacturer:* Bollinger & Mabillard. *Debuted:* 1999, redone 2016. *Location:* Marvel Super Hero Island.

Health advisory. Universal suggests you skip the ride if you're pregnant, have high blood pressure; back, heart or neck conditions; dizziness, height, motion-sickness or strobe issues; or recently had surgery.

Average wait times

9am	10am	11am	Noon	1pm	2pm	3pm	4pm	5pm	6pm	7pm	8pm	9pm
10m	25m	25m	30m	25m	30m	35m	25m	20m	20m	15m	10m	5m

Instant family fun. Hidden in a corner, Universal's spinning ride has short lines, if any.

Storm Force Accelatron

Pounding music, effects spice up overlooked carnival ride

★★★ *EXPRESS* This simple spinning ride serves as a giddy bonding experience that'll leave your family feeling exhilarated. You can't help but smile when you're sliding into each other with abandon, giggling, madly trying to take photos. Much like Disney's spinning teacups, your round capsules twirl on a rotating disc that circles on a platform. Up to five riders grasp a metal wheel mounted in the center, twirling it slowly or quickly or just hanging on. Music pounds, thunder booms, lightning flashes. Kids love the spinning, dizziness and chance to act silly with their parents. Besides attractions at Seuss Landing this is the only ride at the park without a height requirement.

Cheesy graphics in the waiting line tell the ride's backstory—it seems the X-Men's Professor Xavier needs recruits to help weather-controlling heroine Storm defeat mutant villain Magneto, and has built a device that amplifies her powers. He just needs one thing: someone to hop in and spin it, the faster the better, since doing so creates thunder and lightning that Storm can use to defeat Magneto. What? Huh? It doesn't matter.

Tips. *To get extra dizzy:* Spin your wheel first one direction, then the other, as fast as you can. *To avoid getting dizzy:* Hold the wheel tight; stare at its center.

Key facts. *Duration:* 1 minute, 30 seconds. *Capacity:* 48, 12 vehicles, each with space for 4 or perhaps 5. *Access:* Rider Swap available, service animals allowed. *Fear factor:* Spinning. *Queue:* Outdoor, covered. *Debuted:* 2000. *Location:* Marvel Super Hero Island.

Health advisory. Universal suggests you skip the ride if you're pregnant, have abnormal blood pressure; back, heart or neck conditions; dizziness, motion-sickness or strobe issues; or recently had surgery.

Average wait times

9am	10am	11am	Noon	1pm	2pm	3pm	4pm	5pm	6pm	7pm	8pm	9pm
5m	5m	5m	10m	10m	10m	10m	15m	10m	5m	5m	5m	5m

On a clear day you can see... downtown Orlando. Doctor Doom's towers rise 200 feet.

Doctor Doom's Fearfall

Two drop towers toss you up, throw you down

★★★★ *EXPRESS* "Unimaginable fear will be wrenched from your quivering body!" That's why Doctor Doom built this drop-tower, which fuels his Fusion Dynamo machine by extracting human terror. And with that machine, he can vanquish the Fantastic Four! Jeez. What a grinch.

Rings of chairs circle two 200-foot towers. You're strapped in with your feet dangling, then shoot straight up at 40 mph. Adrenaline races as you reach the top and hang there for a beat. Then you fall, faster than you would by gravity alone. The brief ride calms down after the launch, as the doc tosses in a few moments for sightseeing. The ride's queue is the Latverian embassy, the front for his evil headquarters.

Tip. *Where to sit:* On the outside if you have zero fear of heights. *For the biggest thrill:* Look straight up or down as you launch.

Fun finds. ❶ Snap a selfie in Doctor Doom's throne, inside the adjacent arcade, up stairs on a landing. ❷ Silhouettes of the Fantastic Four's bodies are imprinted on the pavement at the entrance.

Key facts. *Duration:* 45 seconds. *Closed by:* Rain or the presence of lightning. *Capacity:* 32 (two towers, each with 16 seats arranged in fours). *Height minimum:* 52 inches. *Access:* Single Rider Line, Rider Swap, test seats available. *Restraint:* Shoulder harness. *Restricted items:* None, but belongings must be in pockets. *Fear factor:* Scary but brief. *Queue:* Indoor. *Debuted:* 1999. *Location:* Marvel Super Hero Island.

Health advisory. Universal suggests you skip the ride if you're pregnant, have high blood pressure; back, heart or neck conditions; dizziness, fog, height, motion-sickness or strobe issues; or recently had surgery.

Average wait times

9am	10am	11am	Noon	1pm	2pm	3pm	4pm	5pm	6pm	7pm	8pm	9pm
5m	25m	30m	35m	20m	15m	20m	20m	15m	15m	15m	10m	10m

© Universal Orlando Resort

"Nice shades." Spider-Man's impressed by your 3-D glasses.

The Amazing Adventures of Spider-Man

Universal's No. 1 simulator? It's tough to argue with Spidey.

★★★★★ ✔ *EXPRESS* You'll laugh during this 3-D dark ride, which combines real sets with video screens. From the brassy braying of Daily Bugle boss-man J. Jonah Jameson to Spider-Man's breezy asides to the over-the-top villains levitating Lady Liberty—this ride tickles your funny bone.

You won't be disappointed in its thrills, either. You spin through nighttime streets, soar past buildings and plunge toward the ground, escaping certain death by a last-minute Spidey-save. Special effects bombard you throughout. Your teeth rattle when Electro shocks your ride vehicle, your skin heats from Doc Ock's flaming tentacle, you get wet when Hydro-Man spritzes you with water.

You're a reporter. *Warning; spoilers ahead.* According to the story, you arrive at the Daily Bugle newspaper as a tourist, looking for a tour. But you don't get it. Instead, pushy J. Jonah Jameson drafts you into a temporary job as a roving reporter, assigning you the job of gathering news about villains who are threatening New York City.

So like all reporters, you don 3-D glasses and go sit in your little gullwing car (hey, just go with it), then head off to get the low-down on the Sinister Syndicate, which you discover has levitated the Statue of Liberty and stolen it with an anti-gravity device (see, making sense...) and will destroy her if the city doesn't agree to total surrender! Ah, but then Spider-Man shows up. He dukes it out with the bad guys as he tries to protect you.

But that's a tall order. The villains—leader Doctor Octopus, Electro, the Hobgoblin,

Average wait times

9am	10am	11am	Noon	1pm	2pm	3pm	4pm	5pm	6pm	7pm	8pm	9pm
5m	25m	25m	20m	15m	15m	20m	20m	20m	20m	15m	15m	10m

© Universal Orlando Resort

Doc Ock brings the heat...

Hydro-Man and Scream—torment you with electrocution, fireballs, floods and exploding pumpkins (perfectly sensible...) as you travel through, under and into the streets of the Big Apple. In the end, you get zapped by the anti-gravity device, causing your car (the Scoop) to float high above the skyscrapers. Spider-Man tries to pull you down to safety, but accidentally sends you plummeting 400 (simulated) feet toward the pavement. But just in time, he throws a web under you and breaks your fall. Whew!

In 2012, the ride was refreshed with 4K film and new projectors, a new audio system with 16-channel surround sound and new lighting and music; its "Spider-Vision" glasses received dichroic-filtered lenses.

Tips. *When to go:* The first hour after the park opens, or use the Single Rider Line. *Where to sit:* In the front for the best view and to get less wet from Hydro-Man.

Fun finds. ❶ In the Daily Bugle office inside the queue, a sign reads "The Bugle! We don't blow it when it comes to the news!" ❷ At the beginning of the ride, the silhouette of a rat creeps by in front of you. ❸ "Nice shades!" says Spider-Man, complimenting your 3-D glasses. ❹ When your car levitates, he says "Hey, we're not insured for that!" ❺ "So, that's all wrapped up," he says at the end of the ride, when all the villains are bound in spiderweb. ❻ While hanging upside down, Spidey gives a thumbs-up sign—then quickly turns his hand upside down, so it's right-side-up to you.

© Universal Orlando Resort

...Electro's got the power.

7 As you slow to a stop near the boarding area, an anti-gravity device sits unattended on the left, shooting its beam into an office; J. Jonah Jameson floats inside. 8 Peter Parker's time card sits next to an old-fashioned time clock, which hangs on the wall just outside the child-swap room. 9 Next to the time clock, a sign reads "Do not read postings on company time!" 10 Marvel Comics founder Stan Lee makes four appearances in the ride. He's the truck driver that nearly hits your Scoop ride vehicle, in the crowd in the Theater District as Spider-Man and Doc Ock battle, on the street again when your Scoop falls to the ground, and standing with the police as Lady Liberty flies back to her perch. Lee's voice bids you farewell at the end of the ride.

Key facts. *Duration:* 4 minutes, 30 seconds. *Capacity:* 12-seat ride vehicles, each with three 4-seat rows. *Height minimum:* 40 inches. *Access:* Single Rider Line, Rider Swap available; closed captioning available, service animals allowed. *Restraint:* Lap bar on a bench seat. *Fear factor:* Sudden acceleration, climbs, drops, tilts and turns; loud explosions, large flame effects and overhead water effects. *Queue:* Indoor. *Debuted:* 1999. *Location:* Marvel Super Hero Island.

Health advisory. Universal recommends that you skip the Spider-Man ride if you're pregnant, have abnormal blood pressure; back, heart or neck conditions; dizziness, enclosed-space, motion-sickness or strobe issues; or recently had surgery.

Will it or won't it? Sometimes the pipe belches water, sometimes it just shoots a spray.

Popeye & Bluto's Bilge-Rat Barges
Elaborate raft ride makes sure you get wet

★★★★ *EXPRESS* You're guaranteed to get soaked on this exhilarating ride. In fact, with its barge wash, overhead leaky pipes, big vents on its walls and all the churning waterways you travel down, you'll likely get drenched. The circular raft spins so much you never know who'll get splashed next.

Like real whitewater rapids, the journey includes abrupt changes in the raft's lift and angle, tilting as much as three feet. You pass amusing scenes—in the Octopus Grotto Popeye wrestles a slimy enemy.

Like most Popeye plots, the story is about his attempt to rescue Olive Oyl from the dastardly Bluto. The villain ends up stretched like a slingshot by his suspenders as Popeye says "I've taken all I can takes, and I can't takes no more!"

Tips. *When to go:* In the afternoon, especially on hot days; consider riding right before you leave the park in case you get drenched and don't want to schlep around in damp clothes. *How to stay dry:* Buy a poncho at a stand near the entrance, take off your shoes and roll up long pants; the raft's covered central console is not watertight, so phones and other electronics should be put in zippered baggies or left in complimentary lockers.

Key facts. *Duration:* 8 minutes. *Opens:* An hour after the park opens. *Closed by:* Rain or the presence of lightning. *Capacity:* 12 per raft. *Height minimum:* 42 inches. *Access:* Rider Swap available. *Restraint:* Seat belt. *Queue:* Outdoor, partially covered. *Debuted:* 1999. *Location:* Toon Lagoon.

Health advisory. Universal suggests you skip the ride if you're pregnant, have abnormal blood pressure; back, heart or neck conditions; dizziness, fog, height or motion-sickness issues; or recently had surgery.

Average wait times

9am	10am	11am	Noon	1pm	2pm	3pm	4pm	5pm	6pm	7pm	8pm	9pm
n/a	5m	5m	10m	15m	15m	20m	15m	20m	20m	15m	10m	5m

Hidden off the park's main walkway, Popeye's playground is often unpeopled.

Me Ship, The Olive

There's lots to do at this interactive playground

★★★ Kids explore the three colorful decks of this cartoon boat, which appears to be tied up at a dock and list slightly to one side. Olive Oyl's giant face peers down from the top; her skinny torso is the boat's figurehead.

The interactive playground has cargo nets, climbing platforms, passageways to crawl through and slides. A slide on the third deck travels down to the second; another goes from the second deck to the first. Bubbling portholes make it appear that the ship actually is sitting in water.

Cartoonish props include bells to ding, buttons to push, buzzers to press, dials to turn, horns to toot and musical instruments to play. Some props spray water. Kids can spin the ship's wheel at the helm of the boat; blowing the whistle produces a satisfying sound. Punching bags hang down, ready for pummeling. The ship's cargo—cans of spinach, of course—is scattered all over the boat.

Swee' Pea's Playpen, an enclosed toddler play area, is tucked on the first-story deck.

The sweeping view from the top deck encompasses the whole park—Hogsmeade, the Lost Continent, Marvel Super Hero Island and Seuss Landing. Don't overlook the opportunity to snap some photos from here that can't be taken anywhere else.

A small elevator stops at all three decks.

Tips. *When to go:* In the afternoon, when your kids need to burn off some steam. *For families:* Watch some Popeye cartoons beforehand to familiarize your children with the sailor man and his friends.

Fun finds. ① Two shark fins circling cargo crates are visible through a hole bashed in the bottom of the boat. ② Aim the second-floor water cannons at the adjacent Popeye & Bluto's Bilge-Rat Barges to drench unsuspecting riders as they float by, strapped in, totally at your mercy. ③ A fully-functional piano sits on the top deck, in the cabin. A bit of sheet music shows a way to play the painted keys; if you do, you'll be rewarded with a fully orchestrated version of Popeye's theme song, complete with his signature toot-toot whistle. ④ Peaceful pathways wind around the ship.

Key facts. *Duration:* 15 minutes. *Closed by:* Rain or the presence of lightning. *Access:* Service animals allowed. *Fear factor:* None. *Debuted:* 1999. *Location:* Toon Lagoon.

Dudley may have won an award, but Nell still has eyes only for his horse.

Dudley Do-Right's Ripsaw Falls

Silly log flume has two little drops, one big one

★★★ *EXPRESS* Bright colors, bonehead puns and goofy vignettes make this log flume ride a fun experience. You're surprised by two false drops before the main one. The story is pure cartoon silliness. Snidely Whiplash tries to kidnap Nell, and Dudley and his horse try to save her. It ends well, with Snidely imprisoned and Dudley earning a medal as Nell flirts with his horse. Anyone under age 50 will probably be in the dark, but that doesn't mean they won't have fun.

It's an intimate ride. You sit low; your legs extend alongside the person in front of you.

Tips. *Where to sit:* In the front to get soaked; in the back to avoid splashes. *To stay dry:* Buy a poncho; a stand sells them.

Fun finds. ❶ A boarding-area sign reads "Please Remove Hats & Antlers." ❷ Snidely's locked up in "Alottapoopoo Island Prison." ❸ His attempt to coax a beaver with keys in its mouth parodies a scene in Disney's Pirates of the Caribbean where jailed pirates lure a dog.

Key facts. *Duration:* 5 minutes, 30 seconds. *Closed by:* Rain or the presence of lightning. *Capacity:* 168. 42 *4-seat ride vehicles, each with four 1-seat rows. Height minimum:* 44 inches. *Access:* Single Rider Line, Rider Swap, test seats available. *Service animals prohibited. Restraint:* Lap bar. *Restricted items:* All loose articles; locker use provided. *Fear factor:* Sudden, dramatic acceleration, drops; riders get wet, possibly soaked. *Queue:* Indoor, overflows into shaded outdoor area. *Top speed:* 45 mph. *Debuted:* 1999. *Location:* Toon Lagoon.

Health advisory. Universal suggests you skip the ride if you're pregnant, have back, blood-pressure, heart or neck conditions; dizziness, fog, height, motion-sickness or strobe issues; or recently had surgery.

Average wait times

9am	10am	11am	Noon	1pm	2pm	3pm	4pm	5pm	6pm	7pm	8pm	9pm
5m	5m	15m	25m	30m	30m	20m	20m	15m	15m	10m	10m	5m

Riders fall under a dynamite shack that explodes with water then fly down a long runout.

© Universal Orlando Resort

Hey, let's go in! Some people think twice about these things. They're never theme-park guides.

Skull Island: The Reign of Kong

Brand-new truck ride combines animatronics, props, video

★★★★★ ✔ *EXPRESS* Mighty King Kong doesn't threaten you on this 3-D ride; instead he protects you. It's good you have him on your side; the place crawls with ravenous prehistoric beasts, including dinosaurs, spiders and otherworldly monsters. When your 1930s expedition through the ruins and temples of Skull Island goes horribly wrong, Kong—the most massive ape that ever lived—is the key to your survival. He bursts on the scene to confront the creatures that are nearly swarming your truck, battling them to confirm his dominance. And as a side effect, keep you alive.

Peter Jackson, director of the 2005 film "King Kong," collaborated with the designers on the look of the huge set. The sculptures in the rockwork, in particular, channel the feel of Jackson's movie. Despite this the attraction has an original story that isn't based on that film, nor the 1933 original, nor the 2017 prequel.

The entranceway of the elaborate queue passes under an archway topped with a giant stone Kong skull. The line winds through a dense jungle littered with an expedition's crates and supplies. An authentic 1930s NBC radio broadcast plays, complete with music from the NBC Orchestra.

In between the songs, transmissions that break in set up the plot of the ride, that you've decided to join the 8th Wonder Expedition Company to explore Skull Island, a mysterious land steeped in legend. Your goal: to research and confirm the existence of living prehistoric creatures. Your first objective: to make it to the communication base camp situated deep in the island's ruins, and rendevous with the expedition team. Radio transmissions from team leader Kate McCaffrey warn of the dangers ahead, while pleading with you to come quickly to help.

Average wait times (estimated)

9am	10am	11am	Noon	1pm	2pm	3pm	4pm	5pm	6pm	7pm	8pm	9pm
10m	40m	45m	50m	30m	50m	50m	70m	50m	40m	25m	15m	10m

© Universal Orlando Resort

One mad monkey. He may not make the best first impression, but he's actually on your side.

The queue continues through the ruins of an ancient temple. You pass evidence of hostile natives, but you can't tell if they are nearby or not. The rhythmic beating of distant drums creates a foreboding atmosphere.

The queue itself adds tension. At first it's made up of large open areas, but it slowly turns into tight, confined spaces.

As you enter the boarding area McCaffrey transmits a message from the expedition's base camp, urging you forward and instructing the truck driver where to go. Apparently the situation in the field is dire, and the team needs your imminent help; the nature of the danger stays shrouded in mystery.

On the ride. *Warning; spoilers ahead.* Once you board the truck it zooms off toward the base camp, bouncing along a degraded road before halting in front of looming, 72-foot-tall temple doors. When they slowly swing open, you see they're bordered by smoking cauldrons and spiked skulls. The truck enters dark, winding caves peppered with predators at every turn. After surviving the caverns, you think you're safe when you emerge into a lush forest.

No such luck. You find yourself in the middle of a battle between towering prehistoric beasts, which attack your truck. All seems lost. Suddenly, with a deafening roar, the mighty giant ape Kong arrives on the scene. Is he friend or foe? He could easily jump in on the attack against your truck and finish you off. Instead, he establishes his dominance as the top predator of Skull Island, and vanquishes your attackers. You see the battle between the fierce beasts in close-up breathtaking detail.

The ride's open-sided 40-foot-long truck is one of the largest, most revolutionary ride vehicles constructed. It uses trackless technology that allows it to move with no one at the wheel. Kong himself is a combination of new fluid animatronics and large-scale 3-D projections. Before tackling Kong, the ride's executive producer Mike West led Universal Creative teams in the creation of the rides "The Simpsons," "Despicable Me: Minion Mayhem," and "Transformers: The Ride 3-D."

Key facts. *Duration:* 5 minutes, 50 seconds. *Capacity:* 25 (5 5-seat rows). *Height minimum:* 34 inches. *Access:* Rider Swap available, open captioning available. *Restraint:* Lap bar. *Fear factor:* Prehistoric creatures threaten you. *Queue:* Outdoor, partially covered. *Debuted:* June 2016. *Location:* Between Toon Lagoon and Jurassic Park.

Health advisory. Universal suggests that you skip the ride if you're pregnant or have abnormal blood pressure; back, heart or neck conditions; dizziness or motion-sickness issues; or recently had surgery.

© Universal Orlando Resort

Facing the park's lagoon, the front of the Discovery Center often seems deserted.

Jurassic Park Discovery Center

It looks like a science center. In some ways it is one.

★★★ This indoor interactive play center is reminiscent of a children's science museum, but on a small scale. Educational exhibits demonstrate topics such as archeology, DNA sequencing and sediment wall scanning. Many stations feature activities you complete on a computer. Life-sized dinosaurs make good photo props, and also allow you to "be-a-saurus" by looking through their eyes using special scopes and making their heads move. Four people can compete against each other in a tongue-in-cheek video-based game to find out who knows the most about dinosaurs; kids often get the highest scores. The peaceful, relaxing spot is nearly always empty.

Some exhibits have themes straight from the "Jurassic Park" movies, such as the idea of using ancient fossilized DNA to bring dinosaurs to life. A computerized "Mr. DNA" station lets digitally create a hybrid between yourself and a dinosaur; at the end, the combined human/dino DNA is deemed too unstable and the experiment is abandoned.

At the hatchery, "scientists" studiously fill out forms and tend to dinosaur eggs behind glass. A scanning device lets you examine the eggs yourself and guess which species is in each egg. Ask an attending technician if a baby dinosaur is ready to hatch. Two or three times an hour an animatronic raptor emerges from its egg. A child from the crowd gets to choose its name.

The outside of the building resembles the Visitors Center from the first "Jurassic Park" film; the entrance rotunda has skeletal dinosaur mock-ups on display.

How best to experience it. Approach this as an educational learning center rather than a theme-park attraction. Sneak behind the building to find a hidden waterfront terrace with beautiful views of the park. It's usually empty, though it sometimes closes for special events.

Fun find. A can of Barbisol shaving cream sits on a low shelf behind glass in the hatchery. In the first "Jurassic Park" film, Dennis Nedry used a can like this to smuggle dino embryos out of the facility.

Key facts. *Hours:* Typically 10 a.m–5 p.m. *Duration:* Allow 15 minutes. *Access:* Closed captioning, service animals allowed. *Debuted:* 1999. *Location:* Jurassic Park.

© Universal Orlando Resort

On Pteranodon Flyers. You sway as you soar through a jungle... if you have a child with you.

Camp Jurassic and Pteranodon Flyers
Great playground has what may be the park's most fun ride

★★★★★ ✔ A kid's delight, this vast playground is the best play area in either park. It recalls the tropical grounds of Jurassic Park. Youngsters can burn off steam by climbing three stories of nets, splashing in fountains and crossing suspension bridges. Kids will especially love the interactive spots. At one, a push of a button makes a spitting dilophosaurus blast water up at a second-story bank of guns, which squirt water back; families can split up and soak each other. Waterfalls are hidden in a dark amber cave; a rope bridge crosses an underground pool. Every 15 minutes or so a geyser erupts in the middle of the pool, splashing people crossing the bridge. The cave has two entrances, so groups can get split up.

The Camp includes the ride Pteranodon Flyers, which circles the area. Only children under 3 feet are allowed on it (drat!), though a parent may accompany them. Topped by a flying dino, the relaxing ride swoops and glides over the treetops, your feet free to dangle.

Key facts. *Duration:* Allow 30 minutes for Camp Jurassic; Pteranodon Flyers takes 80 seconds. *Closed by:* Rain or the presence of lightning. *Access:* Service animals allowed in Camp Jurassic, not on Flyers. *Capacity:* Flyers, 20 (10 2-seat ride vehicles, each with two 1-seat rows). *Height minimum:* Flyers, 36 inches; people over 56 inches tall must be accompanied by a child. *Access:* Flyers, Rider Swap available. *Restraint:* Flyers, seat belt. *Queue:* Flyers, outdoor, partially shaded. *Debuted:* 1999. *Location:* Jurassic Park.

Health advisory. Universal suggests that you skip the ride if you're pregnant or have abnormal blood pressure; back, heart or neck conditions; dizziness, height or motion-sickness issues; or recently had surgery.

Average wait times (Pteranodon Flyers)

9am	10am	11am	Noon	1pm	2pm	3pm	4pm	5pm	6pm	7pm	8pm	9pm
10m	20m	30m	30m	20m	15m	20m	20m	20m	20m	15m	10m	5m

Try to keep your eyes open. It's not easy.

Jurassic Park River Adventure

In for more than a splash, you're "welcome... to Jurassic Park"

★★★★ *EXPRESS* You're in store for one big wet drop. That much is obvious, because you can see the splashdown from outside the ride. What you can't see from there are the gaping jaws of the roaring T-Rex that threatens you just before the drop. On the ride you travel straight toward him, having just passed snarling raptors and acid-spitting dilophosaurs, when you suddenly plunge downhill 85 feet.

So yes, this a thrilling ride that'll leave you shivering—from both the menacing dinos and the stomach-lifting plunge.

The story begins in the queue, on overhead TV monitors. John Hammond, creator and enthusiastic self-promoter of Jurassic Park, introduces the newly opened resort. After his prologue, two slick hosts star in the Jurassic Journal, a show that expounds the joys of the park. They describe and show the Jurassic Park Discovery Center,

Camp Jurassic and the Jurassic Park River Adventure, a (supposedly) serene and tranquil float past different dinosaur habitats.

Suddenly, an emergency announcement breaks in, explaining that River Adventure boats would now bypass the carnivore paddocks due to "technical difficulties."

On the ride. *Warning; spoilers ahead.* In the beginning, the ride is as serene as you've been led to expect. An announcement booms "Welcome to Jurassic Park!" as the towering gates open. You float peacefully beside animatronic herbivores like Stegosaurs and Hadrosaurs. Then everything goes horribly wrong—you veer off course and enter the restricted Raptor Containment zone. Alarms blare, an upset voice over an intercom says we're going the wrong way, and chirruping raptors scurry through the tall grasses. Ahead of you is a giant raptor cage that has

Average wait times

9am	10am	11am	Noon	1pm	2pm	3pm	4pm	5pm	6pm	7pm	8pm	9pm
5m	20m	30m	25m	25m	15m	15m	15m	10m	10m	10m	5m	5m

Clever girl! Across from the Jurassic Park River Adventure, a velociraptor emerges through a broken fence and interacts with you before posing for a photo at the new Raptor Encounter. She seems wild, skulking in the grass, rearing up, making her "Caw! Caw!" signal, sniffing your hair, opening her mouth wide to bite you. Other park visitors look on. A handler tries to keep her under control. Hours are 10 a.m. to 6 or 7 p.m., twice an hour for 20 to 30 minutes.

been ripped open; a wrecked motorboat lies crashed into a dock. As you enter a backstage maintenance facility, your boat floats directly underneath a jittering crate which reads "Danger! Live raptor inside!"; it falls down when you're underneath it, but catches before landing on you. The dark building is populated by dangerous dinos: spitting dilophosaurs, chittering raptors and a huge T-Rex, who is standing right in your way. At the last moment—just before you collide with the T-Rex—your boat plunges down a vertical drop with a huge splash.

Tips. *When to go:* In the afternoon, especially on hot days; the spray will be refreshing. *Where to sit:* In the middle of a back row for the driest experience; in the front for the best view and most legroom. *How to avoid a tight squeeze:* When the lapbar is pulled down across all five riders in a row, press forward a little against the bar; once it's in place you can relax and not be in too tight a squeeze. *How to dry off:* A "personnel dryer" at the exit will dry about four people for $5; you can buy a poncho at a nearby stand. *For families:* The ride has both dinos in the dark to spook you and also a monster of an 85-foot drop.

Fun finds. ❶ The harmless dinos at the beginning of the ride have baggy skin that makes them resemble little old ladies. **❷** You pass a crashed boat as you enter the restricted area; on its deck, two little Compsognathus fight over a ripped "Jurassic Park" employee shirt.

Key facts. *Duration:* 7 minutes. *Closed by:* Rain or the presence of lightning. *Capacity:* 375 (15 25-seat ride vehicles, each with five 5-seat rows). *Height minimum:* 42 inches. *Access:* Single Rider Line, Rider Swap available; assistive listening, closed captioning, service animals not allowed. *Restraint:* Lap bar on bench seat. *Restricted items:* All belongings in hands and pockets, including cameras, car keys, loose change and phones, wallets; locker use provided. *Fear factor:* Threatening dinosaurs, dark scenes, steep 85-foot drop. *Queue:* Outdoor, partially covered. *Debuted:* 1999. *Location:* Jurassic Park.

Health advisory. Universal recommends that you skip the ride if you're pregnant or have heart conditions; abnormal blood pressure; back or neck conditions; dizziness, fog, height, motion-sickness or strobe issues; or recently had surgery.

Sunny playground. Gerald McGrew welcomes visitors to his make-believe zoo.

If I Ran the Zoo

Sunny interactive play area is never crowded

★★★ Kids can enjoy all sorts of interactive fun in this tiny outdoor trail, which is jam-packed with fanciful Seuss-inspired peepholes, ride-on creatures, water-play features, puzzles, games and other silliness. The book that inspired the attraction is about the boy Gerald McGrew and his dream to create a zoo filled with exotic specimens from the most remote regions of the world. Therefore, the attraction is full of bizarre beasts such as the Tizzle-Topped Tufted Mazurka—found on the African island of Yerka—as well as the Natch and the Scraggle Foot Mulligatawny. The maze has two ways to go; make sure you go both directions so you don't miss anything.

Signs in Seussian verse give hints as to what you're seeing, and how to interact. For example, signs at a station overseen by a long-necked creature hint that you're supposed to first put your hand over one doorbell, then over another one; when you follow those directions, the creature's antlers inflate.

Most of the activities are designed for young kids, but parents can join in much of the time. Crawl through a cave in Kartoom—a short tunnel less than 3 feet tall—to find a beast known as the Natch; inside the tunnel you can hear whispers: "You can't catch me!" Slide down the tunnels of Zomba-ma-tant. Turn cranks to make birds appear in the hedges. Play a game by touching the belly of Tic Tac Joe. Climb on a multi-humped cow and pose for a photo. Splash each other in a water-play area which has a cage made of water for capturing wild animals—or children. Step on a Scraggle Foot Mulligatawny and he'll sneeze, shooting water upward.

Tips. *When to go:* Anytime; the play area is never crowded. *How best to experience it:* Read the book "If I Ran the Zoo" with your children beforehand. Take photos; several spots, such as tall Tic Tac Joe, make a good backdrop. The area has no shady spots; if it's sunny have your child wear a hat.

Fun find. Footprints of bears, ducks, monkeys and tiny birds cross the blue pavement at the entrance to the play area.

Key facts. *Duration:* Allow 15 minutes. *Closed by:* Rain or the presence of lightning. *Access:* Service animals allowed. *Debuted:* 1999. *Location:* Seuss Landing.

A huge hat and a rocking pile of home goods hint at the chaos of ride.

The Cat in the Hat

Indoor dark ride spins as it retells the story

★★★★ ✔ *EXPRESS* This indoor dark ride creatively re-tells the beloved story of the mischievous Cat in the Hat and his unforgettable visit to the home of Sally and her brother, using animatronics, video screens, silhouettes and black lights. The attraction is totally faithful to the book, using the same words and art. The queue takes you through a shiny plastic version of the lawn of the house.

Your ride vehicle channels the living room's couch. As the Cat and his Things destroy the home your surroundings get increasingly chaotic, a whirling dervish of furnishings, clothing and dishes that spins your vehicle with it. Eventually the Cat brings out his fixer-upper machine and tidies things up. Then, of course, Mom comes home oblivious and the kids have a dilemma. "Should we tell her about it? Now, what *should* we do? Well… what would *you* do if your mother asked you?"

Tip. *How best to experience it:* Read the book first; the ride carefully re-creates it.

Fun finds. ❶ In the bathroom the pet fish peeks out of the toilet and the faces of the Things are stamped on strewn toilet paper. **❷** As the Things fly kites indoors look up; the fish is above you. **❸** As the Cat fixes things he pours more water into the fishbowl.

Key facts. *Duration:* 6 minutes. *Capacity:* 80 (20 vehicles, each with two 2-seat rows). *Height minimum:* 36 inches. *Access:* Rider Swap available; assistive listening available; service animals allowed. *Restraint:* Lap bar. *Queue:* Indoor, overflows to unshaded outdoor area. *Debuted:* 1999. *Location:* Seuss Landing.

Health advisory. Universal suggests you skip the ride if you're pregnant or have heart conditions; abnormal blood pressure; back or neck conditions; dizziness, motion-sickness or strobe issues; or recently had surgery.

Average wait times

9am	10am	11am	Noon	1pm	2pm	3pm	4pm	5pm	6pm	7pm	8pm	9pm
5m	5m	5m	10m	10m	15m	10m	10m	5m	5m	5m	5m	5m

Hey! I know that one! The Caro-Seuss-el creatures come from the Dr. Seuss books.

Caro-Seuss-el

You board a Seuss beast on this four-row merry-go-round

★★★★ *EXPRESS* No horses circle this carousel—at least none without feathers, fins or other frippery. These odd, whimsical creatures come straight from the Dr. Seuss books. Included are elephant birds from "Horton Hatches the Egg," camels from "One Fish, Two Fish, Red Fish, Blue Fish," cowfish from "McElligot's Pool," and mulligatawnies from "If I Ran the Zoo." Even the purple poles that propel the animals are creative here—curved instead of straight. Two stationary orange carriages have misshapen orange and white wheels and turquoise canopies: each has two simple seats instead of a bench. Even discounting the animals, you get the joy of riding a merry-go-round—the ups and downs, the spinning and the jaunty calliope music.

Many of the animals have interactive elements; some have brass handles that move the creature's head. Elephant birds have reins that move the animal's trunk up and down. Each pink or orange cowfish has a plastic rope around its neck that serves as a hand rest; pulling it down rings a bell and makes the cowfish's ears waggle and its eyes blink.

Tip. *How best to experience it:* Read several Seuss books ahead of time to get familiar; also don't rest your feet in the brass-colored enclosed stirrups, they're too high for most adults and too low for most kids.

Fun finds. ❶ Horton the Elephant sits atop the attraction, cradling the dandelion he found in "Horton Hears a Who." ❷ The ride attendant speaks in rhyme (usually).

Key facts. *Duration:* 2 minutes, 6 revolutions. *Capacity:* 60 (56 animals, two 2-seat carriages). *Access:* Handheld infants, service animals allowed in carriages. *Restraint:* Seat belt on animals. *Queue:* Outdoor, partially covered. *Debuted:* 1999. *Location:* Seuss Landing.

Average wait times

9am	10am	11am	Noon	1pm	2pm	3pm	4pm	5pm	6pm	7pm	8pm	9pm
5m	5m	5m	5m	5m	5m	5m	5m	5m	5m	5m	5m	5m

Pleased to meet you. The Cat in the Hat, Sam I Am and (below) The Lorax.

Oh! The Stories You'll Hear

Sweet little outdoor show is hidden from the crowds

★★★ Suess characters mime their reactions as the Reader (a live human actor) tells the story of either "The Lorax" or "Oh! The Places You'll Go" during this sweet outdoor show. Beforehand they do a little song-and-dance routine; afterward you can pose with them for photos as they hang out in the shade. The characters are some of the most beloved Dr. Seuss stars—the Cat in the Hat, the Grinch, the Lorax, Sam I Am from "Green Eggs and Ham," and Thing One and Thing Two from "The Cat in the Hat." The Grinch skips the show during the Christmas season.

Tip. *How best to experience it:* If few people stick around afterward take time to do so yourself; the Things can be quite playful.

Key facts. *Duration:* 9-minute show with a 15-minute meet-and-greet. *Showtimes:* Scheduled; shows typically begin before noon and continue throughout the afternoon; there are no shows on Sundays but the characters still come out for the meet-and-greets. *Moved indoors by:* Rain or the presence of lightning; which moves it inside the nearby Circus McGurkus Cafe Stoo-pendous. *Access:* Service animals allowed. *Location:* Seuss Landing.

Flying high, a mom and daughter prepare to dip under sprays of water.

One Fish, Two Fish, Red Fish, Blue Fish

Flying fish, spitting fish, and a song that tricks you

★★★★ *EXPRESS* Water squirts at you on this little hub and spoke ride, which puts you into a fish from the eponymous Dr. Seuss book as other fish spit at you. You control the up and down movement of your fish with a lever. It's a kick to try to avoid the streams of water, or on a hot day try to hit them. But whatever you do don't listen to the ride's song—it lies! Supposedly it tells you how to avoid the sprays but if you follow its advice you'll get wet. "Follow me and you'll stay dry." Hah!

Tips. *When to go:* Anytime; the line is rarely long. *How to stay dry:* Move your ride vehicle fish to the very top and watch for the one or two small squirts; duck your fish underneath them as you pass by. *How to get wet:* Keep your ride vehicle fish low or rise to the middle, and sit on the outside of your fish. *How best to experience it:* Sit on the inside and steer your fish so the water hits your seatmate instead of you; if you have kids ride with them in a two-seat two-fish vehicle; letting them steer so they can fly through the squirts.

Fun finds. ❶ The ride attendant always speaks in rhyme (well, usually). ❷ Four Seuss-style fish topiaries are planted in front and to the right of the ride. ❸ The ride's spokes are decorated with green fish that have spinning, spiral-shaped tails. ❹ A star-bellied sneetch from the Dr. Seuss book "The Sneetches" stands atop the hub.

Key facts. *Duration:* 2 minutes. *Closed by:* Rain or the presence of lightning. *Capacity:* 27 (9 2-seat one-fish, 3 3-seat two-fish). *Access:* Service animals allowed. *Restraint:* Seat belt. *Queue:* Outdoor, partially covered. *Debuted:* 1999. *Location:* Seuss Landing.

Health advisory. Universal suggests you skip the ride if you have issues with dizziness, motion sickness or recently had surgery.

Average wait times

9am	10am	11am	Noon	1pm	2pm	3pm	4pm	5pm	6pm	7pm	8pm	9pm
5m	5m	5m	5m	5m	5m	5m	5m	5m	5m	5m	5m	5m

With stars upon thars, trolley riders pop out of the boarding area for a 3-minute tour.

The High in the Sky Seuss Trolley Train
Tour Seuss Landing on your choice of tracks

★★★ *EXPRESS* Four elevated open-air trains slowly tour Seuss Landing on this breezy little ride. The trolleys run on two tracks; each is 15 feet in the air. You'll hear one of four different narrations, all of which are in Seussian prose, none of which relate to the queue and the ride's animatronic scenes, which tell the story of the book "The Sneetches."

Tips. *Where to sit:* In the front seat for the best view. *How best to experience it:* Ride both tracks; the Beach one (on your left as you face the platform) circles over Seuss Landing and its beach, the Star one travels through the Circus McGurkis Cafe Stoo-pendous.

Fun finds. ❶ The queue passes the huge cranking machine from "The Sneetches," which places and removes stars from bellies. Its arms have stars with hanging dollar signs; in the middle a glass window reveals Sylvester McMonkey McBean working on its mechanics. ❷ Each trolley has its name on its back: the Beach ones are Hot-Shot and Oliver Boliver; the Star ones Blinkey and Sneepy. ❸ Seen from the Beach track, the shoreline of Sneetch Beach has a sandcastle, a ball with a star, footprints leading into the water and ❹ the book "If I Ran the Zoo" on a beach towel.

Key facts. *Duration:* 2 minutes, 41 seconds. *Closed by:* Rain or the presence of lightning. *Capacity:* 80 (4 20-seat ride vehicles, each with 10 2-seat rows). *Height minimum:* 40 inches. *Access:* Rider Swap available; assistive listening available; service animals allowed. *Restraint:* Lap bar. *Queue:* Outdoor, covered. *Debuted:* 2006. *Location:* Seuss Landing.

Health advisory. Universal suggests you skip the ride if you're pregnant or have heart conditions; abnormal blood pressure; back or neck conditions; dizziness, motion-sickness or strobe issues; or recently had surgery.

Average wait times

9am	10am	11am	Noon	1pm	2pm	3pm	4pm	5pm	6pm	7pm	8pm	9pm
5m	10m	20m	20m	10m	15m	20m	15m	10m	5m	5m	5m	5m

Maintenance issues. Poseidon is so furious he's let his temple go to ruin.

Poseidon's Fury

A special-effects smackdown from the Greek god of the sea

★★★ *EXPRESS* If you like special effects—fire, water, lasers, smoke—you'll appreciate this guided theatrical presentation. Its best effect is a circular passageway; its walls are formed by a swirling water vortex. Other effects include mist screens, water cannons and mortars which splash around you. The experience culminates with a battle that unfolds onto screens of water and has many explosions.

Taylor's tour. *Warning; spoilers ahead.* Your adventure starts off deep inside the ancient Temple of Poseidon. You're there for a tour, a trip that gets cancelled before it begins when your guide Taylor learns of dangers in the temple and decides to get you out of it. And then, of course, things go wrong. As you try to leave, interference from various gods and goddesses forces you instead to go deeper and deeper into the ruins before you witness a ferocious fight between the god of the sea and his mortal enemy, the evil Lord Darkenon.

A crumbling stone temple houses the attraction; a giant octopus is carved over the entrance. Out front, a looming stone arm grasps a trident. Behind it are the remains of the rest of the statue: all that's left is a pair of sandal-clad feet.

Tips. *When to go:* The first show of the day for the shortest wait. *Where to stand:* In the front of the crowd if you're short or have children; since this is a stand-up attraction it's easy for your view to be blocked by other people if you're in the middle of the crowd.

Fun facts. ❶ The show uses over 200 distinct flame effects and four types of lasers. ❷ Actor Jeremy Irons provides the voice of Poseidon. He voiced Scar in "The Lion King."

Key facts. *Duration:* 25 minutes. *Showtimes:* Continuous; usually begin an hour after the park opens, closing 30 minutes or so before park close. *Access:* Assistive listening available; service animals allowed. *Fear factor:* Loud explosions, large flames, flashing lights, overhead water effects and many instances of total darkness. *Queue:* Indoor. *Debuted:* 1999. *Location:* The Lost Continent.

Health advisory. Universal suggests you skip the show if you're pregnant or have heart conditions; abnormal blood pressure; back or neck conditions; dizziness, motion-sickness or strobe issues; or recently had surgery.

Sindbad jumps a bad guy as he fights to free a princess.

The Eighth Voyage of Sindbad

High-camp stunt show has skilled performers, silly jokes

★★★ *EXPRESS* This campy live-action show features nearly non-stop action and a boatload of special effects; it was refreshed in 2015 to add more stunts and an audience-participation preshow. Its silly story—in an enchanted grotto, dashing swashbuckler Sindbad and his goofy sidekick Kebab work to rescue the saucy Princess Amoura from the monstrous minions of evil witch queen Misteria—hardly matters, as the talented performers are kept so busy kicking, flipping and flying through the air you'll hardly notice it. Kids in particular cheer the extravagant hand-to-hand combat, the many things that go boom and how Misteria catches fire and falls to her watery grave; some also get into it when Sindbad and Amoura slowly kiss to seal the happy ending. Afterward the actors meet viewers and pose for photos.

Preshow. Fifteen minutes before showtime there's an emergency announcement— "Our cast of stunt actors has somehow locked themselves in the gym and can't get out, so we need some replacements. Anyone want to be set on fire?" A stage manager chooses four volunteers… often picking a guy to play Misteria. The hapless group goes through a comical practice session before the regular cast extricates itself just before it's too late.

Tips. *Where to sit:* In the front row just to the right of center to have the evil minions interact with you. *How to be in the show:* When the stage manager asks for volunteers, immediately make a loud fool of yourself. *How best to experience it:* Use the show as a relaxing break from the hustle and bustle of Hogsmeade next door; the open-air amphitheater never fills up so it's easy to get a seat. *If you're a cynic:* Note how the physically fit Sindbad and Amoura try not to stare at each other's chests, how the colors of the backdrop resemble those of fish-tank coral and how Misteria's outfit resembles a Party City version of Disney's Maleficent.

Key facts. *Duration:* 20 minutes, preshow 15 minutes. *Showtimes:* Scheduled; typically four between noon and 6 p.m. *Capacity:* 1,400. *Access:* Assistive listening available, service animals allowed. *Debuted:* 1999, updated 2015. *Location:* The Lost Continent.

Health advisory. Universal suggests you skip this if you have issues with fog or strobes.

© Universal Orlando Resort

Goodbye to you. Hagrid bids you farewell as you pull out of Hogsmeade Station.

The Hogwarts Express — Hogsmeade Station

A magical train takes you to Diagon Alley

★★★★ *EXPRESS* As every Harry Potter fan knows, Hogwarts students arrive and depart the school on the Hogwarts Express, a red steam locomotive pulling passenger cars. Universal has re-created this journey with a real train that travels between Islands of Adventure and Universal Studios Florida (you need a park-to-park ticket or annual pass to board). More than simply transportation, it offers an immersive experience, using special effects and video screens to create distinctly different rides from one park to the other.

On this trip. *Warning; spoilers ahead.* Hagrid waves goodbye from the Hogsmeade platform. Buckbeak soars over Black Lake, skimming a talon on its surface; centaurs gallop through the Forbidden Forest. Fred and George Weasley fly by on broomsticks,

one tosses fireworks which explode into an ad for their store. Harry, Hermione and Ron stop outside your door; Ron presses his face and hands against the frosted glass. Later, spiders on the door freak Ron out until he realizes they're licorice; he eats one. After passing Malfoy Manor, you watch the Knight Bus squeeze and weave through London. Mad-Eye Moody waves you into King's Cross Station.

Key facts. *Duration:* 7 minutes. *Capacity:* 168, 3 train cars each with 7 8-seat compartments. *Access:* Service animals allowed. *Queue:* Indoor. *Debuted:* 2014. *Location:* Hogsmeade; travels to Diagon Alley.

Health advisory. Universal recommends that you avoid riding the train if you have issues with dizziness, enclosed spaces, motion sickness or fog effects.

Average wait times

9am	10am	11am	Noon	1pm	2pm	3pm	4pm	5pm	6pm	7pm	8pm	9pm
10m	10m	10m	15m	15m	20m	20m	15m	15m	20m	10m	10m	5m

Beauxbaton beauty. Elegant girls wave ribbons in rhythm in the Triwizard Spirit Rally.

Hogsmeade live shows

Graceful French girls, tough Bulgarian guys, singing toads

★★★★ ✔ A small raised outdoor stage between the Flight of the Hippogriff coaster and Hogwarts castle hosts two small live shows, both of them worth seeing.

Triwizard Spirit Rally. Students from the Beauxbatons Academy of Magic and Durmstrang Institute wizarding schools perform in the Triwizard Spirit Rally. The show celebrates the foreign institutions participating in the Triwizard Tournament, which took place in "Harry Potter and the Goblet of Fire." The girls perform a graceful, rhythmic dance routine while waving blue ribbons; each ribbon flourish precedes a breathy little "oooo" spoken in unison. The guys do a martial arts-style acrobatic routine as they flip, cartwheel and stamp their staffs on the stage. Afterward, the performers pose for photos.

Frog Choir. As two of them hold fat toads—not frogs—that croak rhythmic bass notes, a quartet of Hogwarts students sings a cappella in an upbeat mini-concert; each student represents one of the school's houses. Conducted by a Hogwarts prefect, the two boys and two girls harmonize to songs from the films. The tunes can include "Hedwig's Theme," "Something Wicked This Way Comes" and "Can You Dance Like a Hippogriff" by the famous wizarding rock band The Weird Sisters. The troupe poses for photos afterward.

The Frog Choir does not appear in the Harry Potter books; it debuted in the 2004 film "Harry Potter and the Prisoner of Azkaban" as a group of about two dozen students with toads, conducted by Prof. Flitwick. Director Alfonso Cuarón added the scene in; author J.K. Rowling loved the idea. In the 2007 film "Harry Potter and the Order of the Phoenix," the choir practices in the castle's Great Hall. Actor Warwick Davis—Prof. Flitwick in the films—conducted the choir at the opening ceremony of The Wizarding World of Harry Potter in 2010.

Key facts. *Duration:* Both shows are 12–15 minutes long. *Showtimes:* Scheduled; the Frog Choir typically at 10:30 a.m., 11:30 a.m., 12:30 p.m., 2 p.m., 3 p.m. and 4 p.m.; the Triwizard Spirit Rally at 10 a.m., 11 a.m., noon, 2:30 p.m., 3:30 p.m., 4:30 p.m., 6 p.m. and 7 p.m. *Access:* No seats; service animals allowed. *Debuted:* 2014. *Location:* Hogsmeade.

Five times you go upside down, regardless of which "dragon" you ride.

Dragon Challenge

Choose your track: intense or super-intense

★★★ *EXPRESS* You'll feel like you've challenged a dragon after riding this intense coaster. It has a pair of intertwined, suspended tracks; you decide which one to take. The red Chinese Fireball one is faster; the blue-green Hungarian Horntail more intense.

Called Dueling Dragons in the park's days before Hogsmeade, the coasters used to launch simultaneously to replicate a duel; after riders were injured that stopped. The reworked ride channels the dragon chasing Harry during the First Task of the Triwizard Championship from "Harry Potter and the Goblet of Fire." The queue passes Triwizard Championship banners and artifacts.

Tip. *Where to sit:* In front for the best view; in back to be whipped around the most.

Key facts. *Duration:* 8 minutes. *Closed by:* Rain or the presence of lightning. *Capacity:* 32 (8 4-seat rows). *Height minimum:* 54 inches. *Access:* Rider Swap, test seat available; service animals not allowed. *Restraint:* Shoulder harness. *Restricted items:* All personal belongings; locker use provided; as you enter the attraction, you pass through an electronic security system much like that at an airport. *Fear factor:* Dramatic acceleration, tilting and dropping; 5 inversions. *Queue:* Outdoor, partially covered; moves indoors. *Chinese Fireball top speed:* 60 mph, 115-foot drop. *Hungarian Horntail top speed:* 55 mph, 95-foot drop. *Track length:* 3,200 feet. *Track type:* Steel tubes filled with gravel and sand. *Manufacturer:* Bollinger & Mabillard. *Debuted:* 2010. *Location:* Hogsmeade.

Health advisory. Universal suggests you skip the ride if you're pregnant or have heart conditions; abnormal blood pressure; back or neck conditions; dizziness, motion-sickness or height issues; or recently had surgery.

Average wait times

9am	10am	11am	Noon	1pm	2pm	3pm	4pm	5pm	6pm	7pm	8pm	9pm
5m	10m	15m	20m	25m	20m	20m	10m	10m	10m	5m	5m	5m

A wicker "training hippogriff" is your vehicle, one with a woven head, wings and talons.

Flight of the Hippogriff

The Wizarding World of Hagrid, with a fun family coaster

★★★★★ ✔ *EXPRESS* Fang's husky barks ringing in your ears, Hagrid's deep British voice surrounding you, Buckbeak bowing you onward—this little coaster immerses you in the world of Harry Potter. Not just the world, but very specifically Hagrid's domain, which for many Potter fans is especially beloved. The environment is so evocative that you can close your eyes on the ride and pretend you're actually soaring on a hippogriff.

Don't think this is a kiddie ride; it's plenty thrilling for adults. You're always in a turn on the brief ride, which is thrilling but not scary, with four short curves but no drops or inversions. Unlike Dragon Challenge it doesn't terrify you and it isn't hard on you physically.

Tips. *Where to sit:* In front for the best view; in back for the wildest ride. *For couples:* Sit together; you'll share a snug bench seat and the constant turning will smush you together.

Key facts. *Duration:* 1 minute. *Closed by:* Rain or the presence of lightning. *Capacity:* 32 (2 16-seat trains, with eight 2-seat rows). *Height minimum:* 36 inches. *Access:* Rider Swap available; service animals not allowed. *Restraint:* Lap bar. *Restricted items:* All personal belongings should be in pockets, including cameras, car keys, loose change, phones, wallets. *Queue:* Outdoor, partially covered. *Top speed:* 29 mph. *Track length:* 1,100 feet. *Track height:* 43 feet. *Track type:* Steel tubes filled with gravel and sand. *Manufacturer:* Vekoma. *Coaster type:* Junior coaster. *Designer:* Universal Creative. *Debuted:* 2010. *Location:* Hogsmeade.

Health advisory. Universal suggests you skip the ride if you're pregnant or have heart conditions; abnormal blood pressure; back or neck conditions; dizziness, motion-sickness or height issues; or recently had surgery.

Average wait times

9am	10am	11am	Noon	1pm	2pm	3pm	4pm	5pm	6pm	7pm	8pm	9pm
10m	10m	10m	20m	20m	20m	25m	30m	30m	25m	20m	15m	15m

Hello Harry! You meet Harry Potter outside the observatory, then on the quidditch pitch.

Harry Potter and the Forbidden Journey

Harry's greatest hits—with a great tour of the castle

★★★★★ ✓ *EXPRESS* This thrilling coaster-simulator condenses some of the most intense elements from the first four Harry Potter films into less than five minutes. A fire-breathing dragon, giant spiders, quidditch, dementors—the scenes come and go so fast you'll get whiplash. Even if it can be hard to keep track of what's happening, it's still a memorable experience that'll leave you smiling.

The focal point of Hogsmeade, the ride combines advanced motion simulation, detailed set pieces, wrap-around video and detailed animatronics to immerse you in its action. While it has no drops, inversions or high speeds, it can still get pretty intense; some of the animatronic creatures are genuinely frightening, and the multidirectional moves of the ride vehicle can easily disorient you. Combined with all the flashy special effects, this makes the attraction difficult to ride twice in a row, especially right after a meal.

Though it's difficult to tell, the ride seems to take place sometime during "Harry Potter and the Order of the Phoenix." School Headmaster Albus Dumbledore is giving muggles (like you) a tour of Hogwarts to teach you about magic firsthand. He asks you to attend a lecture about the school's history, but Harry, Ron and Hermione—the hosts of the attraction—have other plans. They want to give you a proper tour and take you with them to an upcoming quidditch match. Predictably, their attempt to sneak you out goes horribly wrong, and soon you're thrust into a chaotic journey that puts you

Average wait times

9am	10am	11am	Noon	1pm	2pm	3pm	4pm	5pm	6pm	7pm	8pm	9pm
30m	30m	45m	30m	20m	20m	30m	30m	20m	25m	20m	20m	10m

Dumbledore's office, one of many rooms in Hogwarts castle you tour in the queue.

face-to-face with some of the most dangerous creatures in the wizarding world.

Hogwarts castle. Half of the attraction's appeal is in its queue, which winds through Hogwarts. Each of the castle's rooms looks just as it does in the Harry Potter films, and is filled with intricate details to look for while you wait in line.

The queue starts at the base of the castle and weaves through Hogwarts. Upon reaching the Headmaster's office, you're greeted by Dumbledore (an advanced projection), who explains that he's hosting an open house. He finishes his speech by asking you to attend a lecture by the infamously dull History of Magic teacher, Prof. Binns.

Before you can meet up with Binns, Harry, Ron, and Hermione sneak in and invite you to go with them to watch a Gryffindor-versus-Slytherin quidditch match. Before leaving, Hermione tells you to meet up with her so she can send you off to the quidditch pitch. Inside the Room of Requirement, you board a floating "enchanted bench" and begin the ride.

On the ride. *Warning; spoilers ahead.* Once onboard your flying bench, you quickly meet up with Hermione. She sends you through the Floo network up to the castle's highest tower, where you follow Harry and Ron to the quidditch pitch; they ride brooms and are decked out for the game.

Things quickly go wrong as an escaped dragon chases you, separating you from Harry and Ron. A face-to-face encounter with it knocks you off course and into the Forbidden Forest, where a swarm of acromantulas—giant spiders—hunts you from the shadows. You're saved by Hermione, only to run right into the bad-tempered Whomping Willow. Lucky for you, the tree's swinging branches whomp you right into the middle of the quidditch game. It's halfway over by now, and Slytherin is winning. As Harry races Draco Malfoy for the golden snitch, you're suddenly ambushed by a whirlwind of dementors. They chase you into the ruins of the Chamber of Secrets, where one nearly sucks out your soul. At the last minute, Harry swoops in, drives off the creatures with a Patronus charm and leads you to safety. Finally out of danger, you fly back to the castle to see the Gryffindor quidditch team celebrating their miraculous victory over Slytherin. As your journey comes to an end, Dumbledore congratulates you and says that you're free to return to Hogwarts anytime.

The animatronic creatures are probably the most memorable part of the attraction. Particularly noteworthy are the dementors—genuinely frightening, 10-foot-tall figures that swoop fluidly out of the darkness until they're only feet away from you.

A huge array of special effects adds to the immersion. A dragon opens its jaws at you and breathes a burst of red-lit steam, and shadows of giant spiders spritz you with "venom" that's simulated by drizzled water. When a dementor tries to suck out your soul, you hear a thumping heartbeat, the air chills, and the ghostly faces of you and your seatmates are projected onto a cloud of fog.

How best to experience it. Take at least 20 minutes to appreciate the details inside Hogwarts. To do this, you can either meander through the Standby queue—where you'll probably hold up other people in line—or you can ask to to take a self-guided "castle tour." The tour is a separate line that goes through all the same rooms as the regular queue as well as an additional room that's filled with talking portraits. You can take as much time as you want, and are allowed to bring loose articles like bags and cameras. The tour sometimes closes during peak periods. Only take the Single Rider Line if you've already been through the Standby queue. While it usually has a much shorter wait time, it skips most of the castle's rooms and details that set up the ride's plot. If you want to be prepared for the ride photo, wait until you enter the Forbidden Forest; it's taken during the flash of light when Hermione says "Arania Exumai."

Other tips. *When to go:* First thing in the morning or after dark; the detailed Standby queue won't be too crowded. *Where to sit:* On the right to have the dragon breathe fire at you; in the middle to reduce motion sickness slightly. *If you're scared of spiders:* Brace yourself during the Forbidden Forest scene; it's filled with giant spiders that hiss and spit venom; Aragog, the spiders' leader, is particularly detailed and shows up in a sudden flash of lightning.

Fun facts. ❶ Early concepts for the ride included an appearance by Voldemort and a scene based on the giant chessboard scene from "Harry Potter and the Sorcerer's Stone." ❷ In the queue, portraits of the four Hogwarts founders use actors cast specifically for this attraction. ❸ The ride vehicles use advanced Kuka-brand technology to simulate flight, falling and other movement. Each "flying bench" connects to a flexible robotic arm that moves smoothly along a track; it moves in synch with videos shown on wrap-around video screens. These complex mechanics are completely obscured during the ride. ❹ The ride doesn't stop for boarding or departing. This means that when it breaks down, people on the ride get stuck in whatever position they were in when it stopped; some find themselves flat on their backs or surrounded by unsettling dementors.

Key facts. *Duration:* 4 minutes. *Capacity:* 768 in 192 4-seat ride benches. *Height minimum:* 48 inches. *Access:* Single Rider Line, Rider Swap, test seat available. *Restraint:* Shoulder harness. *Restricted items:* All personal belongings must be kept in pockets, including cameras and phones; locker use provided. *Fear factor:* Large, in-your-face animatronic dragon, dementors and giant spiders attack you; a dementor tries to suck out your soul; disorienting motion simulation. *Queue:* Indoor, overflows into a partially shaded outdoor area. *Debuted:* 2010. *Souvenir photos:* $27–$45; purchase not required. *Location:* Hogsmeade.

Health advisory. Universal suggests you skip the ride if you are pregnant or have heart conditions; abnormal blood pressure; back or neck conditions; issues with dizziness, enclosed spaces, fog, heights, motion sickness or strobe effects; or recently had surgery.

Fun finds. ❶ The ride's safety-information signs were created by the Ministry of Magic's Department of Magical Transportation. ❷ Ride attendants dress like house prefects. ❸ As you look at the castle, the covered bridge that crosses the rocky gorge is visible in the distance. On the ride, this bridge is where you get cornered by the escaped dragon. ❹ The plain white building that houses the actual ride is visible behind the castle. ❺ Twin pillars topped by winged boar statues border the start of the line. Twinkling lights spell out the ride's name on the face of each pillar.

The dungeons. ❻ In the queue, the Mirror of Erised stands to the left. ❼ To the right, a greenish statue depicts a hunchbacked witch—a historical figure known as Gunhilda of Gorsemoor. In the books, the statue's hump conceals a secret passage that leads all the way out to Honeydukes. ❽ Prof. Snape's office door is just past Gunhilda's statue. ❾ You can hear a teacher lecturing Neville Longbottom from behind the door to the Potions classroom, to the left of the queue line.

Herbology greenhouses. ❿ Thick vines curl around the frame and rafters of the greenhouses. ⓫ Exotic plants grow from pots hanging over the line. ⓬ Potted mandrakes shift in their pots on a fenced-off shelf towards the end of the greenhouses.

Oxford Corridor. ⑬ A golden statue of the school's architect and first headmaster stands on the right; he holds a long scroll in one hand and a miniature representation of the castle in the other. A lion and a badger rest at his feet. ⑭ The four hourglasses that record house points are set up past the statue. They show Gryffindor in the lead, followed by Slytherin, Hufflepuff and Ravenclaw. ⑮ A statue of Salazar Slytherin glares at people further down the line. ⑯ A bronze griffin statue stands at the end of the corridor. In the films, it marks the entrance to the headmaster's office. ⑰ A tapestry of a unicorn hangs on the wall to the right; in the films, it marks the entrance to the Room of Requirement.

Portrait hall/chamber. ⑱ On the right, a portrait of a former Potions teacher boasts about his expertise in the field. ⑲ Portraits of the four Hogwarts founders hang in the next room. Gryffindor, Hufflepuff and Ravenclaw argue with Slytherin, who's outraged Dumbledore allowed muggles into the castle. ⑳ They lament the news that Hagrid's pet dragon has escaped. "Let's just hope it doesn't burn down the owlery like last time," says Ravenclaw. ㉑ Gryffindor holds his ruby-studded sword, Hufflepuff cradles her golden cup, Ravenclaw wears her silver diadem and Slytherin wears his golden locket.

Headmaster's office. ㉒ Though he warns you about the escaped dragon on school grounds, Dumbledore reassures that all muggles have protective charms placed on them. On the ride, these charms shield from the dragon in question as well as from other dangers, but are ineffective against dementors. ㉓ Dumbledore promises you that Prof. Binns' lecture will "condense hundreds of years of Hogwarts history into a few short hours." ㉔ At one point during his speech, Dumbledore magically makes a book change position on a shelf. ㉕ The Sword of Gryffindor is mounted on the left wall. ㉖ Dumbledore's Penseive sits in its cabinet in the left corner of the room. ㉗ The empty perch of Fawkes the phoenix sits nearby.

Defense Against the Dark Arts classroom. ㉘ A dragon skeleton hangs from the ceiling, just as it does in the second movie. ㉙ The classroom's desks have been removed to make room for the queue line. ㉚ A chalkboard outlines the right way to conjure a Patronus. ㉛ Iconic items from every Defense Against the Dark Arts teacher in the series are scattered throughout the room. These include Quirrell's leather traveling trunks, stacks of Lockhart's autobiography "Magical Me," Lupin's spinal column-shaped candlesticks, Moody's walking stick, stacks of Umbridge's "Dark Arts Defense: Basics for Beginners" textbook and Snape's slide projector. ㉜ Ron tries to send you straight to the quidditch pitch by using magic, but screws up the spell; the attempt triggers a special effect such as snow falling from the ceiling or rain pouring outside the window.

Hall to common room. ㉝ A stained-glass window on the right is replicated from a brief scene with Neville in the 2005 film "Harry Potter and the Goblet of Fire." ㉞ The Fat Lady's portrait urges you to keep walking, chats excitedly about the upcoming quidditch game and expresses concerns about letting so many people inside the Gryffindor common room without the password. ㉟ On a bulletin board to the left, an issue of the Daily Prophet features an article about the upcoming Gryffindor/Slytherin quidditch match.

Gryffindor common room. ㊱ Portraits of an aviator, an etiquette teacher and a quidditch star argue about the proper safety procedures for riding the "enchanted bench" vehicles. ㊲ A copy of Prof. Umbridge's "Dark Arts Defense: Basics for Beginners" textbook lays abandoned on the common room's sofa.

Sorting Hat. ㊳ Past the common room, it recites the safety spiel in its gravelly voice.

The Room of Requirement. ㊴ Dozens of glowing candles float above the boarding area; mirrored walls give the illusion that there are many more candles than there actually are.

On the ride. ㊵ "Those benches can be a bit dodgy. But we haven't lost anyone yet!" Harry says when he and Ron first meet up with you. "Not this week, anyway!" adds Ron. ㊶ Upon entering the Forbidden Forest, you can hear screeching bats and a hooting owl. ㊷ A flash of lightning reveals Aragog, the acromantulas' leader, just feet away from you. ㊸ "Showing off for your muggle admirers, Potter?" sneers Malfoy on the quidditch pitch. ㊹ The Chamber of Secrets is in ruins: the basilisk's curled skeleton lies abandoned. ㊺ While flying over the Black Lake, you pass through a flock of owls carrying student mail. ㊻ Past the owls, the dragon from earlier flies by the castle. ㊼ As your bench settles down, Dumbledore reminds you to pick up your stored belongings, "lest you want them confiscated by Mr. Filch."

Exitway. ㊽ Monitors urging you to "View Ride Photos To The Left!" point with a jagged arrow shaped like Harry's lightning-bolt scar.

Universal CityWalk

IF YOU DRIVE TO UNIVERSAL ORLANDO, or take a bus or other ground transportation to get to it, you walk through this combination dining, entertainment, nightclub and retail district on your way to its theme parks; if you arrive via water taxi your boat docks here. Popular with locals as well as tourists (the authors of this book come here at least once a week), CityWalk is also a destination all its own, with national brands that run the gamut from Starbucks to Emeril's, Hard Rock Cafe to Blue Man Group. The 30-acre area opened in 1999 as part of a massive expansion of Universal's Florida project that also added a second theme park, Islands of Adventure, hotels and a huge parking complex. CityWalk includes a 20-theater movie house, a 36-hole miniature golf course, a few nightclubs, dozens of restaurants and a handful of stores. Partiers can hit a variety of spots until 2 a.m., some clubs and restaurants have live music, some have DJs. Among other benefits it offers a convenient place to eat dinner after a day at the parks.

Restaurants. There are some good ones here, with memorable food and interesting decor. Prices can be high, but not always.

The Cowfish. ✔ Like burgers? Like sushi? Either way, this restaurant is for you. It's not the fanciest restaurant at Universal, not by a mile, but it is the most inventive and quirky, and it serves up dishes that might be some of the most unique you've ever had. Expect sushi that's more innovative than you're accustomed to at a mid-priced spot (even if not exactly Japanese), and hamburgers crafted with as much concern about the beef as the stuff piled on top of it. *Sunday–Thursday 11 a.m. to 11 p.m.; Friday, Saturday to midnight. $14–$25 (children $7). Seats 642 inside, 74 on a second-floor patio.*

NBC Sports Grill & Brew. ✔ It's tough to miss this expansive sports bar and grill—its bright-as-day stadium screen towering over the entrance stretches more than 120 feet, playing the greatest moments in NBC Sports history. Inside, TV screens air live sporting events, but the audio is muted; you hear upbeat pop and rock. A monster menu offers over 75 dishes, from the requisite burgers and wings to filet mignon and grilled shrimp. The quality of the food may surprise you. Chefs make good use of open-fire grills, adding a wonderful charred flavor to many dishes. The salmon is noteworthy—it's grilled on a cedar plank that's soaked overnight to let the cedar flavor infiltrate the fish and keep it moist. Skip the ridiculously huge banana cake for dessert; instead go for the dense but fluffy New York cheesecake or the apple crumble with spicy raisins and butterscotch. Specialty drinks include a pineapple-flavored Crimson Derby and a manly Kentucky Gold—whiskey, orange juice and bitters. Over 8 dozen bottled and draft beers include craft brews and an exclusive IPA. *On the Studios walkway. Noon–1:30 a.m. $10–$45 (children $7). Seats 625 inside; 36 outside on shaded tables. 407-224-2353.*

Antojitos Authentic Mexican Food. This colorful, boisterous eatery serves chimichangas, tacos, fajitas and the like, with handmade tortillas and guacamole made tableside; its tequila drinks are varied and exceptional. Second-floor tables offer private spots to eat. *On the elevated southern walkway, next to Jimmy Buffett's Margaritaville. 11 a.m. to 11 p.m. Sunday–Thursday; Friday, Saturday to midnight. $13–$22 (children $7). Seats 580 inside; 44 outside on a shaded patio. 407-224-2804.*

Bob Marley: A Tribute to Freedom. ✔ This laid-back Jamaican eatery serves jerk chicken and grilled mahi-mahi at reasonable prices. The front re-creates Bob Marley's home in Jamaica. Memorabilia and photos from his life decorate the walls. Most of the covered seating is open to the elements, with no air conditioning. *On the elevated southern walkway, across from Cowfish. 4 p.m.–2 a.m. $10–$18 (children $7). Seats 400 inside.*

Bubba Gump Shrimp Co. The menu features Southern-style shrimp dishes but also offers burgers, fish and ribs. A walk-around costumed shrimp waves to passing visitors outside the restaurant. A gift shop sells "Forrest Gump" souvenirs including a "Stupid is as stupid does" T-shirt. *Across from the Cineplex. 11 a.m. to midnight, $10–$23 (children $6). Seats 302. 407-903-0044.*

Emeril's Restaurant Orlando. This sophisticated, white-tablecloth eatery serves po-boys, cheeseburgers and pizza for lunch; for dinner they offer fish, steaks and vegetarian dishes. The tall ceilings and wood floors

make for a noisy atmosphere. No sleeveless shirts for men and boys ages 12 and over. *On the walkway to Islands of Adventure, next to Jimmy Buffett's Margaritaville. Lunch 11:30 a.m.–3 p.m., $13–$18 (children $6–$8); dinner 5 p.m.–10 p.m. Sunday–Thursday, to 10:30 p.m. on Friday and Saturday, $21–$40 (children $8–$18). Seats 676 inside, 154 outside on covered terrace. 407-224-2424.*

Hard Rock Cafe. The world's largest Hard Rock Cafe serves hamburgers, sandwiches, steaks, ribs and flatbread from its expansive menu; there's a ton of rock memorabilia. *Across the lagoon, next to Islands of Adventure. 11 a.m.–midnight. $14–$35 (children $7). Seats 1,200 inside; 30 outside on unshaded tables. 407-351-7625.*

Jimmy Buffett's Margaritaville. This amiably tacky spot serves fish, sandwiches, tacos and steaks as well as, of course, cheeseburgers and margaritas. Many screens show Buffett videos; the tourist-trap decor features fake stuffed sharks; real surfboards, fishing and boating stuff—every cliché you can think of about Florida in one convenient spot. One of three bars has a volcano, its lava made from margarita mix. *On the Islands of Adventure walkway. 10:30 a.m. to midnight Sunday–Thursday; Friday and Saturday to 1 a.m. $14–$27 (children $8–$10). Seats 898 inside; 208 outside on shaded tables. 407-224-2155.*

Pat O'Brien's Orlando. This New Orleans-style eatery, a franchisee of the famous Big Easy spot, serves Cajun and Creole dishes: jambalaya, po-boy sandwiches, crawfish etouffee. Desserts include bags of beignets. The famous Hurricane drink comes in its souvenir glass. *On the elevated southern walkway. 4 p.m.–2 a.m. $10–$18 (children $7). Seats 589 inside, 206 on terrace. 407-224-2106.*

Vivo Italian Kitchen. ✔ No fancy flourishes here, just fresh comfort food such as fettuccine carbonara, chicken Marsala, risotto with short ribs. Reasonable prices belie the quality of ingredients; the mozzarella is hand-pulled. Sit at the food bar around the kitchen to watch cooks hang fresh pasta. *On the central walkway, next to Cowfish. 5 p.m.–11 p.m. $13–$27 (children $7). Seats 420 inside; 47 outside on shaded tables. 407-224-2253.*

Fast-food spots. There's a Burger King, but dig a little deeper and you'll find a sweet sandwich spot, a very good pizza place and other fine eateries that won't break your budget.

Burger King Whopper Bar. The chain's signature burger offered with unusual toppings. Chicken sandwiches. Food court atmosphere. Shares seating with Moe's and Panda Express. *On the elevated northern walkway next to the AMC Universal Cineplex. 10:30 a.m.–11 p.m. Thursday through Sunday; Friday and Saturday to 1 a.m. $8–$10 (children $6–$7). Seats 88 inside.*

Bread Box Handcrafted Sandwiches. ✔ These hot melts, cold deli sandwiches and salads are made with tender loving care. Fries come with all orders. The triple-decker grilled 3-cheese is perfect comfort food. Two tables have swinging bench seats. The diner-like atmosphere is bright, cheery and comfortable. You order at the counter; they bring you your food. Unlike many CityWalk counter-service spots, it has its own bathroom. Bread Box is one of the authors' favorite CityWalk spots; if you see an old guy or a young girl with a camera or a hard-working woman with a laptop, come say Hi. *On the elevated northern walkway next to the AMC Universal Cineplex. 10:30 a.m.–10 p.m. Thursday through Sunday; Friday and Saturday to 1 a.m. $8–$12 (children $8). Seats 146 inside. 407-224-2556.*

Cinnabon. Cinnamon rolls, like in the mall. *Central walkway. 7:30 a.m.–11:30 p.m. Sunday–Thursday, Friday and Saturday to 12:30 a.m. $3–$6. Seats 14 inside; 24 outside on shaded tables.*

Cold Stone Creamery. Hand dipped ice cream, shakes and other ice cream treats. *Central walkway, next to Starbucks. 10:30 a.m.–midnight Sunday–Thursday; Friday and Saturday to 1 a.m. $5–$8. Seats 16 outside on covered tables.*

Fusion Bistro & Sake Bar. Bento boxes, mako rolls and sashimi. Ordering window with outdoor seating. *On the elevated northern walkway next to the AMC Universal Cineplex. 11 a.m.–midnight to 2 a.m. $7–$12. Seats 200 outside on shaded tables in shared outdoor courtyard.*

Hot Dog Hall of Fame. ✔ Hot dogs (and mustards) from baseball stadiums around the country. Best is the Chicago dog, a Vienna sausage topped with onions, tomatoes and banana pepppers; finish it off with Boetje's, a stone-ground mustard made in Illinois for more than a century. A huge screen above the ordcring counter shows sporting events. *On the elevated southern walkway next to Emeril's. 11 a.m.–10 p.m. Sunday–Thursday; Friday and Saturday to 1 a.m. $9–$15. Seats 64 outside on shaded tables, a separate section lines up 18 authentic stadium seats from ballparks throughout the country,* each marked with a plaque indicating its years of use.

Lone Palm Airport. Tropical tiki bar serves Cuban sandwiches, wings, hot dogs, burgers. Tucked behind it is a real seaplane, the Hemisphere Dancer, owned by Jimmy Buffett. The singer piloted the craft through the Caribbean; it's the inspiration for the song "Jamaica Mistaica." *On the walkway to Islands of adventure across from Jimmy Buffet's Margaritaville restaurant. 10:30 a.m.–11 or midnight. $6–$17. Seats 84 outside on shaded tables.*

Menchie's Frozen Yogurt. You make your own frozen yogurt or sorbet treat at this tiny spot which has more than two dozen toppings. *On the elevated northern walkway next to the AMC Universal Cineplex. 11 a.m.–10 p.m. Thursday through Sunday; Friday and Saturday to 11 p.m. $4–$9 (children $5–$6). 59 cents per ounce; typical order costs $4–$6. Seats 11 inside.*

Moe's Southwest Grill. Made-to-order burritos, quesadillas, tacos. Food court atmosphere. Shares seating with Panda Express and the Whopper Bar. *On the elevated northern walkway next to the AMC Universal Cineplex. 10:30 a.m.–11 p.m. Thursday through Sunday; Friday and Saturday to 1 a.m. $4–$9 (children $5–$6). Seats 88 inside.*

Panda Express. Orange chicken, Kung Pao chicken and broccoli beef. Food court atmosphere. Shares seating with Moe's and the Burger King Whopper Bar. *On the elevated northern walkway next to the AMC Universal Cineplex. 10:30 a.m.–11 p.m. Thursday through Sunday; Friday and Saturday to 1 a.m. 10:30 a.m.–11 p.m. Thursday through Sunday; Friday and Saturday to 1 a.m. $8–$10 (children $6). Seats 88 inside.*

Red Oven Pizza Bakery. ✔ Don't expect fancy. You're going to sit outside, you're not going to spend much and you're going to eat pizza. But do expect to fall in love with this place, because these pizzas are fantastic. Imagine—a pizza for two for 12 bucks and it tastes like it was just thrown together at an Italian farmers market and then seared to perfection in some old firey oven. That's what you get here, a spot you'd probably walk right by if you didn't know better, because it sits out on the CityWalk entranceway with no more presence than the Starbucks next door. But it's worth a stop, for its crackly crusts that come out just a little charred and its wonderful toppings such as roasted portobello mushroom, buffalo mozzarella

© NBCUniversal

NBC Sports Grill & Brew.

and sweet fennel sausage. There's even a good dessert pizza: pear and fig. Servers bring your pie to your table and refill your beverages constantly, earning their tips. *On the central walkway from the parking garage, next to Cold Stone Creamery. 11 a.m. to midnight Sunday–Thursday; Friday and Saturday to 1:30 a.m. $12–$14. Seats 120 outside on shaded tables.*

Starbucks. ✔ Breakfast sandwiches, other sandwiches, pastries and—of course—coffee. Crowded after the parks close. A high ceiling and nice lighting make for a comfortable atmosphere. *On the central walkway near the AMC Universal Cineplex. 7 a.m.–midnight Thursday through Sunday; Friday and Saturday to 1 a.m. $4–$8. Seats 56 inside; 88 outside on covered tables. 407-244-2910.*

Auntie Anne's Pretzels. Pretzels and pretzel dogs. *Studios walkway, in front of NBC Sports Grill & Brew. 9 a.m.–9:30 p.m. $4–$7. No seats.*

Dippin' Dots. Ice cream in cups, sundaes and floats. *Islands of Adventure walkway. 11 a.m.–11 p.m. $5–$6. No seats.*

Icon. Or as most people call it, "The Giant Coke Bottle with the Video Screen." Foot-long hot dogs and foot-long corn dogs, turkey legs, pretzels. Outdoor stand. *In the Coke bottle on the central walkway. 9 a.m.–2 hours after park close. $9–$13. No seats.*

Bars. Over a dozen small outdoor stands serve as full-service bars. All offer specialty cocktails; some have beer on tap. Most have seats that circle their stands, with perhaps a few tables nearby. Two locations of Fat Tuesday (one by The Groove, one by the water on the walkway to Universal Studios) specialize in flavored frozen daiquiris. *3 p.m.–11:30 p.m. or midnight.*

Clubs. Whether you're a college kid here on Spring Break or all-grown-up and respectable, CityWalk has a place you can party.

CityWalk's Rising Star. ✔ It's karaoke, but in a way that you may have never seen before: singers perform with a live band complete with backup singers, on a big stage with spotlights, strobe lights and a smoke machine. A huge song list includes tunes geared to guys (The Jet's "Are You Gonna Be My Girl," Young MC's "Bust a Move"), tunes geared to women (Britney Spears' "Hit Me Baby, One More Time," Ke$ha's "Tik Tok") and dozens that could be performed by anyone (Poison's "Talk Dirty to Me"). The result is a lively environment where almost everyone cheers the singers along and sings along with them—regardless of whether they're talented or talent-free. The club's also a good people-watching spot, a two-level venue where many dress to the nines. *On the elevated southern* *walkway, across from The Groove. 8 p.m.–2 a.m. Cover charge $7. Seats 420. 407-224-4233.*

Red Coconut Club. 1950s Vegas. 1950s Havana. 1960s Tiki Room. They blend together here. Couches look vintage; bar stools look like bongos. Intimate tables hide on two levels; three lively bars are easy to find; a high ceiling tops the dance floor. On Saturday nights DJs drive a Latin beat: bachata, merengue and salsa mixed with reggae, rap and pop; Thursday is Latin night. Live bands perform Thursdays through Saturdays. A calm outdoor balcony offers a change of pace. Happy hour typically runs to 9 p.m. *On the elevated southern walkway across the AMC Universal Cineplex. 7 p.m.–2 a.m. Monday–Saturday, opens at 8 p.m. Sunday. Cover $7. Ages 21 and up; casual chic dress code, no hats or tank tops. Smoke free. 407-224-2425.*

The Groove. Meant to be a steampunk-era theater that's slowly being renovated, this multi-level club swirls lights over its high-energy dance floor. Resident and guest DJs spin pulsating music in an open format. Multiple bars. *On the elevated southern walkway next to Antojito's. 9 p.m.–2 a.m. Cover $7. Ages 21 and up; casual chic dress code, no hats or tank tops. 407-224-2166.*

Other entertainment. Not a dancer? Want to dine, then dance in the same spot? Have children with you? You've got options galore.

AMC Universal Cineplex. Twenty-screen movie theater features all-stadium seating with high-backed rocking chairs, digital projection and sound systems and an IMAX auditorium. Concession stands include a full bar. *On the central walkway. Hours vary. Tickets $10 (children $8) after 4. IMAX $15 (children $12). Discounts for military, seniors, students and movies before 4 p.m. 407-354-3374 box office; press 0 for movie times.*

Blue Man Group. ✔ They never speak. Never smile. But their whole show is full of wit, an irreverent Harpo Marx humor that creates a pretension-free spectacle. There's nothing quite like it; the closest thing is the Muppets' performance of the nonsense song Mahna Mahna that aired on a 1969 "Ed Sullivan Show." But even that sells it short. Because at times it's also a rock concert, a dance party, a joyful piece of performance art both high-tech and low that involves everyone in the theater. You'll leave happy; your kids will too. And you'll all have an expanded vocabulary, ready to use phrases such as "Minneapolis and St. Paul" and "happy walrus

with no tusks" in ways you never considered before. It's one of seven permanent Blue Man shows in the world. *At the 1,015-seat Sharp Aquos Theatre, next to the Universal Studios theme park. 90-minute shows at 6 and 9 p.m. Tuesday through Saturday. Reserved seats $60–$100 (children $30–$70). Pricier options include a backstage tour; meal-and-show deals. 1,015 seats. Tickets available 6 months early at blueman.com or at the Blue Man Group box office: 8 a.m.–7 p.m. 407-258-3626.*

Bob Marley: A Tribute to Freedom. ✔ Live reggae band plays every night starting at 9 p.m.; the band plays for 45 minutes then takes a 30-minute break while a DJ takes over. The music continues until 1:30 a.m. There's a $7 cover charge after 9 p.m.

Hard Rock Live Orlando. This live concert venue features musical and comedy acts; audio, lighting and video is high-tech. Full bar and concession stand. *Ticket prices vary by act. Seats 3,000. 407-351-5483.*

Hollywood Drive-In Golf. ✔ Two 18-hole mini-golf courses—The Haunting of Ghostly Greens and Invaders from Planet Putt—are themed to 1950s horror and sci-fi movies. You putt past a cemetery, under a giant spider, around an alien robot, through the gaping mouth of a huge space worm and into the basement lab of a haunted house. Edge-lighting lines nighttime play. *At the end of the moving walkway from the parking garages. 9 a.m.–2 a.m. One course $15 (children $13), two courses $27 (children $23). Discounts for AAA members, Florida passholders, residents, military and seniors. 407-802-4848.*

Jimmy Buffett's Margaritaville. A live band plays on the indoor stage; a guitarist entertains on the outdoor Porch of Indecision. *10 p.m. to midnight Sunday–Thursday; Friday and Saturday to 1 a.m. $7 cover charge after 10 p.m. 407-224-2155.*

Pat O'Brien's Orlando. Dueling pianos in Pat O's Piano Bar. *On the elevated southern walkway. 5 p.m.–2 a.m. $7 cover charge after 9 p.m. 21 and older after 9 p.m.*

Shopping. First you get your Dr. Seuss T, then you get your tattoo. Looks good, right?

Element. One of four Element stores in the world, with a huge assortment of the brand's eco-friendly dresses, footwear, hats, pants, shirts, skirts, shorts, tops; also handbags, shoulder bags. Exclusive skateboard decks, wheels. *Studios walkway next to the NBC Sports Grill & Brew. 8:30 a.m.–11 p.m.; Friday, Saturday to midnight. 407-224-3663.*

Bob Marley: A Tribute to Freedom.

Fossil. Watches; also handbags, jewelry, sunglasses, wallets. *At the center of CItyWalk, 9 a.m.–11 p.m., Friday and Saturday to midnight. 407-226-1705.*

Fresh Produce. Casual loose-fitting womenswear; Vera Bradley bags and luggage, Crocs footwear. *Studios walkway. 10 a.m.–11 p.m. 407-363-9363.*

Hart & Huntington Tattoo Co. Asian, fantasy, realistic and traditional tattoos for ages 18 and up; apparel and accessories. *North walkway across from Menchie's Frozen Yogurt. 10 a.m.–midnight. 407-373-0718.*

The Island Clothing Store. Resort wear from Lacoste, Lilly Pulitzer, Tommy Bahama. Designer sunglasses. *Studios walkway. 8 a.m.–11 p.m. 407-224-2165.*

P!Q. Quirky novelties, toys. *Studios walkway. 10 a.m.–11 p.m. 407-224-2305.*

Quiet Flight Surf Shop. Casual fashion apparel from Billabong, Element, Hurley, Nixon, Quicksilver, Quiet Flight, Roxy, Volcom and other brands. Sandals, sunglasses, swimwear. Merges with Island Clothing Co. into one long shop. *Central walkway, the first store on your right as you enter CityWalk. 8 a.m.–11 p.m. 407-224-2125.*

Universal Studios Store. Universal-branded items as well as Dr. Seuss, Harry Potter, Simpsons, Spider-Man, SpongeBob, Woody Woodpecker gear; candy; DVDs.

Islands of Adventure walkway. 9:30 a.m.–11 p.m. 407-363-8000.

Other shops. Five restaurants have their own shops: Bubba Gump, Margaritaville, Hard Rock, Bob Marley's and Pat O'Brien's.

Tickets. Most clubs have a $7 cover charge; a $12 Party Pass gives you unlimited club-to-club access to Bob Marley: A Tribute to Freedom (after 9 p.m.), Rising Star, The Groove, Margaritaville (after 10 p.m.), Pat O'Brien's (after 9 p.m.) and the Red Coconut. For $15 you also get a movie ticket at the Cineplex. If you already have a multi-day park ticket or a Premier annual pass you get a Party Pass at no extra charge.

Ticket packages. The Meal & Movie Deal gives you a movie ticket for the AMC Universal Cineplex and a meal at Bob Marley: A Tribute to Freedom, Fusion Bistro Sushi & Sake Bar, Jimmy Buffett's Margaritaville or Pat O'Brien's; the meal is from a limited menu; price is $22. The Meal & Mini Golf Deal gives you one round of miniature golf at the Hollywood Drive-In Golf and a meal at one of the same four restaurants from the Meal & Movie Deal; again, the meal is from a limited menu; price is $24. The Meal & Blue Man Group Deal gives you admission to a Blue Man show and a limited-menu meal at one of the restaurants above. It starts at $75.

Accommodations

WITH THE OPENING OF ISLANDS OF ADVENTURE in 1999, Universal Orlando became a destination expansive enough to fill on-site hotel rooms. A partnership with Loews Hotels opened the Loews Portofino Bay Hotel that same year, followed by the Hard Rock Hotel in 2000 and the Loews Royal Pacific Resort in 2001. Cabana Bay Beach Resort, Universal's first value-level property, opened in 2014. A moderate hotel, the Loews Sapphire Falls Resort, debuted in the summer of 2016.

Why stay at a Universal hotel? Staying on-site at one of these properties gives you special benefits. One of the biggest: the ability to enter one of the two Universal theme parks an hour before it opens to experience The Wizarding World of Harry Potter virtually crowd-free. The upscale Hard Rock Hotel, Loews Portofino Bay and Loews Royal Pacific also provide guests with free Universal Express Unlimited passes for both Universal theme parks. These passes let you bypass the standby lines at all attractions that accept them, which is most all of them. And you can use it at all of your favorites as many times as you wish.

Other benefits. All hotel stays include complimentary transportation to CityWalk, charging privileges at the theme parks and CityWalk and delivery of merchandise to your hotel room, free parking at the CityWalk garages and the ability to "pool-hop" at hotels. You'll get priority seating at certain restaurants in the parks and at CityWalk. All hotels also provide transportation to SeaWorld and its Aquatica water park, the Universal-owned Wet 'n Wild water park (until it closes at the end of 2016) and participating golf courses (with complimentary golf clubs and range balls for foursomes).

You can take advantage of these benefits from the moment you arrive at your hotel until midnight on the day you check out. You can register at your hotel as early in the morning of your first day as you like, check your bags, pick up your Universal Express

Unlimited passes (if eligible), and head over to the parks for Early Park Admission. On the morning you check out, you can hang around all day, swimming in the pools until late at night. Check-in times for all Universal hotels is 4 p.m., check-out is 11 a.m.

Cabana Bay Beach Resort. Universal's only value resort is also its largest (lobby shown at left). Neon signs welcome you; a retro theme recalls iconic beach resorts from the 1950s and 1960s. Both sophisticated and kitschy, it's sort of a "Mad Men" meets "Happy Days" vibe. Vintage cars sit outside the lobby.

Rooms. Colorful period decor; bright retro accents feature abstract artwork. Each family suite includes two flat-screen TVs, a fold-out sofa, a kitchenette and bathroom area designed for use by three people at a time. *Rooms: 400 sq ft. Sleep 4. 2 queen beds, small refrigerator. Suites: 430 sq ft. Sleep 6. 2 queen beds, full-size pull-out sofa, kitchenette with small refrigerator, microwave, sink.*

Swimming pools. The hotel has two huge pools. The Cabana Courtyard's 10,000-square-foot zero-entry pool has a 100-foot-long dive tower waterslide with a sand beach. Nearby are outdoor billiard tables, chess and checker tables, bag toss games, a large fire pit and an interactive kids play area; poolside cabanas are available for rent. The Lazy River Courtyard's 8,000-square-foot zero-entry pool has an expansive sand beach, a lazy river with waterfalls and cannons for interactive fun, plus two fire pits.

Restaurants and food. Comfortable food court Bayliner Diner has stations for burgers, deli sandwiches, desserts, international offerings, pizza and salads. Large TVs play retro commercials. Power outlets are available for charging phones and tablets, including one beside each booth. *Breakfast 7–11 a.m. weekdays, weekends 7 a.m.–noon; $5–$8 (children $5). Lunch and dinner 11 a.m.–11 p.m. weekdays, weekends noon–11 p.m.; $5–$13 (children $5). Seats 808. Pizza delivery available Sunday–Thursday noon–midnight; to 1 a.m. on Friday and Saturday.*

Galaxy Bowl. The hotel's only table-service spot serves burgers, sandwiches, pizza, wings, draft beer and has a full bar. You can eat while you bowl, or just sit in the lounge and nosh while watching music videos or sports one of the big screen TVs. The 10-lane bowling alley channels the Hollywood Star Lanes seen in the 1998 film "The Big Lebowski," with lanes illuminated by colorful lights at night. Bowling costs $15 (children $9) for 60 to 90 minutes; the price includes shoe rental. *Noon–midnight. Entrees $6–$10. Seats 40.*

The Hideaway Bar & Grill. This pool bar serves a basic grill menu of sandwiches and salads. *11 a.m.–10 p.m., drinks served to 11 p.m. $8–$12. Seats 40 outside.*

Other amenities. Arcade, fire pits, fitness center. Laundromat, laundry service. Children's programs: Organized activities include arts and crafts, hula-hoop contests, pool games, nightly poolside movies with s'mores kits available for roasting over fire pits. Characters often stop by the lobby on Fridays for meet-and-greets.

Key facts. *Rooms:* Rack $129–$214, discounted to $90. *Suites:* Rack $175–$210, discounted to $119. *Type:* Universal Prime Value Resort with clustered buildings. *Size:* 900 rooms, 900 suites. *Built:* 2014. *Universal transportation:* Shuttle buses. *Parking:* $12 per day; day guests $8 for 5–30 minutes; $20 for 24 hours. *Phone:* 407-503-4000. *Fax:* 407-503-4010. *Address:* 6550 Adventure Way, 32819.

Hard Rock Hotel. Just a short walk away from the Universal Studios Florida theme park, this upbeat pet-friendly resort books to capacity faster than any other Universal play to stay. It's especially popular with young adults and families with teenagers. The outside has a California Mission vibe with white stucco walls and burnt siena roof tiles, much like the building on the cover of the Eagles album "Hotel California." The lobby's chrome and marble looks more modern, with stark white walls. Check out the hotel's collection of rock memorabilia—including Elvis' jumpsuit and Elton John's boots—worth well over a million dollars. The front desk has a flyer to help you take a self-guided tour of the plethora of costumes, musical instruments and posters. On the last Thursday of the month, the lobby bar hosts a live rock concert called Velvet Sessions. For a schedule of artists and ticketing information, visit www.velvetsessions.com. The "Sound of Your Stay" program lets you borrow one of 20 Fender electric guitars with an amplifier and headphones if you're in the mood to jam; it's free with a $1,000 credit card deposi.

Rooms. Pale pastel furniture, light gray walls; refurbished 2015. Plush bedding with extra pillows. Cotton bathrobes. Club level available. *Rooms: 375–500 sq ft. Sleep 5. 2 queen beds, small refrigerator. 1–3 bedroom suites: 800–2,375 sq ft. Sleep 3–13.*

© Universal Orlando Resort

Cabana Bay Beach Resort.

Swimming pools. A 12,000-square-foot pool features an underwater stereo sound system and Florida's longest (at 260 feet) resort water slide. A sandy palm-lined beach leads to the pool's zero-entry edge. Nearby are two whirlpool spas, a sand volleyball court and a children's interactive play area with fountains. Several times a week a live band plays poolside, or a DJ spins tunes. Poolside cabanas are available for rent.

Restaurants and food. The Hard Rock has two table-service restaurants, a poolside bar and grill and an ice-cream parlor that's also a small market. Room service is 24 hours.

The Palm Restaurant. Modeled off its famed New York sister steakhouse, The Palm offers prime cuts of beef and live jumbo Nova Scotia lobster. Dark woods and white tablecloths highlight a sophisticated atmosphere. *5 p.m.–9 p.m. Sunday, Monday; 5 p.m.–10 p.m. Tuesday–Saturday. $30–$60 (children $10–$19). Seats 204. No flip-flops, shorts, swimwear or tank tops. Reservations: 407-503-7256.*

The Kitchen. This casual, rock music-themed restaurant serves Southern cuisine and comfort food, with character dining twice a week. Specialties include eggs Benedict at breakfast, flatbreads and burgers at lunch, crab cakes and boneless short ribs for dinner. Walls are hung with food-themed memorabilia from the hotel's celebrity guests. A separate "Kid's Crib" offers bean-bag chairs and TVs for children. A magician performs Fridays from 6 p.m. to 9 p.m. *7 a.m.–11 p.m. $15–$37. Character breakfast Tuesdays from 8 a.m.–11 a.m., $19 (children $13); character dinner Saturdays from 6 p.m.–9 p.m., $32 (children $28); characters vary. Seats 294.*

BeachClub. Poolside grill and full bar serves sandwiches, salads. *11 a.m.–9 p.m.; drinks until 10 p.m. $7–$12. Seats 24 outside.*

Emack & Bolio's Marketplace. Ice cream treats are named after rock songs—Bye Bye Miss America Mud Pie, Jumping Jack Grasshopper Pie, Sweet Dreams Are Made of This Smoothie—at this Boston-based spot. It also has Starbucks coffee, pastries, grab-and-go items, pizza after noon. *Opens 6:30 a.m., closing time varies. $4–$13. Seats 44.*

Other amenities. Arcade, concierge, fitness center, pets allowed, his-and-hers saunas. Laundromat, laundry service. Meeting space (6,000 sq ft, ballrooms). Business center. Children's programs: Organized activities include weekly "dive-in movies." Various characters often mingle with guests in the lobby, posing for photos and signing autographs. Camp Lil' Rock, a fully supervised kids babysitting camp, serves children ages 4 to 14. The camp rotates between the Hard Rock Hotel, Loews Royal Pacific Hotel and Loews Portofino Bay Hotel; it's run by the

© Universal Orlando Resort

Cabana Bay Beach Resort. A family suite.

outside organization Kids Nite Out. Camp hours are 5 p.m.–11 p.m. Thursday through Sunday; 5 p.m.–midnight Friday and Saturday. $15 per hour plus $15 per meal per child. **Key facts.** *Rooms:* Rack $289–$494, discounted to $175. *Type:* Universal Premier Resort with one sprawling eight-floor building. *Size:* 650 rooms, 29 suites. *Built:* 2001. *Universal transportation:* Water taxis and shuttle buses. *Parking:* $20 per day; valet $27; day guests $22; valet $32. *Phone:* 407-503-2000. *Fax:* 407-503-2166. *Address:* 5800 Universal Blvd, 32819.

Loews Portofino Bay Hotel. Large rooms and bathrooms, good restaurants, evening entertainment and a waterside setting distinguish Universal's flagship resort, which is also pet-friendly. Inspired by Portofino, Italy; designers worked with Portofino's mayor to portray the feel of the Mediterranean seaside getaway— cobblestone streets, sidewalk cafes, Venetian glass chandeliers. Italian sport cars and Vespa scooters are parked out front. Nightly live music (6:30 p.m. on the hotel's Harbor Piazza)blends classic opera and pop—"popera." **Rooms.** A luxurious Italian decor has muted colors, Italian marble sinks; showers have adjustable spray nozzles. Despicable Me kid's suites have missile beds inspired by

those of Gru's daughters; the door to the kid's area looks like a security vault. Cotton bathrobes. Club level available. *Rooms: 450–490 sq ft. Those with a king bed sleep 3, those with 2 queens sleep 5. Small refrigerator. 1–4 bedroom suites: 650–2,725 sq ft. Sleep 4–18.*

Swimming pools. The resort houses three themed swimming pools. The Beach Pool features a Roman aqueduct-themed water slide, a sand beach, two hot tubs and a children's pool and play area. Private cabanas (available for rent) border a serene Villa Pool; a secluded Hillside Pool is quiet and relaxing.

Restaurants and food. Portofino Bay offers three table-service restaurants, a pizza deli, two outdoor spots, a gelateria and a Starbucks. Room service is 24 hours.

Mama Della's Ristorante. Casual family-style dining features dishes from the Italian regions of Tuscany, Naples and Piemonte, including pasta, seafood and meats. Musicians stroll tableside. *5:30 p.m.–10 p.m. $21–$39 (children $7). Seats 248. No flip-flops, shorts, swimwear or tank tops.*

Bice Ristorante. Elegant, chic restaurant serves pasta, seafood and meats. *5:30 p.m.–10 p.m. $19–$48. Seats 156. No flip-flops, shorts, swimwear or tank tops.*

Trattoria del Porto. This casual restaurant is themed to colorful Italian country festivals. A children's play area holds a large-screen

© Universal Orlando Resort

Hard Rock Hotel.

TV that plays cartoons. *Breakfast 7 a.m.–11 a.m., Monday through Friday; to noon on weekends. $7–$17 (children $7). Dinner 5 p.m.–varies, $12–$25 (children $8). Character dining Fridays 6:30 p.m.–9:30 p.m. Seats 224.*

Sal's Market Deli. Brick-oven pizza, sandwiches and salads. *11 a.m.–11 p.m. $12–$16 (children $7). Seats 54.*

The Thirsty Fish. This harborside Italian wine bar serves savory cicchetti (small plates of food), also pizza and sandwiches. It also sells cigars and cigarettes, which can be smoked in this outdoor location. Live jazz music plays Thursday–Saturday. *8 p.m.–11 p.m. Opens 6 p.m. $7–$15. Seats 48.*

Splendido Bar & Grill. Casual poolside bar serves pizza, burgers, salads. *Opens at 11 a.m. $7–$17. Seats 38 outside.*

Gelateria. Breakfast sandwiches, pastries, cereals, gelato, smoothies. *Sunday–Thursday 6 a.m.–10 p.m., Friday–Saturday 6 a.m.–11 p.m., $2–$7. Seats 28.*

Starbucks. *6 a.m.–8 p.m. Seats 14.*

Other amenities. Arcade, bocce ball courts, concierge, fitness center, jogging trails, pets allowed, tennis courts. Full-service Mandara Spa. Laundry service. Conference center (42,000 sq ft, 2 ballrooms). Business center. Children's programs: Organized activities include ping pong tournaments, pool basketball, hula hoop contests, arts & crafts, weekly poolside movies. Various characters often mingle with guests in the lobby, posing for photos and signing autographs. Campo Portofino, a fully supervised kids babysitting camp, serves children ages 4 to 14. The camp rotates between the Hard Rock, Royal Pacific and Portofino Bay hotels; it's run by the outside organization Kids Nite Out. Camp hours are 5 p.m.–11 p.m. Thursday through Sunday; to midnight Friday and Saturday. $15 per hour plus $15 per meal per child.

Key facts. *Rooms:* Rack $304–$494, discounted to $254. *Type:* Universal Premier Resort with interconnected buildings. *Size:* 705 rooms, 45 suites. *Built:* 1999. *Universal transportation:* Water taxis and shuttle buses. *Parking:* $20 per day; valet $27; day guests $22; valet $32. *Phone:* 407-503-1000. *Concierge:* 407-503-1200. *Fax:* 407-503-1202. *Address:* 5601 Universal Blvd, 32819.

Loews Royal Pacific Resort. Why stay here? Perhaps because it's the least expensive hotel that offers complimentary Universal Express passes; perhaps because you can walk from it to Islands of Adventure; perhaps you like Disney's Polynesian Resort but prefer Universal's theme parks. Other selling points include a relaxing atmosphere, a fun pool, a good choice of restaurants and a pet-friendly room policy. Themed to the South Seas, the

© Universal Orlando Resort

Loews Portofino Bay Resort.

hotel features lush tropical landscaping and waterfalls, staffers greet you with "Aloha." To enter the lobby, you cross high over a stream on a covered bamboo bridge decorated with carved wooden frogs. Light streams through tall windows into the A-frame lobby, which is furnished in teak and circles an expansive outdoor fountain and reflecting pool that's scattered with carved elephants. A torch-lighting ceremony with Polynesian dancing, fire-juggling and music entertains poolside at sunset a few nights a week.

Rooms. An island decor has neutral walls and carpets with floral and dark-wood accents, earth-tone linens; refurbished 2015. Beds have 300-thread count sheets. Cotton bathrobes. Club level available. *Rooms: 335 sq ft. Sleep 5. 2 queen beds, small refrigerator. 1, 2-bedroom suites: 670–2,010 sq ft. Sleep 3–8.*

Swimming pools. The Royal Pacific's serene lagoon-style swimming pool is huge and themed to resemble an ocean liner; unfortunately it doesn't have a water slide. Tropical palms and foliage surround a "Royal Bali Sea" interactive play area for kids which includes water cannons for battles. Nearby are a white sand beach, two hot tubs and a beach volleyball court; complimentary ice water flavored with lemons, oranges or strawberries sits poolside. Private cabanas surrounding the pool are available for rent.

Restaurants and food. The Loews Royal Pacific Resort offers two full-service restaurants, a sushi-bar lounge and a weekly luau. Room service is available 24 hours a day.

Emeril's Tchoup Chop. Subdued lighting, tall ceilings, painted concrete floors and an open kitchen make for a relaxed, comfortable setting. It serves bold Asian and Polynesian fusion dishes, including beef, duck, rice and noodle bowls, seafood, pork, sushi and vegetarian offerings. The menu changes frequently. *Lunch 11:30 a.m.–12:30 p.m., $8–$18 (children $8); dinner 5 p.m.–10 p.m., $24–$34 (children $8). Seats 150. No flip-flops, shorts, swimwear or tank tops. Reservations: 407-503-2467.*

Islands Dining Room. Tropical surroundings enhance the relaxed atmosphere at this restaurant, which offers a breakfast buffet, dinner and both breakfast and dinner character meals. Some nights offer the Wok Experience, an all-you-can-eat Pan-Asian stir fry. Cuisine is American for breakfast, Pan Asian for dinner. *Breakfast 7 a.m.–11 a.m. weekdays, 7 a.m.–noon on weekends; $12–$17 (children $7). Character breakfast Sundays 7 a.m.–noon. Dinner 6 p.m.–10 p.m., $16–$30 (children $7). Character dinner Monday, Wednesday and Thursday 6:45 p.m.–9:15 p.m.; characters vary. Seats 248, 44 outside on a patio.*

© Universal Orlando Resort

Loews Royal Pacific Resort.

Jake's American Bar. Dim lounge serves sandwiches, burgers, flatbreads; dinner adds duck, seafood, steak; full bar. *11 a.m.–2 a.m.; limited menu after 11 p.m. Lunch $7–$17, dinner $7–$35. Seats 104, 17 at the bar.*

Orchid Court Lounge & Sushi Bar. This lobby lounge serves a continental breakfast plus pancakes; an expansive sushi and sashimi menu at dinner; Asian-inspired regular dinner menu with sandwiches, burgers, spring rolls. It has a full bar. Diners overlook a serene orchid garden. *Breakfast weekdays 6–11 a.m., 6 a.m.–noon on weekends; $2–$10. Sushi bar 5–11 p.m., $4–$120, regular dinner menu $8–$18. Cocktail lounge 5 p.m.–midnight. Seats 44, 10 at the bar.*

Bula Bar & Grille. This poolside bar serves up burgers, sandwiches, tacos; frozen treats are offered seasonally. Bula means "welcome" in Fijian. *Dining weekdays 11 a.m.–8 p.m., 11 a.m.–9 p.m. on weekends. Bar 11 a.m.–10 p.m. $11–$17 (children $7). Seats 38 outside at covered tables.*

Wantilan Luau. Universal's only dinner show offers authentic Polynesian food in a covered pavilion with live Hawaiian music, traditional hula and fire dancers and storytellers. Audience members are invited to learn the hula. The all-you-can-eat buffet of Polynesian specialties features a pit-roasted suckling pig. A children's buffet offers less adventurous chicken fingers, macaroni and cheese and pizza. *Reservations required: 407-503-3463. Every Saturday night; registration begins at 5 p.m., seating at 6 p.m. $63 (children $35 for ages 3–11). Price includes gratuity and beer, mai tais and wine for adults aged 21 and older. Priority seating adds $7 (children $5) and gives you a table near the front. Seats 264.*

Other amenities. Arcade, concierge, fitness center, jogging trails, pets allowed, elaborate dog-walking area, ping-pong tables, his-and-her saunas, shuffleboard court. Weekly luau. Laundromat, laundry service. Convention center (132,000 sq ft of total meeting and function space, 2 ballrooms, 15 breakout rooms), connected to the new Loews Sapphire Falls Resort by a walkway, creating a massive meeting space with more than 247,000 square feet between the two properties. Business center. Children's programs: Arts and crafts, hula-hoop contests, ping-pong tournaments, pool basketball and weekly movies shown poolside. The Mariner's Club, a fully supervised kids babysitting camp, serves children ages 4–14. The camp rotates between the Hard Rock Hotel, Loews Royal Pacific Hotel and Loews Portofino Bay Hotel; it's run by the outside organization Kids Nite Out. Camp hours are 5 p.m.–11 p.m. Thursday through Sunday; 5

Loews Sapphire Falls Resort.

p.m.–midnight Friday and Saturday. $15 per hour plus $15 per meal per child.

Key facts. *Rooms:* Rack $244–$424, discounted to $199. *Type:* Universal Preferred Resort, three connected Y-shaped wings. *Size:* 949 rooms, 51 suites. *Built:* 2001. *Universal transportation:* Water taxis and shuttle buses. *Parking:* $20 per day; valet $27; day guests $22; valet $32. *Phone:* 407-503-3000. *Fax:* 407-503-3010. *Address:* 6300 Hollywood Way, 32819.

Loews Sapphire Falls Resort. This pet-friendly resort hotel opened in the summer of 2016, after this book went to press. Blending traditional Caribbean styling with modern American touches, it channels a leisurely estate in the tropics. The lobby displays the ruins of a stone turret. The hotel is nestled into a chunk of land between the Royal Pacific and Cabana Bay hotels.

Rooms. A pale blue decor has light wood furniture and island-inspired artwork. Beds have 300-thread count sheets. *Rooms: 321 sq ft. Sleep 5. 2 queen beds, small refrigerator. 1, 2-bedroom suites: 529–1,353 sq ft. Sleep 3–5.*

Swimming pools. Surrounded by cascading waterfalls, a 16,000-square-foot zero-entry pool has two sand beaches and a water slide. Nearby sits a huge hot tub, fire pit and children's play area with pop-up jets. Private cabanas are available for rent.

Restaurants and food. The table-service Amatista Cookhouse serves a Caribbean breakfast, lunch and dinner from an open kitchen, with both indoor and outdoor seating. A lobby lounge, the Strong Water Tavern features a wall of vintage rums, a rum specialist, a ceviche bar and daily rum tastings; its patio overlooks the lagoon. Small marketplace New Dutch Trading Co. offers ready-to-go meals, beverages, fresh-baked breads and homemade jams. Poolside bar and eatery Drhum Club Katine has a small-plate menu focusing on fresh fish. Hotel room service is available 24 hours a day.

Other amenities. Arcade, concierge, fitness center, pets allowed. Laundromat, laundry service. Convention center (115,000 sq ft, ballroom, 16 breakout rooms), connected to the Royal Pacific by a walkway, creating a massive meeting space with more than 247,000 square feet between the two properties. Business center. Children's programs: Organized activities include arts and crafts, pool games.

Key facts. *Rooms:* Rack $179–$284. *Type:* Universal Preferred Resort. *Size:* 917 rooms, 83 suites. *Built:* 2016. *Universal transportation:* Water taxis and shuttle buses. *Parking:* $20 per day; valet $27; day guests $22; valet $32. *Phone:* 407-363-8000. *Fax:* 407-503-5000. *Address:* 6601 Adventure Way, 32819.

© Universal Orlando Resort

Characters

BEYOND THOSE IN SHOWS AND PARADES, more than 80 costumed characters appear at Universal Orlando, all eager to pose for a photo with you and sign an autograph (some don't sign because of costume limitations). Most stand in designated areas; some freely roam. All are easy to meet; only a few have waiting lines of more than a dozen people. A Photo Connect photographer is often on hand, though you're welcome to take photos yourself or have the photographer snap a few for you with your camera or phone.

Types of characters. Universal has two types of characters, "face" and "fur." The costume of a face character, such as Popeye, shows the face of a performer who talks with fans. The costume of a fur character, such as Woody Woodpecker, covers the performer entirely and usually includes an oversized head. Fur characters interact through mime.

Character meals. An assortment of stars roam the dining rooms of a few Universal restaurants, posing with patrons while they eat.

How to help your child interact. Though face characters rarely intimidate young children, the huge heads of the fur folks sometimes do. To help your child feel comfortable talk with her beforehand so she knows what to expect; buy her an autograph book. When it's her turn don't push her; the characters are trained to be patient. Approach fur characters from the front; many can't see to their sides.

Agnes Gru. The youngest and most trusting adopted daughter of "Despicable Me" star Felonius Gru, this 6-year-old has brown eyes and a black ponytail; she wears blue overalls. She loves unicorns. Especially fluffy ones.

Where to meet her. Alongside the exit to Despicable Me Minion Mayhem into the store Super Silly Stuff (you can enter through the store), in front of the nearby Universal Studios Store after the 9:30 a.m. Minions dance routine (most days), Production Central; after Despicable Me Character Parties in front of Mel's Drive-In and at the Superstar Character

Velma Dinkley. Above left: Fred Jones, Daphne Blake, Scooby-Doo, Shaggy Rogers.

Olive Oyl and Popeye

Breakfast (Thr.–Sat. 9–11:15 a.m., Café La Bamba), Hollywood Blvd.; Universal Studios.

Baby Jaguar. Rescued as an infant by Diego in the 2005–2011 animated series "Go, Diego, Go!" this wild cat became the boy's best friend.
Where to meet him. After Dora the Explorer Character Parties in front of Mel's Drive-In and at the Superstar Character Breakfast (Thr.–Sat. 9–11:15 a.m., Café La Bamba), Hollywood Blvd.; Universal Studios.

Barney. "Super dee-duper!" Chances are that's what this big purple T-Rex will think of your encounter with him; it's what he thinks of nearly everything. So unfailingly friendly, kind and optimistic he is often gleefully attacked as being too one-dimensional; in 2002 TV Guide named his 1992-2009 preschooler program "Barney & Friends" one of The Worst TV Shows of All Time.
Where to meet him. After each performance of A Day in the Park with Barney, in the theater and then inside Barney's Backyard Playground, Woody Woodpecker's KidZone, Universal Studios.

Bart Simpson. His first name an anagram of "Brat," this 10-year-old mischievous underachiever fits the bill perfectly. The oldest child of Homer and Marge in the long-running animated television series "The Simpsons," he was conceived by creator Matt Groening as a boy with every negative trait of Tom Sawyer, Huckleberry Finn and Eddie Haskell from the 1958–1963 Universal TV series "Leave it to Beaver." He wears a red shirt, blue shorts.
Where to meet him. With other Simpsons on Hollywood Blvd. and in Springfield near Kwik-E Mart, Universal Studios.

Beetle Bailey. Skinny and freckled, this lazy U.S. Army private always conceals his eyes with his cap or helmet. He's the namesake of the syndicated comic strip "Beetle Bailey" started in 1950 by cartoonist and World War II vet Mort Walker, who as of 2015 was still producing it at age 92. Stuck in basic training, Beetle takes frequent naps and avoids chores.
Where to meet him. At Toon Lagoon, Islands of Adventure.

Betty Boop. *"You can feed me bread and water, or a great big bale of hay, but don't take my boop-oop-a-doop away!"* That's what she sang in her early 1930s cartoons, when she was a flapper in a strapless red dress so small it showed her cleavage and her garter belt, when she had a boyfriend who was a literal dog (as was she in her first cartoon, a black poodle). The voice that squeaked out of her bow-shaped red lips was that of a sassy New

Betty Boop

Yawker, who introduced her cartoons with a wink at the audience and a shake of her hips. Soon the industry's Hays Code ensured no one ever took her boop-oop-a-doop away, as it refused to let her future cartoons be distributed unless she ditched her career (too racy), her outfit (too sexy) and her boyfriend (too beastial). Today the resulting homebody Boop is long forgotten but bawdy Betty lives on, an attitude icon for women.

Where to meet her. In front of her stores (in Toon Lagoon, Islands of Adventure and on Rodeo Drive, Universal Studios).

Bluto. More brawn than brain, this bloated bearded bad boy is the nemesis of sailor Popeye. Almost always angry, he punctuates what he says with bear-like growls of additional comments that can't be understood. Like the Sailor Man he longs for Olive Oyl.

Where to meet him. Seasonally near Popeye & Bluto's Bilge-Rat Barges, Toon Lagoon, Islands of Adventure.

Boots. An impulsive monkey in red footwear, Boots is the best friend of Dora in the 2000–2015 animated TV series "Dora the Explorer."

Where to meet him. After Dora the Explorer Character Parties in front of Mel's Drive-In, Hollywood Blvd.; Universal Studios.

Bullwinkle. A master of misunderstanding the obvious, Bullwinkle J. Moose is a delightfully kindhearted dimwit, the sidekick of Rocky the Flying Squirrel on the 1960s prime-time variety show "Rocky and His Friends," which due to the moose's popularity was renamed "The Bullwinkle Show" after its second season. As the duo thwarts the schemes of Pottsylvanian spies Boris Badenov and Natasha Fatale, Bullwinkle often breaks the show's fourth wall, acknowledging its audience (*Rocky:* "What game can you play with girls?" *Bullwinkle:* "Hmm... this is a kid's show... why Parcheesi, of course!"). Hosting other segments, he demonstrates his supposed expertise as "Mr. Know-It-All," acts out famous poems in "Bullwinkle's Corner" and as a magician continues to try to pull a rabbit out of his hat—"Nothing up my sleeve... Presto!"—only to fail miserably. A brown moose with yellow antlers, he appears at Universal wearing his red sweater from his collegiate alma mater, Wossamotta U.

Where to meet him. Seasonally at Toon Lagoon, Islands of Adventure. Also on Hollywood Blvd., Universal Studios.

Bumblebee. Like other Transformers this sentient robot can morph into a particular vehicle or weapon; in his case a yellow-and-black Chevy Camaro. Nearly everyone's favorite Transformer, he's a plucky, brave Autobot (a good guy), one of leader Optimus Prime's most trusted lieutenants though he isn't the strongest or most powerful. He communicates by tuning his radio to play appropriate music and audio clips, even when he meets fans at Universal (it's very cool).

Where to meet him. Behind Transformers 3-D, Production Central, Universal Studios.

Captain America. Punching Adolf Hitler in the face on the cover of his debut comic book ("Captain America," released in December 1940) this classic Marvel Comics superhero fights for truth, justice and the America Way much like DC Comic's Superman, who had debuted two years earlier but was far less political. Similar to Clark Kent, scrawny fine arts student Steve Rogers is Cap's alter ego, a young man rejected by the U.S. Army to fight in World War II but nevertheless so dedicated to his country that he volunteers to take an experimental serum which gives him super-human strength. Equipped with a bulletproof shield and a red-white-blue uniform he designed himself, he fights the Axis powers until a failed mission leaves him frozen in ice. Later he's brought back to life by the Avengers and becomes their leader.

Where to meet him. On Marvel Super Hero Island, Islands of Adventure.

Carlos. This streetwise Easter chick leads a coup against the Easter Bunny in 2011's "Hop."

Where to meet him. After Hop Character Parties at Mel's Drive-In; at the Superstar Character Breakfast (Thr.–Sat. 9–11:15 a.m., Café La Bamba); Universal Studios.

The Cat in the Hat. Pure id in a top hat, a revolutionary with no concern for what's right or wrong and no sense of guilt, the Cat in the Hat is the titular character of the iconic 1957 children's picture book by Dr. Seuss. He shows up at the home of a boy and girl one afternoon when their mom's away and proceeds to Party Rock—destroying the house with help from companions Thing One and Thing Two as he shows the kids a few tricks to entertain them.

Where to meet him. Mon.–Sat. after the stage show "Oh the Stories You'll Hear," typically 10:30 a.m.–4:30 p.m. on the half hour (no show at 1:30 p.m.), Sunday no shows but

Marilyn Monroe

characters still appear, Seuss Character Zone, Seuss Landing, Islands of Adventure.

Curious George. An inquisitive brown monkey who gets into trouble whenever his owner leaves the house but also always saves the day, Curious George starred in seven children's books in the 1940s, 1950s and 1960s. They were written by Margret Rey and illustrated by her husband Hans Augusto Rey, the first book soon after the Jewish couple escaped the Nazi invasion of Paris by mere hours, carrying the "Curious George" manuscript with them as they rode bicycles to the Spanish border.
Where to meet him. At Curious George Goes to Town, Woody Woodpecker's KidZone, on Hollywood Blvd., Universal Studios.

Cyclops. Why is he always wearing those weird ruby quartz glasses? Because it's the only way this tortured hero can control the powerful beams of energy that shoot out of his eyes. Scott Summers' vision was normal until as a young boy he saw his parents die in a plane crash. Placed in an orphanage, as a teenager he was taken in by paraplegic professor Charles Xavier, and later became the first of his X-Men, a group of human-mutant superheroes, adopting the name "Cyclops."
Where to meet him. At Marvel Super Hero Island, Islands of Adventure.

Daphne Blake. Neon go-go-boots match the minidress of this teen redhead in the 1969–1970 animated sitcom "Scooby-Doo Where are You!" At first clumsy and danger-prone, she soon learns to take care of herself, through karate as well as skills such as opening locks with her makeup accessories. She assumes Freddy is her boyfriend; he doesn't object.
Where to meet her. With other Scooby stars on Hollywood Blvd., Universal Studios.

Diego. Taking a scientific approach to reach his goals, 8-year-old Diego Marquez uses gadgets and gizmos to save and protect animals in the 2005–2011 animated series "Go, Diego, Go!" He's a cousin of Dora the Explorer.
Where to meet him. After Dora the Explorer Character Parties in front of Mel's Drive-In and at the Superstar Character Breakfast (Thr.–Sat. 9–11:15 a.m., Café La Bamba), Hollywood Blvd.; Universal Studios.

Doc Brown. Wide-eyed, absent-minded Dr. Emmett Lathrop Brown invents a time machine out of a DeLorean sports car in the Universal movie trilogy "Back to the Future." With help from his lab assistant Marty McFly, he travels from 1985 to 1955 and then to 2015. Later stuck in the 1880s, he builds a second time machine out of a steam locomotive.
Where to meet him. At the "Back to the Future" train and car outside Springfield, roams to Hollywood Blvd., Universal Studios.

Doctor Doom. Archenemy of the Fantastic Four, Doctor Victor von Doom turned evil in college, after a machine he built to rescue his mother's soul blew up in his face. Though the incident left only a few minor scars on his face, his vanity led him to order a metal mask for himself, which he applied before it had fully cooled, disfiguring himself horribly. An arrogant genius, inventor and sorcerer, he can exchange minds with others, absorb and fire bolts of energy and travel through time.
Where to meet him. On Marvel Super Hero Island, Islands of Adventure.

Donkey. He's a talking donkey who annoys everyone he meets—because he's a chatterbox, a coward, afraid of spiders, afraid of getting sick, loves to break out into song and totally lacks tact. Still, he sees the bright side of everything and loves both sweets (especially waffles) and his sweetie (Dragon, with whom he has six kids). Voiced by Eddie Murphy, Donkey is the sidekick to Shrek in the 2001–2010 "Shrek" animated movies.
Where to meet him. Alongside Shrek 4-D at shaded Donkey's Photo Finish, Production Central, Universal Studios.

Dora the Explorer. This young Hispanic American goes on an adventure in every episode of the 2000–2015 television series "Dora the Explorer," one of the first animated children's programs to encourage viewers to play along with its characters. Though obstacles get in her way, with the help of her monkey Boots, her talking purple backpack and her viewers she always overcomes them.
Where to meet her. After the Dora the Explorer Character Parties in front of Mel's Drive-In and at the Superstar Character Breakfast (Thr.–Sat. 9–11:15 a.m., Café La Bamba), Hollywood Blvd.; Universal Studios.

Dudley Do-Right. Stupid but steadfast, this cheerful Canadian Mountie always gets his man yet never his distressed damsel Nell Fenwick, who despite his continued rescuing has eyes only for his horse. Yes, *his horse.*

Bumblebee

Felonius Gru and two Minion recruits

That storyline was repeated in all 46 "Dudley Do-Right Of The Mounties" television cartoons of the 1960s, which aired as segments of "Rocky & His Friends," "The Bullwinkle Show" and "The Dudley Do-Right Show." The cartoons were a parody of the Northern, an early type of Western melodrama which took place in the Canadian North and had its conflict resolved by Mounties using reason and a sense of fair play. Dudley himself channels operatic baritone Nelson Eddy's performance as Mountie Sergeant Malone in the 1936 Northern "Rose-Marie"; as such he often breaks out into Eddy's signature song, the folk tune "Shortnin' Bread" ("*Mama's little baby loves shortnin', shortnin'…*").

Where to meet him. Seasonally near the ride Dudley Do-Right's Ripsaw Falls, Toon Lagoon, Islands of Adventure.

E.B. This rebellious teen would rather be a drummer than follow the footsteps of his Easter Bunny father in the 2011 comedy "Hop."

Where to meet him. After Hop Character Parties at Mel's Drive-In; at the Superstar Character Breakfast (Thr.–Sat. 9–11:15 a.m., Café La Bamba); Universal Studios.

Edith Gru. Always wearing her striped pink knit cap with ear flaps and tassels, even in bed, Edith is the adopted middle child of Felonius

Gru in the "Despicable Me" films. She shares with her stepdad a dark sense of humor.

Where to meet her. Alongside the exit to Despicable Me Minion Mayhem into the store Super Silly Stuff (you can enter through the store), in front of the nearby Universal Studios Store after the 9:30 a.m. Minions dance routine (most days), Production Central; after Despicable Me Character Parties in front of Mel's Drive-In and at the Superstar Character Breakfast (Thr.–Sat. 9–11:15 a.m., Café La Bamba), Hollywood Blvd.; Universal Studios.

Felonius Gru. "Lightbulb!" That's what this former supervillain and current jelly maker shouts out whenever he gets an idea. The main character in Universal's "Despicable Me" comedies, he's a smart bald man who's the boss of the Minions, the adoptive father of three girls and a heck of a dancer.

Where to meet him. Outside the Universal Studios Store after the 9:30 a.m. Minions dance routine (most days), Production Central; after Despicable Me Character Zone Parties and at the Superstar Character Breakfast (Thr.–Sat. 9–11:15 a.m., Café La Bamba), Hollywood Blvd.; Universal Studios.

Fiona. The only princess who belches, farts and can sing so high birds explode. Voiced by Cameron Diaz in four "Shrek" movies

Agnes, Margo and Edith Gru

(2001–2010), Fiona was locked in a castle until the green ogre rescued her in the first movie, and was plagued by a curse that transforms her back and forth between a beautiful human girl and an ogress—her natural state.
Where to meet her. Near Shrek 4-D at the shaded Donkey's Photo Finish, Production Central, Universal Studios.

Fred Jones. Often building elaborate Rube Goldberg-style traps for villains which his friends set off by mistake, blond "Freddy" is one of the teenage mystery solvers on the 1969–1970 animated sitcom "Scooby-Doo Where are You!" He has a thing for redhead Daphne, but also an eye for other ladies. He wears a white shirt with a red ascot.
Where to meet him. With other Scooby stars on Hollywood Blvd., Universal Studios.

The Green Goblin. Four men have assumed the alias of this evil-grinning pointy-eared supervillain—rich industrialist Norman Osborn, his embittered son Harry, Harry's psychologist Bart Hamilton and Phil Urich, the son of a journalist who works at the New York City newspaper The Daily Bugle. All expose themselves to a mysterious goblin serum, which increases their intelligence at the price of their sanity. A major nemesis of Spider-Man, the Green Goblin has green

skin, a belted purple suit and an arsenal of Halloween-themed weapons, including boomerang-like razor bats, pumpkin bombs and grenades that release ghost-like gasses.
Where to meet him. Marvel Super Hero Island, Islands of Adventure.

The Grinch. He's a mean one, this green Seussian Scrooge. The protagonist of the 1957 book "How the Grinch Stole Christmas!" he lives on a cliff high above chipper Whoville, and becomes so irritated by its Christmas festivities that, dressed like Santa Claus, he steals all of its food, presents, trees and decorations—only to see its residents cheerfully celebrate anyway. In 1966 the book was adapted into an animated television special; Jim Carrey starred as the Grinch in a live-action Universal movie in the year 2000.
Where to meet him. Mon.–Sat. after the stage show "Oh the Stories You'll Hear," typically 10:30 a.m.–4:30 p.m. on the half hour (no show at 1:30 p.m.), Sunday no shows but characters still appear, Seuss Character Zone, Seuss Landing, Islands of Adventure. Also at the Grinch & Friends Character Breakfast (the "live-action" Grinch), various mornings in December only, Circus McGurkus Cafe Stoo-pendous; as well as in the bookstore All the Books You Can Read, Seuss Landing, Islands of Adventure.

Bart and Homer Simpson

Hello Kitty. No, she's not a cat. According to her creator, Japanese company Sanrio, she's Kitty White, a little girl who loves to dress up like a cat, a white one with black eyes and whiskers but no mouth. She lives in London with her twin sister Mimmy and pet Persian cat, Charmmy Kitty. As a cat Kitty wears girly outfits; all include a bow over her left ear.

Where to meet her. Inside the Hello Kitty store, Rodeo Drive, Universal Studios.

Homer Simpson. The head of the Simpson family, this incompetent Springfield nuclear plant inspector loves to toss back a few Duffs after work at Moe's Tavern. Lazy, irresponsible and impulsive, he's decent at heart. Named for Simpsons creator Matt Groening's own father Homer, his middle initial J. is a nod to Bullwinkle J. Moose.

Where to meet him. With other Simpsons on Hollywood Blvd. and in Springfield near Kwik-E Mart, Universal Studios.

Krusty the Clown. Jaded and cynical, the host of "The Krusty the Clown Show" on "The Simpsons" is an exuberant goof when he's on the air; off-camera an alcoholic chain-smoker who will merchandise anything to make a buck—Krusty swabs, Krusty Burgers, Krustyland. Homer Simpson in clown-face, Krusty is based on a real TV clown Simpsons

creator Matt Groening watched as a child: Rusty Nails of Portland, Oregon.

Where to meet him. In Springfield near Kwik-E Mart, Universal Studios.

Lisa Simpson. She's a Buddhist, member of MENSA (her IQ: 159), vegetarian and mighty mean saxophone player. Eight-year-old Lisa Simpson may look like the rest of her family, but otherwise she's on a different wavelength. She likes to read and dreams of one day having a pony.

Where to meet her. With other Simpsons on Hollywood Blvd. and in Springfield near Kwik-E Mart, Universal Studios.

The Lorax. This small orange creature with a big yellow moustache tries to save a forest of Truffula trees in the 1971 Dr. Seuss book "The Lorax," though he can't convince the human Once-Ler to stop chopping them down.

Where to meet him. Mon.–Sat. after the stage show "Oh the Stories You'll Hear," typically 10:30 a.m.–4:30 p.m. on the half hour (no show at 1:30 p.m.), Sunday no shows but characters still appear, Seuss Character Zone, Seuss Landing, Islands of Adventure.

Lucy Ricardo. As portrayed by Lucille Ball in the definitive 1951–1960 sitcom "I Love Lucy," this chatty, childlike housewife is

Fiona, Donkey and Shrek

married to band leader Ricky Ricardo (Ball's husband Desi Arnaz) and is always scheming to break in to showbiz herself—posing as a celebrity on Hollywood Blvd. while a tourist like you takes her picture is apparently her latest idea. She has orange-red hair, red lipsticked lips and big star-struck eyes.

Where to meet her. On Hollywood Blvd. and Rodeo Dr., Universal Studios.

The Man in the Yellow Hat.
The patient guardian of mischievous monkey Curious George, Ted Shackleford first befriended the animal when he brought him home from Africa as his pet. Besides his wide-brimmed hat he wears a yellow long-sleeved shirt, yellow pants and brown boots. Absent-minded and awkward, he constantly loses his hat.

Where to meet him. At Curious George Goes to Town, Woody Woodpecker's KidZone, on Hollywood Blvd., Universal Studios.

Marge Simpson. This sensible homemaker cares for her kids and heads off disasters caused by her husband. She wears a strapless green dress with a red bead necklace; her blue beehive is a nod to how Simpsons creator Matt Groening's mom Marge wore her hair.

Where to meet her. With other Simpsons on Hollywood Blvd. and in Springfield near Kwik-E Mart, Universal Studios.

Margo Gru. The oldest adopted daughter of Felonius in "Despicable Me," Margo has brown hair tied in a ponytail, glasses, a brown jacket, plaid skirt, red sneakers and a T-shirt with the face of The Lorax. Intelligent and sarcastic, she often outsmarts her stepdad.

Where to meet her. Alongside the exit to Despicable Me Minion Mayhem into the store Super Silly Stuff, in front of the Universal Studios Store after the 9:30 a.m. Minions dance routine (on most days), Production Central; after Despicable Me Character Zone Parties and at the Superstar Character Breakfast (Thr.–Sat. 9–11:15 a.m., Café La Bamba), Hollywood Blvd.; Universal Studios.

Marilyn Monroe. Raised in an orphanage, as a teenager Norma Jeane Mortenson began her career as a brunette pin-up girl; soon her red lips, hourglass figure, switch to blond hair transformed her into the singular sex symbol of the 1950s. Her hip-swinging moves earned her the nickname "the girl with the horizontal walk." Innocent and girlish, vulnerable and naive, she often used a breathy, little-girl voice in her films though she spoke normally offscreen. An iconic image of the last century is of Monroe standing over a subway grate as a passing train causes her white halter dress to billow up in the air; a scene from the 1955 movie "The Seven Year

SpongeBob SquarePants

Itch." The Universal character appears in that white dress in the park.

Where to meet her. On Hollywood Blvd. and Rodeo Dr., Universal Studios.

Marty McFly. This quick-witted 17-year-old travels through time with Doc Brown in the "Back to the Future" trilogy. He wears jeans, a checked long-sleeved shirt, a jean jacket, an orange Gore-tex vest and white tennis shoes.

Where to meet him. Seasonally near the "Back to the Future" locomotive and DeLorean movie props, near Springfield; also on Hollywood Blvd.; Universal Studios.

Megatron. This silver sentient robot is the leader of the villainous Decepticons in the Transformers world. The nemesis of Optimus Prime, he has a growling voice and hatred of humans; he transforms into large trucks.

Where to meet him. Behind Transformers 3-D, Production Central, Universal Studios.

Men in Black. Aloof and dignified, these employees of a secret organization devote themselves to policing and monitoring extraterrestrial activity on Earth. They wear black suits, white shirts and Rayban sunglasses.

Where to meet them. In front of Men in Black Alien Attack, World Expo; also on Hollywood Blvd.; Universal Studios.

The Minions. Rambunctious and playful, these small yellow pill-shaped creatures have either one eye or two and wear metal goggles, blue overalls and black gloves. Driven by their desire to serve supervillain Felonius Gru, they understand English but don't speak it; jabbering instead in their own language. They love bananas. Minions in the park include:

Bob. The most immature Minion, Bob is short, bald and has two eyes, one brown; one green. Seeing him in the park is rare, but he does show up at special occasions.

J.J. Rarely seen except at the park, J.J. is the identical twin of the better known Jerry.

Jerry. A short plump Minion, Jerry has two eyes and short spiky hair. He's easily frightened but loves to play his guitar.

Kevin. The only Minion knighted by the British Empire, tall "Sir Kevin" is the Minion leader. He has two eyes that are often half shut and a sprout of hair. He likes golf.

Stuart. His hair neatly parted down the center, Stuart is medium height and has one eye. He plays the guitar and loves to laugh.

Tim. Often smirking or frowning, tall two-eyed Tim has a temper. He's the twin of Kevin.

Tom. Often surprised, tall Tom appears with his eyes wide open and his mouth ajar.

Where to meet them. Along the exit to Despicable Me Minion Mayhem near Super Silly Stuff, occasionally outside the store.

Dora the Explorer and Diego

Olive Oyl. Popeye's stick of a girlfriend has big feet and a black bun of hair tied with a red bow, a red shirt, a black skirt with a red hem and black heels. She often gets kidnapped by Bluto, which she secretly likes. Created in 1919, she was a main character in the comic book Thimble Theater before Popeye appeared and changed its name; her older brother was Castor Oyl, her mom Nana Oyl (banana oil) her dad Coal Oyl (kerosene). **Where to meet her.** At Toon Lagoon, Islands of Adventure; also on Hollywood Blvd., Universal Studios.

Optimus Prime. The leader of the good-guy Autobots in the "Transformers" world, Optimus Prime dukes it out with bad-guy Megatron and his villainous Decepticons. Transformers are sentient robots with the ability to transform into various vehicles or weapons; Optimus Prime can transform into a Kenworth W900 truck (or, in the films, as a modified Peterbilt 379). He is silver with royal blue accents and red flames. **Where to meet him.** Behind Transformers 3-D next to Mel's Drive-In, Universal Studios.

Patrick Star. This dimwitted pink starfish is SpongeBob's best friend in "SpongeBob SquarePants." He sports thick eyebrows and lime pants dotted with lavender flowers.

Where to meet him. After the SpongeBob Character Parties on Hollywood Blvd. in front of Mel's Drive-In; at the Superstar Character Breakfast (Thr.–Sat. 9–11:15 a.m., Café La Bamba); Universal Studios.

Phil. The sidekick to Carlos in Universal's 2011 animated comedy "Hop," this good-natured Easter chick loves music; work… not so much. **Where to meet him.** After Hop Character Parties at Mel's Drive-In; at the Superstar Character Breakfast (Thr.–Sat. 9–11:15 a.m., Café La Bamba); Universal Studios.

The Pink Berets. This beret-wearing trio is the all-bunny royal guard of E.B., the prodigal son of the Easter Bunny in the 2011 Universal animated comedy "Hop." Armed and dangerous, brown-eyed leader Fluffy has a tracking device, Patch has blow darts, blue-eyed baby Bit has an inhaler she thinks is a weapon. **Where to meet them.** After Hop Character Parties outside Mel's Drive-In; at the Superstar Character Breakfast (Thr.–Sat. 9–11:15 a.m., Café La Bamba); Universal Studios.

Popeye. "Yuk-yuk-yuk-yuk-yuk," he laughs. "I yam what I yam," he proclaims. An elephant is an "elephink." No one else speaks like Popeye, the sailor man who first appeared in comic strips in 1929. Also known for his

Phil and Carlos

squinting right eye, oversized forearms and skinny upper arms, Popeye is violent and uncivilized, but also introspective and with high moral fiber. He often rescues his girl-friend Olive Oyl from his rival Bluto. In early comics he always had superhuman strength; in later cartoons he has it after downing a can of spinach (hence the line in his theme song, *"I fights to the finish when I eats me spinach"*). He rarely smokes a corncob pipe; instead he toots it like a tugboat's steam whistle.

Where to meet him. At Toon Lagoon, Islands of Adventure; also on Hollywood Blvd., Universal Studios.

Private Zero. This buck-toothed, big-eared farm boy is the redheaded best friend of Beetle in the comic strip "Beetle Bailey." Earning his nickname, he misunderstands everything and takes commands extremely literally. Told to "make it snappy" he'll use mouse-traps and snapping turtles to decorate an effort.

Where to meet him. Seasonally in Toon Lagoon, Islands of Adventure.

Rocky the Flying Squirrel. "Hokey smoke!" That's what this gliding rodent proclaims when he finds himself in a jam, before using his wits to get him and moose buddy Bullwinkle out of it in serials that headlined the 1959–1964 animated television show "Rocky and His Friends" (later renamed "The Bullwinkle Show"). Rocky has brown fur and wears a leather flying helmet.

Where to meet him. Seasonally at Toon Lagoon, Islands of Adventure.

Rogue. Born with the ability to absorb and sometimes remove the memories, strength and superpowers of anyone she touched; as a teenager she wore body-concealing clothing that made that impossible. As an adult she gained control of her powers, first as a villain with the Brotherhood of Evil Mutants, later as one of the heroic X-Men. A white streak runs through her long brown hair.

Where to meet her. At Marvel Super Hero Island, Islands of Adventure.

Sam I Am. Relentless in his demand that a poor bystander try green eggs and ham in the 1960 Dr. Seuss children's book "Green Eggs and Ham," he is turned down no matter if he offers it on a house, with a mouse, in a box, with a fox, with a goat, on a boat… the options go on forever. Eventually the bystander gives in and is shocked at the results. "Say! I like green eggs and ham! I do! I like them, Sam-I-am!" In 1965 the book was banned in the People's Republic of China for "its portrayal of early Marxism." A short cat with no ears or tail, Sam wears a yellow shirt and red hat.

Bullwinkle

Doc Brown

Where to meet him. Mon.–Sat. after the stage show "Oh the Stories You'll Hear," typically 10:30 a.m.–4:30 p.m. on the half hour (no show at 1:30 p.m.), Sunday no shows but characters still appear, Seuss Character Zone, Seuss Landing, Islands of Adventure.

Scarlett O'Hara. A vain, spoiled black-haired beauty, she stomps on people to save herself and her family plantation Tara in 1939's Civil War epic "Gone With the Wind."
    Where to meet her. Seasonally along Hollywood Blvd., Universal Studios.

Scooby Doo. Here's betting Frank Sinatra never thought one of his legacies would be the 1969–1975 cartoon television series "Scooby-Doo, Where Are You!" But it is, as that show's star is named after a throwaway line in Sinatra's 1966 hit "Strangers in the Night," a scat improvisation of its title ("scooby-dooby-doo..."). Possessing no characteristics of an actual Great Dane beyond his size, Scooby is cowardly, has a sloping chin, spots and bow legs. He speaks, though, in broken English, putting the letter "R" in front of most every word *("roast revery word")*. His owner is teenage amateur

detective Shaggy Rogers; Scooby sticks closely by him.
    Where to meet him. With other Scooby stars on Hollywood Blvd., Universal Studios.

Shaggy Rogers. Named for his unkempt sandy-blond hair, this '70s slacker is the owner of Great Dane Scooby Doo in "Scooby-Doo, Where Are You!" He wears a green v-neck T-shirt, brownish red bell bottoms and sports the starting tufts of a goatee. A secret coward, he's also friendly. Always hungry, he often seems to be, as it was said in the '70s, "one toke over the line." His voice often breaks when he speaks.
    Where to meet him. With other Scooby stars on Hollywood Blvd., Universal Studios.

Shrek. This misanthropic ogre lives peacefully by himself in a swamp before falling for and marrying ogress princess Fiona in the first film in the "Shrek" movie series. Afterward, he gets friendly. Overweight with green skin and antenna for ears, he's strong, loves onions and speaks in a Scottish brogue.
    Where to meet him. Near Shrek 4-D at the shaded Donkey's Photo Finish, Production Central, Universal Studios.

Wolverine

Cyclops

Sideshow Bob. A palm tree. That's what his hair looks like—a curly red palm tree. A recurring character in "The Simpsons" TV series, Sideshow Bob got his stage name when he was the non-speaking sidekick to Krusty the Clown on "The Krusty the Clown Show." Insulted by the role, the self-proclaimed genius and champion of high culture plotted Krusty's downfall and framed the clown for a crime, only to be exposed by Bart and sent to prison.
 Where to meet him. In front of the Kwik-E Mart in Springfield, Universal Studios.

Spider-Man. What happens when a shy, nerdy high-school student is bitten by a radioactive spider? A superhero is born! One who can cling to most surfaces, has superhuman strength and can shoot strong spider-web strings from his wrists. Debuting in comic books in 1962, the alter ego of Peter Parker was something new: a flawed teenage superhero, one with everyday problems. He later joined the Avengers and the Fantastic Four. He wears a red and blue suit that covers him from head to toe, with a spider silhouette on his chest. He's the only fully masked character at Universal Orlando who speaks.

 Where to meet him. Usually inside his own meet-and-greet spot at Marvel Super Hero Island, Islands of Adventure.

SpongeBob SquarePants. This happy-go-lucky sea sponge is the star of the Nickelodeon series "SpongeBob SquarePants," which first appeared in 1986 and still airs today. As fans know, he "lives in a pineapple under the sea" and "absorbent and yellow and porous is he" (he looks like a kitchen sponge, with blue eyes, two buck teeth and freckled cheeks; his outfit is a white shirt with a red tie, brown short pants with a black belt). A resident of ocean village Bikini Bottom, he lives with his pet snail Gary, near best friend Patrick and co-worker Squidward. He works as a fry cook at the local fast-food joint The Krusty Krab, where he gleefully flips Krabby Patties.
 Where to meet him. After the SpongeBob Character Parties in front of Mel's Drive-In on Hollywood Blvd.; at the Superstar Character Breakfast (Thr.–Sat. 9–11:15 a.m., Café La Bamba); Universal Studios.

Squidward Q. Tentacles. He's like the grumpy guy at work who everyone avoids. Except SpongeBob. Squidward lives next to

Storm

Doctor Doom

SpongeBob in Bikini Bottom, in an Easter Island head. Despite his name he's not a squid but an octopus, with a large frowning head, a big droopy nose and yellow eyes with rectangular red pupils. His skin is turquoise; which clashes with his orange shirt.
   Where to meet him. After the SpongeBob Character Parties in front of Mel's Drive-In on Hollywood Blvd.; at the Superstar Character Breakfast (Thr.–Sat. 9–11:15 a.m., Café La Bamba); Universal Studios.

Storm. The ultimate weather girl, Storm was born with the ability to control the weather. She can also manipulate the air in a person's lungs and the pressure inside their inner ear, causing an evil-doer intense pain. She descends from an ancient line of African princesses, all of whom had white hair and could do magic. Strong and serene, she can fly, too, and pick locks and pockets and excels at hand-to-hand combat. When using her powers her eyes turn solid white.
   Where to meet her. At Marvel Super Hero Island, Islands of Adventure.

Thing 1 and Thing 2. Chaos. That's what these creatures cause in the 1957 Dr. Seuss

book "The Cat in the Hat." Once the Cat releases them from a box to show young Sally and her brother, they knock things over without regard, fly kites in the house, play with the mom's new polka-dot dress. The Things wear red jumpsuits labeled "Thing 1" and "Thing 2"; otherwise you couldn't tell them apart. Their hair is wild, shaggy and bright blue.
   Where to meet them. Mon.–Sat. after the stage show "Oh the Stories You'll Hear," typically 10:30 a.m.–4:30 p.m. on the half hour (no show at 1:30 p.m.), Sunday no shows but characters still appear, Seuss Character Zone, Seuss Landing, Islands of Adventure.

Vector. A spoiled son of a wealthy banker, upstart supervillain Victor "Vector" Perkins becomes Felonius Gru's nemesis in 2010's "Despicable Me" after he tries to hijack Gru's plan for stealing the moon. He wears glasses and an orange tracksuit, has a pot belly on a scrawny body, and in the park believes himself to be quite a dancer.
   Where to meet him. Outside the Universal Studios Store after the 9:30 a.m. Minions dance routine (most days), Production Central; after Despicable Me Character Parties in front of Mel's Drive-In and at the

Winnie Woodpecker

Superstar Character Breakfast (Thr.–Sat. 9–11:15 a.m., Café La Bamba), Hollywood Blvd.; Universal Studios.

Velma Dinkley. This pageboy brunette brainiac has one big problem; she always loses her glasses. In the 1969–1975 television cartoon series "Scooby-Doo, Where Are You!" she's often crawling on the floor searching for the chunky frames, only to find them at the feet of whichever bad guy was terrorizing the teens that week. The resident genius of Mystery Inc., she at first solves the group's mysteries by herself, though later Freddy helps her. She wears a baggy orange sweater, a red skirt, knee-length orange socks and sensibly black Mary Janes. Over time she became the GenX version of baby-boomer "Gilligan's Island" character Mary Ann—the wholesome girl male viewers preferred over her more outgoing cohort—in Velma's case go-go-booted blonde Daphne Blake, in Mary Ann's case breathless movie star Ginger Grant.
Where to meet her. With other Scooby stars on Hollywood Blvd., Universal Studios.

Winnie Woodpecker. Appearing in only one Woody Woodpecker theatrical cartoon but many television ones, sometimes Winnie is Woody's girlfriend, sometimes just his friend. As for looks she's his twin except for having blue eyes instead of green, long eyelashes, forward-bent headfeathers and wearing a yellow skirt as a fashion statement. As for personality she's much less nutty.
Where to meet her. With Woody at the Universal Studios gate and on Hollywood Blvd.

Wolverine. He feels bad when he uses deadly force; he feels bad about nearly everything. Marvel's most brooding superhero, Wolverine has bone-like claws that slide out from the back of his hands, the senses of a wild animal, superhuman strength and the ability to regenerate his body parts. He masks his eyes, and wears a yellow and navy blue outfit.
Where to meet him. At Marvel Super Hero Island, Islands of Adventure.

Woody Woodpecker. Crazy! Demented! That was the first Woody, in 1940. Soon he grew saner, a bird who only went nuts when it made sense. His look evolved too, into more-or-less that of a pileated woodpecker. His catchphrase ("Guess who?") and laugh ("ha-ha-ha-HA-ha!") come from voice artist Mel Blanc, who went on to be Bugs Bunny. Woody is the mascot of Universal Orlando; his image appears throughout the resort.
Where to meet him. At the Universal Studios gate and on Hollywood Blvd; also at Port of Entry, Islands of Adventure.

Woody Woodpecker

Special events

A Celebration of Harry Potter. This three-day event is held in late January or early February. Actors from the series sign autographs and answer questions; past stars have included Rupert Grint, Bonnie Wright and Matthew Lewis. Demonstrations have included a Props Showcase with propmaster Pierre Bohanna and dueling lessons with choreographer Paul Harris. Booths and displays showcase art and props from the films and offer art for sale. Past booths have included the work of artists Miraphora Mina and Eduardo Lima; the Sorting Hat has appeared too, determining what Hogwarts house visitors belong in.

If you go. Attendance is free with park admission. Most autograph sessions and presentations take place on the Music Plaza Stage at Universal Studios. Expect three sessions per day, each with more than one actor. Each requires a ticket which must be picked up in person; the distribution point is near the Blue Man Group Theater and typically opens at 7:30 a.m. Tickets are limited to one per person per day and are first-come, first-served.

Mardi Gras. This New Orleans-style family-friendly event takes place at the Universal Studios park on most Saturday and some Friday evenings in February, March and April.

Parade. Dancers, stiltwalkers and other performers add zest to the park's Mardi Gras parade, which features floats designed by Blaine Kern Studios, the creator of the floats in the New Orleans parade since 1947. The floats are updated yearly but always include a riverboat and a huge one dedicated to "King Gator." Riders toss beads and doubloons. Annual passholders can often ride on a float if they're at least 48 inches tall, either at least 18 years old or accompanied by an adult, and sign up on Universal's website at least a week early.

Food. Andouille sausage, beignets, jambalaya, red beans and rice and shrimp gumbo are offered after 4 p.m. at booths in a special French Quarter Courtyard of the park.

Left © Universal Orlando Resort; right © NBCUniversal Media

One Direction performs in front of the Universal Studios Florida Music Stage in 2014.

Music. Barenaked Ladies, the B-52s, Fall Out Boy and Diana Ross have all appeared in the event's nightly concerts, which feature major pop, rock, R&B and country artists at the Music Plaza Stage in front of the Hollywood Rip Ride Rockit coaster. A smaller stage in the French Quarter Courtyard features blues and Zydeco bands direct from Louisiana, a tradition Universal started after Hurricane Katrina struck the Big Easy in 2005.

If you go. Universal's Mardi Gras celebrations occur rain or shine and are included with park admission. The park's rides and attractions close when the parade begins.

Concert series. Famed singers and artists perform live at Universal Studios from mid-May to mid-June; fall shows are in November. Past concerts have featured Pitbull, Jason Derulo and the Goo Goo Dolls. Performances take place on the Music Plaza Stage.

If you go. Attendance is free with regular park admission. Shows do not have seating; to score a good spot to stand close to the stage arrive three to six hours before showtime.

Rock the Universe. Live performances by top Christian acts are the main draw of this Universal Studios event, which takes place on a Saturday and Sunday in mid-September. Past shows have featured Jeremy Camp, Kari Jobe and Switchfoot. All park attractions stay open except those in Diagon Alley; the Hollywood Rip Ride Rockit roller coaster plays Christian rock songs. A candlelighting ceremony adds a solemn tone Saturday night; a worship service does Sunday morning.

If you go. Admission requires a separate ticket. In 2015, prices for single-night tickets were $60; full-weekend tickets with daytime access to both parks were $160; Universal Express passes added $15–$20 per night. The park closes for regular visitors at 6 p.m.; attendees can arrive anytime after 4 p.m.

Halloween Horror Nights. Scream-worthy haunted houses, "scare zones" and risqué shows filled with fanservice make up this delightfully dark Halloween celebration. Universal's signature event, it takes place on about 30 evenings from mid-September through October at the Universal Studios park; each year has its own theme and experiences. Pulsing ambient rock and metal enhance the vibe, as do a variety of alcoholic party drinks. Bars are set up throughout the park; bloody nurses coyly sell blood bags filled with jello shots of rum and passion fruit.

Outdoor scare zones. Nearly 200 imaginatively costumed "scare-actors" wander the park's darkened streets, leaping forward, backward and sideways as they startle one

Little Bo Peep has eaten her sheep. Below: a nurse has a shot for you.

person after another. A third of them carry chainsaws, engines on and revving.

Haunted houses. Most as thoroughly executed and immersive as any major theme-park attraction, eight to 10 houses are set up inside soundstages and other structures backstage, occupied by murderers and other vicious beings who for the most part are out to kill whoever stops by. Party-goers brave enough to do so walk through dark forboding scenes in a single-file line, constantly getting startled by live actors who pop out of nowhere. The houses change each year; most are based on well-known horror films and television

The Dollhouse of the Damned, from 2014. Below: The Freddie vs. Jason house, 2015.

shows; sometimes one is in 3-D. Waits for the most popular houses can reach three hours.

Theatrical shows. Not at all scary, the irreverent Bill & Ted's Excellent Halloween Adventure is a raunchy good-natured local fave that takes vicious jabs at politicians, pop-culture icons and the Walt Disney Co. Hosted by the two most excellent dudes from the 1989 movie "Bill and Ted's Excellent Adventure," it takes place in the Fear Factor Live theater and can run to 40 minutes. Halloween Horror Nights also has a second live show—for years a tribute to The Rocky Horror Picture Show, in 2015 and maybe future years an updated

Dr. Frank N. Furter and Janet. At left: Posters promote haunted houses over the years.

fan favorite: the Carnival of Carnage, a gory game of on-stage executions of park visitors (OK, actors) hosted by crude madman Jack the Clown and busty gal pal Chance, spiced up with darkly sensual dancing Harlequins.

Tips. *When to go:* On a Wednesday (always the least busy night of a week), a Thursday (the second least crowded) or a Sunday. Halloween night isn't crowded, neither are any nights that follow it. Don't go the first week; Universal often tweaks a few things after it. *To save money:* Buy your tickets in advance; if you're also buying a Halloween Horror Nights Express pass (see Options, below) go on a less crowded night and they'll cost less. *To get the most for your money:* Arrive at Universal before 5 p.m., pick up an event map (it shows the location of every house, show and scare zone) and look over it while you wait at the turnstiles. When the night begins immediately take in a house or two; save the others for after 11 p.m. In between explore the scare zones, eat, drink, go on the rides and see the shows (either the first or last Bill and Ted show; others can have waiting lines of up to an hour). Stay at the event until it closes; to stretch out your night step in a line for your last house just before closing time; you'll still get in. If you're already in the park on the night you go, stay in it after it closes to regular visitors at 5

p.m. by heading to one of its Stay and Scream holding areas; wait at the KidZone one and you'll get into the houses near it as early as 5:30 p.m. Another option: Make reservations to eat at Finnegan's restaurant at 5 o'clock or so; you'll get into the party at the same time as those who are first in line out front. *To see all the houses:* Buy a Halloween Horror Nights Express pass, take an RIP Guided Tour or go more than one night (see below). *To maximize being scared:* Scream! Loudly! Whenever any scareactor frightens you—you'll attract others. Move slowly through the scare zones, taking in everything, paying little attention to the people around you. In the houses, take long looks to your sides and behind you to get a good look at everything in them. *To minimize being scared:* Strut through the scare zones looking straight ahead. Don't be distracted—the scareactors target visitors looking at their phones, texting or engaged in conversations. In the houses, continually look forward and keep an eye on the person in front of you, otherwise it can be easy to get disoriented; in some houses you'll lose track of the pathway, making you an easy mark. Have a drink or two, and remember that though they can get uncomfortably close, none of the actors on the streets or in the houses are allowed to touch you. *To stay comfortable:* Wear soft shoes, not sandals;

Jack's harlequins perform in black ruffs, patent leather corsets, cheap tutus and torn fishnets.

Jack and Chance. He channels Pennywise ("It") and the Joker, she the Joker's girl Harley Quinn.

you'll be on your feet all night. *To fully appreciate a haunted house:* Learn what the houses are ahead of time, pick out the ones you most want to see and watch their movies or television shows before you visit. *To fully appreciate the total experience:* Consider a behind-the-scenes tour (see Options below).

If you go. The park closes for regular visitors at 5 p.m. on event nights; the party kicks off at 6:30 p.m. (ticket-holders can enter at 6 p.m.) and runs to 1 or 2 a.m. Many rides stay open, typically Hollywood Rip Ride Rockit, Transformers The Ride 3-D, Revenge of the Mummy, Harry Potter and the Escape from Gringotts, Men in Black Alien Attack and The Simpsons Ride. Costumes and masks are prohibited; alcohol can't be brought in. No food, drinks, bottles, recording, flash photography, flashlights or laser pens are allowed in the houses. As its horror is quite graphic and its shows adult, Universal advises that children under the age of 13 shouldn't attend Halloween Horror Nights; it's rare to see one.

Admission requires a separate ticket; the event is not included with any park ticket except a Premier annual pass. Expect tickets to cost about $100, less if you're a Florida resident, annual passholder or have already bought a regular park ticket; tickets include admission to some CityWalk clubs. Multi-night tickets are often great deals.

Options. Express passes ($70-$120) let you skip the regular lines at all houses and major rides and get reserved seats at the Bill & Ted show. They often sell out. Four-hour guided "RIP" tours (8 p.m., $140 per person) give you and up to 12 other people front-of-line access to each house and reserved Bill & Ted seats. Private RIP tours ($1400 for a group of up to 10) include those things plus skip-the-line access to two rides. Past backstage tours have included Arcane Insights (Halloween Horror Nights creative types lead you through the event, with a stop at a house's makeup or wardrobe area and a seated Q&A session, $210 plus event admission) and Unmasking the Horror (daytime lights-on tours of three houses, $60). To see what special experiences are offered on your night call 1-866-346-9350 or email vipexperience@universalorlando.com.

Christmas. A special parade and a touching stage show spread holiday cheer at both parks starting in late November. Many buildings are decorated, vintage Christmas tunes and a towering tree brighten Universal Studios.

Macy's Holiday Parade. Giant balloons from the famous Thanksgiving Day parade in Manhattan—including a blinking string of Christmas lights—feature in this jolly Universal Studios procession of floats, costumed characters and local high school bands.

Cindy-Lou Who helps the Grinch realize the true meaning of Christmas in Universal's stage show "Grinchmas." Below: Materialistic tree decorator Martha May temporarily woos some male Whos to her view of the holiday as she belts out "Mister Santa."

Santa and Mrs. Claus bring up the rear, which stops in front of the park's Macy's facade for Santa to magically light the park's Christmas tree. The parade begins daily at 5 p.m. in front of Mel's Drive-In, traveling clockwise down the route of the Universal Superstar Parade. Reserved viewing areas are available for young families, annual passholders and visitors with disabilities. If you like, you can walk in the parade and help guide the

A chorus line of Santa's helpers celebrates his tree lighting in the Macy's parade.

balloons. Volunteers must speak English, be at least 18 years of age, at least 48 inches tall, at least 125 lbs. and able to walk the mile-long parade route for up to an hour. Sign up at least two hours before the parade kicks of; in recent years the sign-up spot was near the E.T. Adventure attraction.

Grinchmas. The Grinch steals the spotlight with his snarky quips, but this musical stage-show version of "How the Grinch Stole Christmas" will still touch you deeply—the story is just so good, and Universal's production of it here is just so well done. The entire cast sings live; among it are Broadway veterans; a real dog plays the Grinch's pet Max. Based, of course, on the Dr. Seuss book and television special, the show also includes elements from Universal's live-action movie.

The 30-minute show is performed six to eight times a day in a soundstage between the two parks; the walkway to it comes from Islands of Adventure, next to the Circus McGurkus Cafe Stoo-pendous in Seuss Landing. On peak days people start lining up more than a hour before showtime; they're seated row-by-row in the order they arrive.

Seuss Landing. Whimsical trimmings, colorful tinsel and faux snow decorate this Islands of Adventure land; button-nosed Whos roam its walkways and sing Christmas carols with children. The Grinch—reformed

and wearing his Santa suit—signs autographs and poses for pictures inside the All the Books You Can Read shop and stars in a character breakfast at Circus McGurkus Cafe Stoo-pendous on some mornings. Expect to pay about $27 for adults, half that for children.

Other festivities. At Universal Studios the Blues Brothers and Barney perform Christmas shows; Mannheim Steamroller performs some nights on the Music Plaza Stage.

If you go. Festivities begin and decorations are put up in November; the parks return to normal in the beginning of January. All holiday events except the Seuss character breakfast are included with park admission. The parks get very crowded starting the week before Christmas; things get back to normal soon after New Year's Day.

Eve. One of Orlando's better New Year's Eve deals, this CityWalk event features a huge outdoor dance party; six bars and clubs have "party zones" with entertainment of their own. An unlimited buffet offers shrimp, prime rib and tenderloin; at midnight there's a champagne toast and small display of fireworks.

If you go. Eve offers regular and VIP tickets; the latter gives you access to private bars and seating areas. Expect tickets to be $100–$200 per person; buy them early for the cheapest rates. Party-goers must be at least 21.

Universal Orlando A–Z

Access policies and services. Universal has many policies regarding disabled guests:

Hearing issues. Except where indicated the devices below are available for use at Guest Services; they require a deposit. Assistive Listening is available at these attractions at Universal Studios: A Day in the Park with Barney, Animal Actors On Location, Fear Factor Live, Men in Black Alien Attack and Terminator 2 3-D; at Islands of Adventure The Cat in the Hat and The Eighth Voyage of Sindbad. Transcripts of some attractions are available for loan. In queues that have material presented on video monitors, personal transmitters turn on closed captions; at many theatrical attractions, attendants can supply handheld acrylic panels that reflect captions from an LED display on a back wall. American Sign Language interpreters translate live shows daily, guide maps list their times. Telecommunication Devices for the Deaf are available at Guest Services and park

First Aid centers. Amplified handsets and text typewriters are provided at pay-phone locations throughout each park.

Mobility issues. All shopping and dining facilities are wheelchair accessible; most attraction queues are except the one at Pteranodon Flyers at Islands of Adventure. Each attraction has its own boarding requirements and accommodations, however if someone can transfer to a ride vehicle (either by themselves or with the help of someone in their party) Universal lets them. Outdoor stage shows have areas reserved for visitors in chairs. Pay telephones in reach of wheelchair visitors are throughout the parks.

Manual wheelchair access. Some attractions let a visitor in a standard manual wheelchair (or mobility scooter) stay in it throughout the experience. At the Universal Studios park these are A Day in the Park with Barney, Animal Actors On Location, Curious George Goes to Town, Despicable Me Minion Mayhem, E.T. Adventure, Fear

Factor Live, Fievel's Playland, The Hogwarts Express at King's Cross Station, Men in Black Alien Attack, Shrek 4-D, Terminator 2 3-D and Universal Orlando's Horror Make-Up Show. At Islands of Adventure: Camp Jurassic, Caro-Seuss-el, The Hogwarts Express at Hogsmeade Station, If I Ran the Zoo, Jurassic Park Discovery Center, Me Ship The Olive, One Fish Two Fish Red Fish Blue Fish, Poseidon's Fury, The Cat in the Hat and The Eighth Voyage of Sindbad. At other attractions, specific vehicles help visitors transfer from a chair. At Universal Studios, these are Despicable Me Minion Mayhem, Harry Potter and the Escape from Gringotts, Kang & Kodos' Twirl 'n' Hurl, Men in Black Alien Attack and Woody Woodpecker's Nuthouse Coaster. At Islands of Adventure: Dudley Do-Right's Ripsaw Falls, Flight of the Hippogriff, Jurassic Park River Adventure, Popeye & Bluto's Bilge-Rat Barges and Storm Force Accelatron.

Motorized-chair and scooter access. With the exception of the Hogwarts Express, no attraction queue or ride vehicle at Universal Orlando allow motorized wheelchairs or mobility scooters (electric convenience vehicles, or ECVs). At rides which accommodate manual wheelchairs, visitors may transfer from their motorized chair or scooter into one.

Rentals. Universal rents manual wheelchairs for $12 a day; mobility scooters for $50 a day ($65 with a canopy) plus a $50 deposit; Guest Services (407-224-7554) reserves chairs and scooters. If you don't reserve one arrive early to rent a scooter without a canopy; they often sell out before noon. Rental locations are in the central rotunda of the parking structure (wheelchairs only) and at the far left of the entrance to each theme park. Manual wheelchairs are free to use in the parking garages; they're at the central rotunda. Outside companies that rent wheelchairs and scooters include Apple Scooter (800-701-1971), Best Price Mobility (866-866-3434), Buena Vista Scooter Rentals (866-484-4797), CARE Scooter Rentals (800-741-2282) and Scooterbug (800-726-8284).

Restrooms. All park and CityWalk restrooms have wheelchair-accessible stalls. Companion restrooms are located throughout each park, including First Aid stations.

Transportation. Universal shuttle buses and water taxis can accommodate wheelchairs and mobility scooters.

Vision issues. Guide map information, attraction scripts and restaurant menus are available in large type and Braille at Guest

Services. Many attractions can accommodate a visitor with a white cane or provide a receptacle in which to place the cane in the ride vehicle; at some rides the cane will need to be collapsed. At other rides the cane must be held by an attendant after the visitor is seated; the attendant will return it in the unload area. At Universal Studios, these attractions are E.T. Adventure, the Fievel's Playland water slide, Harry Potter and the Escape from Gringotts, Hollywood Rip Ride Rockit, Men In Black Alien Attack, Revenge of the Mummy and Woody Woodpecker's Nuthouse Coaster. At Islands of Adventure: Caro-Seuss-el, Doctor Doom's Fearfall, Flight of the Hippogriff, Harry Potter and the Forbidden Journey, The Incredible Hulk Coaster and Pteranodon Flyers.

Other issues. Here's a quick review of Universal's other policies and services for disabled visitors; for more detailed information check out the complimentary Rider's Guide for Rider Safety and Guests with Disabilities, available at Guest Services.

Attractions Assistance Pass. This pass is for visitors who are unable to withstand extended waits at attractions due to a disability. At each ride or show, showing it lets a visitor board the ride quickly (often through its Universal Express line) or, if the posted wait time at that moment is more than 30 minutes, return after that time and board then. Once that reservation is used, the user can reserve another time at another attraction in the same manner. At least that's the official policy. In reality attendants often have the freedom to let an AAP holder board their ride quickly regardless of its wait time, so they can treat more seriously impaired visitors with appropriate compassion. The pass is free, good for parties up to six people, valid for 14 days and available at Guest Services. A doctor's note is not required.

Body braces and casts. Visitors with body braces or casts cannot ride Dragon Challenge or The Incredible Hulk Coaster. At other attractions, the brace or cast must fit comfortably in the ride vehicle and not interfere with the functioning of the restraint.

Oxygen devices. Oxygen tanks are permitted at these attractions at Universal Studios: A Day in the Park with Barney, Animal Actors On Location, Curious George Goes to Town, Despicable Me Minion Mayhem (stationary seating only), Fear Factor Live, Fievel's Playland (except water slide), The Hogwarts Express King's Cross Station, Shrek 4-D (stationary seating only), Terminator 2 3-D (stationary seating only) and Universal Orlando's Horror Make-Up Show. At Islands of Adventure: Camp Jurassic (except at Pteranodon Flyers), The Eighth Voyage of Sindbad, The Hogwarts Express Hogsmeade Station and the Toon Amphitheater. Oxygen concentrators and related devices are often permitted at attractions if they can be secured and don't interfere with its restraint.

Parking. The parking complex has handicapped parking spaces convenient to its moving walkways for vehicles that display Accessible Parking Permits.

Prostheses. Visitors must remove all prosthetic limbs before riding Hollywood Rip Ride Rockit at Universal Studios and Dragon Challenge and Pteranodon Flyers at Islands of Adventure. Visitors should secure or remove all prosthetic limbs before riding the following attractions at Universal Studios: Harry Potter and the Escape from Gringotts, Revenge of the Mummy and Woody Woodpecker's Nuthouse Coaster. At Islands of Adventure: Doctor Doom's Fearfall, Dudley Do-Right's Ripsaw Falls, Flight of the Hippogriff, Harry Potter and the Forbidden Journey, The Incredible Hulk Coaster and the Jurassic Park River Adventure. Visitors with prosthetic arms or hands must be able to grasp a ride's restraint. At some attractions, certain arm, hand, joint and leg elements are required to ride.

Service animals. Trained and leashed (or harnessed) service animals are allowed throughout Universal Orlando, in all restaurants, shops and attraction queues. They can also accompany their owners on some rides and shows. Portable kennels are available. Visitors with service animals will often enter an attraction through its Universal Express entrance. Each park has designated walking areas for service animals. At Universal Studios, these are in the Central Park area across from Cafe La Bamba and in World Expo between Men in Black Alien Attack and Fear Factor Live. At Islands of Adventure, they're on Marvel Super Hero Island between The Amazing Adventures of Spider-Man and Doctor Doom's Fearfall, in the Jurassic Park area behind the Pizza Predattoria fast-food spot and on Seuss Landing behind the ride One Fish Two Fish Red Fish Blue Fish.

Alcohol. Visitors cannot bring alcoholic beverages into either Universal park or CityWalk, though those of legal age (21 in Florida) can carry open containers of purchased alcoholic beverages. Drinks served in restaurants, however, cannot be taken elsewhere.

Birthdays. Guest Services hands out buttons that read either "It's My Birthday" or "I'm Celebrating." Universal staffers will notice and comment on the button all day; at Islands of Adventure the Lost Continent's Mystic Fountain may sing the wearer a personalized birthday song. Button wearers at Ollivanders Wand Shop in the Wizarding World of Harry Potter are likely to be picked to have a wand choose them.

Business facilities. Four Universal Orlando hotels—the Hard Rock, Loews Portofino Bay, Loews Royal Pacific and Loews Sapphire Falls—have convention and conference centers, with more than 295,000 square feet of combined meeting space. Attendees get discounted room rates and park tickets.

Childrens policies and services. The resort has many policies regarding kids:

Childcare. Three Universal-owned hotels offer an evening childcare center: Loews Portofino Bay Hotel (Campo Portofino, 407-503-1200), Hard Rock Hotel (Camp Lil' Rock, 407-503-2200) and Loews Royal Pacific Resort (The Mariner's Club, 407-503-3200). Each is stocked with arts and crafts, books, computer desks, games, a movie room, toys and videos; one counselor overlooks 8 to 10 children. ($15 per hour per child, $15 per meal. Children must be toilet trained, no pull-ups, 4–14 years old. 5 p.m. to 11:30 p.m. Sunday through Thursday; to midnight on Friday and Saturday. Reservations required.)

Babysitters. Universal works with in-room childcare provider Kids Nite Out (407-828-0920, kidsniteout.com) to supply babysitting and childcare for kids ages 6 weeks to 12 years, including those with special needs. Caregivers bring toys, activities, books, games and arts and crafts. Rates start at $18 per hour with a 4-hour minimum, plus a $10 transportation fee.

Child swap. This complimentary service (also known as rider swap) allows two parents or guardians of a child too small or unwilling to experience a ride to wait in line once while the other watches the child, then switch. To use the service notify an attendant.

Family Service Centers. These quiet spots have private nursing areas, changing rooms with tables and unisex bathrooms and kitchens with microwave ovens and sinks, and sell supplies and over-the-counter medications. They're located next to the two First Aid stations in each park—at Universal Studios near its entrance by Lost and Found and on Canal Street between the New York and San Francisco areas; at Islands of Adventure in the Port of Entry near Guest Services and near the Sindbad show in The Lost Continent.

Infant care. Diaper-changing stations are in men's and women's restrooms throughout Universal. Moms can nurse babies anywhere on Universal property without hassle; the Family Service Centers have specialized chairs set aside for nursing.

Discounts. Universal offers reduced prices for children ages 3 to 9 for park tickets and food. Children younger than age 3 are admitted free into Universal theme parks.

Equipment rentals. Universal offers cribs, rollaway beds and strollers. Outside companies rent those items and more and often handle delivery and pickup.

Strollers. Each theme park offers strollers for rent, to the left side of its entrance. Single strollers rent for $15 a day; single kiddie strollers $18 a day; double strollers $25 a day; double kiddie strollers $28 a day. Made of molded plastic, Universal's strollers are not designed for infants. For an infant stroller contact Baby's Away (407-334-0232), Kingdom Strollers (407-674-1866), Magic Strollers (866-866-6177) or Orlando Stroller Rentals (800-281-0884).

Other equipment. Baby's Away and All About Kids rent car seats, high chairs, playpens and the like. Most local car-rental companies offer infant or child safety seats ($7–$15 per day) with advance notice.

Height requirements. Some attractions require guests to be a particular height to be allowed to ride. Any child who meets the minimum height requirement for an attraction, but does not meet the 48-inches ride-alone height must be accompanied by a "supervising companion"—someone who is 14 years of age or older and meets all other attraction ridership requirements. At all attractions, children under 48 inches tall must be able to sit upright and unassisted. Children less than 48 inches tall must be accompanied by a supervising companion at all times.

Lost children. Lose your child? Tell the closest Universal employee. He or she will instantly spread the news throughout the park and advise you on what to do next. Typically theme park attendants who come across lost children take them to the Guest Services location at the entrance to that park. Some parents introduce their children to an attendant first thing when they arrive at a theme park, and point out the worker's distinctive name tag. Other parents use a permanent marker to write their cellphone number on the child's arm.

Restaurants. Most Universal eateries have kids' menus and high chairs; a few offer character meals. Expense-account spots near Universal (many on Sand Lake Road, promoted on signs atop taxis and recommended by non-Universal concierge in exchange for free meals) often aren't child-friendly.

Dining plans. The Universal Quick Service Dining Plan (adults $20, children $13) gives you a credit-card-like pass that's good for 1 quick-service meal (entree and beverage), 1 snack, 1 beverage. More than 100 restaurants and snack stands accept it; a few spots at CityWalk do. Use it to get expensive meals and snacks and you'll save about 30 percent.

Available only to on-site hotel guests who buy it as part of a Universal Vacation Package, the Universal Dining Plan (adults $52, children $17) gives you a table-service meal, quick-service meal, snack and non-alcoholic beverage per nightly stay. At the Universal Studios park it's good at Finnegan's Bar & Grill, Lombard's Seafood Grille and the Superstar Character Breakfast at Cafe La Bamba; at Islands of Adventure Confisco Grille, Mythos Restaurant and The Grinch & Friends Character Breakfast at Circus McGurkus (seasonal); at CityWalk Antojitos Authentic Mexican Food, Bob Marley A Tribute to Freedom, Cowfish, Jimmy Buffett's Margaritaville, Pat O'Brien's, Red Oven Pizza Bakery and Vivo Italian Kitchen.

Early entry. Each day at least one of the Universal park opens its Wizarding World of Harry Potter area an hour early for its on-site hotel guests (Universal Studios also opens Despicable Me Minion Mayhem); at peak times of the year both parks open early. To find out which park is open early on a particular day call Universal Guest Services at 407-224-4233; it usually knows a month in advance. Hotel concierge staff also should know. Universal also lets its annual passholders in early on many days; details are on the annual passholder section of the Universal website (universalorlando.com).

Guest Services. Each theme park has a walk-up Guest Services window outside its entrance as well a walk-in office inside; CityWalk's window is tucked in between its Coldstone ice cream parlor and Red Oven Pizza Bakery. Staffers make dining reservations, reprint and upgrade park tickets, sell annual passes, help with transportation problems, check on lost items (for items lost that day) and answer general questions. International visitors can exchange currency amd pick up guide maps printed in German, Spanish and Portuguese.

Kennel. A daytime kennel for dogs and cats (407-224-9509, fax 407-224-9516) is housed near Universal's parking garages at the corner of its RV and camper parking lot at the intersection of Universal Blvd. and Hollywood Way; follow signs for parking. Water is provided; owners must provide food and may bring blankets and toys. The kennel doesn't take reservations; it runs on a first-come, first-served basis. Walks aren't provided, so owners should plan to stop by and walk their pets at least once during a day. It opens at 8 a.m. and is locked and unattended two hours after the last theme park closes, however, pets can stay until 3 a.m. to be picked up.

Boarding a pet is $15 per day for each pet (50 percent off for premier annual passholders for the first pet). Cats and small dogs (up to 38 lbs.) stay in indoor, air-conditioned kennels (3 feet by 2 1/2 feet) that are solid metal with a chain-link front. Larger dogs (over 38 lbs.) stay outside in fully covered, fan-cooled kennels (7 feet by 4 feet) with cement floors and chain-link fencing. Proof of up-to-date vaccinations (rabies, bordetella and DHPP for dogs; rabies, calicivirus, panleukopenia and rhinotracheitis for cats) is required.

Lockers. Multi-use lockers can be rented at each theme park. At Universal Studios, they're outside the park to the far right of the entrance just past Guest Services as well as just inside the front gate near the exit turnstiles. At Islands of Adventure they're inside the front gate and outside the exit turnstiles at Group Sales. Lockers cost $8 a day for a space 17 inches tall by 9.5 inches wide by 17 inches deep. Larger "family-size" lockers (17 inches tall by 12.5 inches wide by 25 inches deep) cost $10 a day; super-sized ones (23 inches tall by 15.5 inches wide by 35 inches deep) also rent for $10 a day but are outside the front gates. Other lockers are at attractions that don't allow loose articles (Harry Potter and the Forbidden Journey, Dragon Challenge, Hollywood Rip Ride Rockit, Revenge of the Mummy, Harry Potter and the Escape from Gringotts, and Men in Black Alien Attack); these lockers are free for the amount of time spent at the attraction (you're given at least 45 minutes, time may vary), though you can choose to pay to use the locker for additional time ($2 per hour, $14 daily maximum). At Islands of Adventure, short-term lockers are near the park's three rides that get riders wet—Dudley Do-Right's Ripsaw Falls, Popeye & Bluto's Bilge-Rat Barges and the Jurassic Park River Adventure. Their rates are $4 for 90 minutes and $3 for each additional hour, with a $20 daily maximum.

Lost and found. Universal has multiple Lost and Found centers, one at each theme park, at CityWalk and at every on-site hotel. At the Universal Studios theme park Lost and Found is located just inside the entrance at the far right, a walk-up counter under a sign that reads Studio Audience Center. At Islands of Adventure it's inside the Guest Services office; at CityWalk it's also at the Guest Services office. Universal hotels have their own Lost and Found offices; check with the concierge desk. Items are held for 30 days except credit cards, which are shredded after 3 days, and cellphones, which are held 90 days. Items lost at the Universal Studios park are held there; those lost at Islands of Adventure and CityWalk are held at Islands of Adventure (the CityWalk office sends them over there after 24 hours). If you identify your item over the phone (407-224-4233, option 2), Universal will ship it to you free of charge.

Medical services. Medical care at Universal is close at hand; on property or just minutes away. Universal hotels can arrange in-room appointments and prescription deliveries.

First Aid. Each theme park has two Health Services stations manned by either registered nurses or paramedics who handle minor medical incidents (at no charge) and contact Orlando emergency personnel for more serious matters. At Universal Studios the main First Aid center in the New York area of the park behind Louie's Italian restaurant across from the upcoming Fast and Furious attraction; a satellite facility is at the front of the park next to Lost and Found. At Islands of Adventure First Aid is next to The Eighth Voyage of Sindbad show in Sindbad's Village in The Lost Continent (look for the Red Cross across from Oasis Coolers); a satellite facility is inside the Guest Services building to the right of the main entrance turnstiles.

Money. Nearly every Universal restaurant, snack stand and shop accepts credit and debit cards as well as cash. Visitors will need cash for some tips, however, as well as highway tolls, parking fees, pressed-coin machines and some taxi and limo services.

Credit and debit cards. Universal accepts American Express, Diners Club, Discover, MasterCard and Visa cards. On-site hotels also accept Carte Blanche and Japan Credit Bureau (JCB). As American Express is Universal's official card, holders get access to the Amex VIP Lounge in Universal Studios (daily noon to 5 p.m), behind the Classic Monsters Cafe near Shrek 4-D. Each card allows six people to enter; entry requires showing a valid card and a park pass. Inside is free bottled water, snacks, phone-charging stations and a Universal concierge.

Currency exchange. Foreign currency can be exchanged for U.S. dollars at theme park Guest Services windows and Universal on-site hotel concierge desks.

Gift cards. Cards good throughout both parks and CityWalk are available in $5 denominations up to $500. They never expire. You can reload more funds to your card at most shops and restaurants in both parks (reloading must be done in person); cards cannot be redeemed for cash; lost cards can't be replaced. Cards are available in designs based on Universal characters as well as Happy Birthday and Congratulations designs. They're sold throughout Universal's hotels, parks and CityWalk as well as online at universalorlando.com/giftcards.

Wizarding Bank Notes. Available only at the Gringotts Money Exchange in Universal Studio's Diagon Alley, this whimsical scrip is accepted at all Universal parks, shops, hotels and valet-parking spots. Popular as souvenirs as well as currency, it comes in denominations of $10 and $20; the exchange rate is always $1 for $1.

Obese visitors. Visitors of nearly all shapes and sizes can experience most of what Universal has to offer with no problem.

Bench seats. On some attractions an obese person should take a bench seat alone to fit comfortably. To do so easily when an attendant at the loading area asks how many are in your party say "1" and then the number of the rest of your party, such as "and 3."

Getting around. A parkgoer can walk 5 or 10 miles a day, which can be tough on anyone who isn't fit; overweight visitors should pace themselves and take breaks. Universal offers mobility scooters that many obese guests rent; they often sell out on crowded days.

Lap bars. Many rides have lap bars that are designed to fit snugly. A large person should *not* share a lap-bar seat with a dramatically smaller person; the lap bar will stop and lock based on the large tummy, leaving the smaller person relatively unrestrained.

Seat-belt rides. Pull the seatbelt out all the way before sitting down. Hold it out while you sit, then fasten the buckle. Ask a family member to help attach the buckle if needed. Universal attendants aren't allowed to help.

Test seats. At several rides you can check out one of its seats before getting in line.

Theater seats. For attractions with armrests, obese guests may find it easier to sit on the front edge of a seat and then slide back, or sit sideways and then turn to squeeze in.

Parking. Visitors traveling to a Universal theme park or CityWalk park their car in one of two adjacent parking garages (6000 Universal Blvd.). Moving sidewalks lead from the garages, to a security check which as of December 2015 includes metal detectors.

Rates. Daily rates are $20 for cars, motorcycles and taxis and $22 for buses, campers and tractor-trailers. Preferred parking ($30, free for Preferred Annual Passholders) gets you a spot closer to the moving walkways. Florida residents park free after 6 p.m. with proof of residency (i.e., a driver's license); others pay $5. Everyone parks free after 10 p.m. Once your pay a parking fee, its receipt is good for free parking the rest of that day.

Security. Universal officers can be contacted via call boxes throughout the garages.

Valet parking. Before 6 p.m., valet parking is $20 for 2 hours, $40 for more than 2 hours, and $50 for Red Carpet; it's typically sold at the parking gates before noon, at a CityWalk drop-off point afterward. After 6 p.m., rates lower for staying longer for 2 hours ($35) and for Red Carpet ($45, guarantees access to your vehicle in less than 5 minutes; if there is a line at the valet you get to skip it and hand your ticket to the next attendant). Preferred annual passholders get valet parking for $15 (excluding nights of special events); Red Carpet for $25. Premier annual passholders get free valet parking (except on special-event nights); Red Carpet valet for $15. Tesla and Clipper Creek charging stations are available for valet-parking visitors with electric vehicles.

Vehicle assistance. If you run into car trouble, battery jumps are provided throughout the garages. For help, raise your hood.

Photography. Whether it's one in a phone or a fancy DSLR, a camera can capture spontaneous moments that create treasured memories. Whatever shots you snap take turns being the photographer; if mom takes all the pictures none will include mom. Consider giving children their own cameras.

Photo Connect. Universal photographers take shots of you throughout the parks but you pay only for images you later choose to buy with this service; you don't have to buy any. Photographers are stationed at park entrances, icons and character spots; they link their shots to a free Photo Connect card. You can see and buy shots at shops at the front of each park or online for up to 45 days. Photos can be purchased either a la carte starting at $20 per image, or by buying a Star Card package ($70 for 1 day, $90 for 3 days, $140 for 14 days) which gives you unlimited digital photos, discounts on additional prints and videos and a lanyard to hold a card. They're sold online at universalphotoconnect.com and at Guest Services offices (prices are $10 higher on-site). A Photo Connect photographer will take a photo with your camera free of charge.

Shopping. Universal has more than 60 stores. To order merchandise from outside the resort call 888-762-0820 or go online to universalorlando.com/merchandise.

Package Pickup. Universal will transport any purchased merchandise from a park store up to the front of the park at no charge for a visitor to pick up later. At Universal Studios the pickup location is It's a Wrap; at Islands of Adventure it's Ocean Traders. Visitors staying at a Universal hotel can have their purchases delivered to their rooms the following day at no charge.

Smoking. Universal parks have designated smoking areas; there are none in The Wizarding World of Harry Potter.

Taxes. All area hotels charge sales tax and a 6-percent resort tax on rooms. Universal Orlando sits in Orange County; its combined state and local sales tax rate is 6.5 percent.

Telephones. Pay telephones are located throughout the parks near restrooms and next to the entrance and exit turnstiles. At CityWalk phones are next to Guest Services.

Telephone numbers. *Dining reservations:* 407-224-4233. *General info:* 407-363-8000. *Guest Services:* 407-224-4233. *Hotel reservations:* 888-273-1311; meeting attendees/individual call-in for group blocks: 866-360-7395. *Lost and Found:* 407-224-4233 (option 2). *Merchandise info:* 888-762-0820. *Ticket info:* 407-224-7840. *Vacation packages:* 877-801-9720; hard of hearing TDD 800-447-0672.

Theme park policies. Universal has policies regarding dress and what a visitor can bring into one of its theme parks or CityWalk, though the policies aren't heavily publicized and enforcement can vary.

Dress code. Unacceptable attire includes clothing that has offensive language or content or that represents the wearer as a Universal employee or an emergency worker. All visitors must wear shirts and shoes.

Items allowed in theme parks. Visitors can bring a lot into a Universal theme park:

Coolers. Those that don't have wheels, are soft-sided and are smaller than 6 inches long by 8.5 inches wide by 6 inches high are OK.

Food. Visitors can bring in any snacks, foods or beverages (except alcoholic) that do not require heating and are not in glass containers. Picnic lunches are not acceptable.

Medications. Visitors can bring in any necessary medication. Medication coolers may be stored in a locker or at Guest Services.

Umbrellas. Most any umbrella is allowed at Universal unless it's a beach umbrella.

Items not allowed. Prohibited items include alcoholic beverages, beach umbrellas, coolers larger than 8.5-by-6-by-6 inches or that are hard-sided, folding chairs, food than requires heating or refrigeration, glass containers (excluding baby food jars), pets (service animals are OK), pulled items such as children's wagons, weapons, or wheeled items (inline skates, skateboards, shoes with built-in wheels, wheeled backpacks and coolers) except scooters, strollers and wheelchairs. Eating or drinking, flash photography and smoking inside any attraction or its waiting area is not allowed.

Operating hours. Park hours vary; during slower seasons they're typically 9 a.m. to 5 p.m.; at busy times such as holidays they're often 8 a.m. to 11 p.m. For particular days call

407-363-8000 or go to universalorlando.com/Resort-Information/Theme-Park-Hours.

Tickets. Universal sells theme-park tickets that are good from one to 4 days as well as yearly; Florida residents save on daily passes and can pay for annual passes monthly.

Single-park admission. As of January 2016, a one-day ticket to one park costs $102 for adults, $97 dollars for children ages 3 through 9. A two-day ticket is $150 for adults, $140 for children. A three-day ticket is $160 for adults, $150 for children. A four-day ticket is $170 for adults, $160 for children. Prices typically increase once per year.

Two-park admission. To go to both parks in the same day your ticket will cost about $50 more, depending on how many days it's valid.

Tickets expire 14 days after their first use. Children under 3 are admitted free. For more ticket prices or to buy tickets from Universal, go to universalorlando.com/Theme-Park-Tickets/General-Admission.

Orlando FlexTicket. This ticket provides unlimited admission to five theme parks for 14 days: Universal Studios, Islands of Adventure, the Universal-owned Wet 'n Wild (which closes at the end of 2016), SeaWorld and SeaWorld's Aquatica water park. An adult ticket costs $370, a child ticket is $355. Adding Busch Gardens Tampa Bay adds $20.

Annual passes. Three Universal annual passes include admission to both theme parks and discounts. A Power Pass ($240) has blockout dates around the holidays. A Preferred Pass ($335) adds free self-parking after the first visit. The top level, a Premier Pass ($480) also includes complimentary valet and preferred self-parking, a complimentary Halloween Horror Nights ticket, free CityWalk club access, Universal Express Pass privileges after 4 p.m. and eight complimentary bottles of water. The passes are discounted for Florida residents and members of the U.S. military. Florida residents can buy annual passes and pay for them monthly, without interest, after a down payment of about half the total amount.

Blue Man Group tickets. Adult tickets range from $70 to $115; child tickets $30 to $52.50. Details at 407-BLUE-MAN.

Tours. In Universal's VIP Experience ($330 per person for one park, $350 for two parks) a knowledgable guide leads you and up to nine other people (whether they're part of your party or not); the tour includes backstage access, priority front-of-the-line access to 8 to 10 attractions, reserved seating for shows, complimentary valet parking, a continental breakfast, some park history and discounts at select dining and merchandise locations.

A Personal VIP Experience for a private party of up to 5 people is way more expensive ($2600–$2900 per party for a one-park tour, $2900–$3200 per party for a two-park tour, $4800–$5000 per party for a two-day two-park tour). This tour is often used by celebrities.

Visitors meet at the VIP Experience Lobby, which is next to Universal Studio's Guest Services office at that park's entrance. Visitors under 18 years of age must be accompanied by an adult; theme park admission is required. Taking a tour is the only way to skip to the front of the line at either of the two major Harry Potter attractions, though both have Single Rider Lines. To book a tour call 407-363-8295 or 866-346-9350. For details visit viptours@universalorlando.com.

Transportation. Shuttle buses are complimentary to Universal hotel guests to the parking hub. Water taxis connect the hotels (except Cabana Bay) to the parks and CityWalk, using a dock near the bridge to the Universal Studios park as a hub. The boats depart every 15 minutes, starting an hour before a park's Early Entry begins and running until a half hour after CityWalk shuts down at 2 a.m. Each leg of a trip takes about 20 minutes.

From Orlando International Airport. Mears Transportation (407-423-5566) will take you to Universal by taxi ($45–$55), town car ($60–$70), van ($70–$80) or shuttle bus ($20 per adult, $15 per child; $32 round-trip per adult, $24 per child; children under 3 ride free. SuperStar Shuttle offers transfers to Universal hotel guests who book their stay through Universal Vacations at $35 round trip per person; children under 3 ride free).

Waiting lines and how to avoid them. A downside to any theme park is that you often have to wait in long lines to experience its attractions, as the number of people the park will admit far exceeds the capacity of its rides and shows. Here's a primer on waiting lines at the Universal Orlando parks:

Learning wait times. A sign at each ride displays its current wait; so does the Universal Orlando app. To get a sense what a ride's wait time will be in advance see the Average Wait table in the ride's review in this book.

It reflects the ride's wait for each hour of the day as it appeared on the app throughout 2014 and 2015; if a review doesn't have such a table the attraction typically doesn't have a wait.

Single Rider Lines. Don't mind going on a ride by yourself? A Single Rider Line offers an easy way to lessen your wait; during peak periods using one can cut it by at least 30 minutes. Attractions at Universal Studios with Single Rider Lines are Harry Potter and the Escape from Gringotts, Hollywood Rip Ride Rockit, Men in Black Alien Attack, Revenge of the Mummy, Transformers The Ride 3-D; at Islands of Adventure The Amazing Adventures of Spider-Man, Dudley Do-Right's Ripsaw Falls, Dr. Doom's Fearfall, Harry Potter and the Forbidden Journey and the Jurassic Park River Adventure.

How they work. When ride attendants can't fill a vehicle from a queue without breaking up a group, they take a person from its Single Rider Line. Groups wait in it together but will be split up. It skips a lot of the queue (which often introduces a ride's story and may contain much of its experience); people in it often can't specify where they sit in a vehicle.

Universal Express passes. These optional passes let you bypass the line at an attraction by entering a separate line that's much shorter; most attractions honor it. They come in two types: a standard pass good for one admission at each attraction and an Unlimited pass good for unlimited admissions. Prices vary; from $35 per day for a one-park standard pass during a slow season to $150 for a two-park unlimited pass during holidays. The passes are sold at the front of each park, at shops and kiosks inside them and online at universalorlando.com. If you stay at a Universal luxury hotel (the Hard Rock, Portofino Bay or Royal Pacific) you get an Unlimited pass for the duration of your stay at no extra charge. Passes are limited and can sell out; Halloween Horror Nights has its own.

Attractions that take them. At Universal Studios: A Day In The Park with Barney, Animal Actors on Location, Despicable Me Minion Mayhem, E.T. Adventure, Fear Factor Live, Hollywood Rip Ride Rockit, Men in Black Alien Attack, Revenge of the Mummy, Shrek 4-D, The Simpsons Ride, Terminator 2 3-D, Transformers The Ride 3D, Universal Orlando's Horror Make-Up Show and Woody Woodpecker's Nuthouse Coaster. At Islands of Adventure: The Amazing Adventures of Spider-Man, The Cat In The Hat, Caro-Seuss-el, Doctor Doom's Fearfall, the Dragon Challenge coaster, Dudley Do-Right's Ripsaw Falls, The Eighth Voyage of Sindbad, Flight of the Hippogriff, The Incredible Hulk Coaster, Jurassic Park River Adventure, One Fish Two Fish Red Fish Blue Fish, Popeye & Bluto's Bilge-Rat Barges, Poseidon's Fury, Skull Island Reign of Kong and Storm Force Accelatron. *Note: Rides that don't accept Express passes include some of Universal's most popular: Harry Potter and the Forbidden Journey, Harry Potter and the Escape from Gringotts and the Hogwarts Express train.*

Weather. Florida's subtropical climate creates mild winters but summers that are hot and humid. Between May and August, visitors can get exhausted with little effort; temperatures in direct heat are usually about 12 degrees warmer than those in the shade and can easily reach 100 degrees. Daily afternoon heat indexes during those months usually exceed 105 degrees. Brief afternoon thunderstorms are common. Universal does not offer refunds due to weather or rain checks.

Rain gear. Universal sells clear plastic ponchos; adult sizes cost about $10; children sizes $7. Small collapsible umbrellas go for about $15. Rain gear isn't always displayed.

Weddings. Couples can tie the knot and have their reception at the Loews Portofino Bay Hotel, Loews Royal Pacific Resort or Hard Rock Hotel. For details contact Universal Events at 888-266-2121.

Youth groups. Universal offers activities and competitions for youth groups of 15 or more. Participants get discounted group rates for both accommodations and theme-park tickets. Opportunities include:

STARS Marching Opportunities. Students perform at Universal year-round, including during the Macy's Holiday Parade. Optional performance workshops are available.

STARS Stage Performances. Jazz bands, show choirs, concert choirs, orchestras and dance teams can perform on one of several stages in and around the Universal Studios theme park and CityWalk.

Universal education programs. These programs give students real-world learning experiences at Universal parks. Hands-on courses include a Business Learning Series, It Starts With a Hero, Ride Design: Innovation in Motion, Culinary Arts: Recipe for Success and a variety of education tours. Details are online at universalorlandoyouth.com.

Opposite page artwork © Universal Orlando Resort

THE WIZARDING WORLD OF Harry Potter™

A FIELD GUIDE

BY MICAELA NEAL

© Universal Orlando Resort

Entrance arch, Hogsmeade.

INTRODUCTION

SEVEN BOOKS FORM the heart of the Harry Potter saga. Blending fantasy with the obscure British boarding school genre, these coming-of-age novels are geared to children and teenagers but have fans of all ages. Despite their length (they average 586 pages), the series exploded in popularity soon after its release. Its basic plot is simple. On his 11th birthday, a seemingly normal boy learns that he's actually a young wizard. He receives an invitation to attend the Hogwarts School of Witchcraft and Wizardry, where he becomes best friends with two other students his age, Ron Weasley and Hermione Granger. Meanwhile, the evil wizard Voldemort—who had disappeared after murdering Harry's parents and attempting to kill the infant Harry—seeks to destroy Harry and rule the wizarding world. It's up to Harry to stop him.

A MAGICAL COMMUNITY.

In the series, a magical community lives in secret among the rest of the populace. Non-magical people (muggles) are kept ignorant of the day-to-day lives of witches and wizards. Magical people can cast spells, brew potions and form bonds with magical creatures. While the ability to perform magic is genetic (it can't be learned by muggles) young witches and wizards need to practice their spells and other abilities to use them correctly, so they attend schools like the Hogwarts School of Witchcraft and Wizardry.

In the seventeenth century, witch hunts and stake burnings drove the wizarding community into hiding. In 1689, an International Statute of Secrecy was enstated to keep the world hidden and safe, and muggles' knowledge of magic faded into obscurity. Overall, the wizarding community is rather ignorant about the rest of the world. Much of its culture and fashion seems stuck around the late 1700s, the time when it went into hiding. Since magic makes electricity go haywire, the only technology the magical world uses is in primitive gadgets like gramophones.

A FIELD GUIDE

Some magical people are called "muggle-borns," meaning they come from non-magic families. However, they're just as magically talented as any other witch or wizard. Some older, wealthier wizarding families view muggles as inferior, and look down on anyone who associates with them. They believe in "blood purity," that magical blood is inherently purer than non-magical blood. People with no muggle ancestors are considered "pure-bloods," those with mixed bloodlines are "half-bloods." Muggle-borns are "mud-bloods," an offensive slur. There's no basis for this concept, as wizards and witches have been around so long that they all have muggle blood in their history.

The story takes place from 1991 to 1998, following Harry during his years at Hogwarts. Readers who come from the same generation as the author of this text (i.e., who are in their twenties or early thirties) grew up with the characters over the 10-year span of the books' release, from 1997 to 2007. The books are:—

1. "Harry Potter and the Sorcerer's Stone"
   ("Philosopher's Stone" outside the United States)
2. "Harry Potter and the Chamber of Secrets"
3. "Harry Potter and the Prisoner of Azkaban"
4. "Harry Potter and the Goblet of Fire"
5. "Harry Potter and the Order of the Phoenix"
6. "Harry Potter and the Half-Blood Prince"
7. "Harry Potter and the Deathly Hallows."

An eighth installment called "Harry Potter and the Cursed Child" is a West End play set to debut in 2016; it takes place 19 years after the main series, and stars a middle-aged Harry and his son, Albus. Three other books are based on the series:—

1. "Fantastic Beasts and Where to Find Them"
2. "Quidditch Through the Ages"
3. "The Tales of Beedle the Bard."

The series was written by Joanne Rowling; she used the pseudonym "J.K." at the suggestion of her publisher, who was convinced that obscuring her gender would make it easier to attract readers. She doesn't actually have a middle name—the "K" comes from her grandmother, Kathleen.

The seven main books have been adapted into movies. The first was released in 2001 after the fourth book was published; the last book was divided into two films that came out in 2010 and 2011. Released starting in 2016, a film trilogy of "Fantastic Beasts and Where to Find Them" takes place in the 1920s; it follows the adventures of author and magi-zoologist Newt Scamander. More information is on the series website, Pottermore.

THE WIZARDING WORLD OF HARRY POTTER.
The Wizarding World of Harry Potter is unlike any other theme park area. When you're there it's often easy to forget you're at a theme park; the atmosphere can be so immersive it's almost as if the world of the books and movies has come to life. It consists of two distinct areas of Universal Orlando: one (Hogsmeade and Hogwarts castle) in its Islands of Adventure park, the other (London and Diagon Alley) in its Universal Studios Florida park. They're connected by a train. The designs stick true to the look and feel of the movie series, including many thoughtful, easy-to-miss details. Both are treated like the places they are in the series rather than theme park lands. As a result, attractions and other important tourist spots tend to blend right in with the rest of the place; the entrance to Diagon Alley is completely unmarked. Another nice touch: there are no meet-and-greet locations for iconic characters, because signing autographs and posing for photos would be completely out of character for them.

Hogsmeade Village.

Many clerks, docents and ride attendants appear to be wizards and witches, dressing in robes and carrying wands in their belts. Throughly trained on Potter lore, they stay in character; they're often confused by things like smartphones. Many come from the United Kingdom; their authenic accents add to the atmosphere. Shops only stock appropriate wizarding merchandise, no Minions or Spider-Man shirts or anything with a Universal logo. And each shop only offers merchandise that makes sense for it—the wandmaker Ollivanders only sells wands, not dragon plushies or toy brooms.

J.K. Rowling personally tested and approved all the food and drinks served at the Wizarding World. Counter-service restaurants offer British and Scottish dishes inspired by the books; Universal spent three years creating the menus. The areas don't sell normal soft drinks; instead they offer choices like gillywater, pumpkin juice, butterbeer and actual beer. Want a bag of potato chips? It'll be a British brand.

Much of the architecture is modeled directly off of the film sets; original details expand on them. Both Hogsmeade and Diagon Alley were designed with the help of Stuart Craig and Alan Gilmore, the head production designers for the films. Universal also recruited Miraphora Mina and Eduardo Lima—designers who spent 10 years creating the signs and other graphics for the movies. Everything has a used, weathered look, with faded print on vintage wood. All the weathering is artificial; in truth everything is made to withstand long-term exposure to Florida weather, including hurricanes.

The Wizarding World areas are easily the most popular spots in each theme park. Some visitors come to Universal Orlando solely for its Harry Potter experience; many wear wizard robes or Hogwarts house colors.

HOGSMEADE.

Hogsmeade debuted at Islands of Adventure on June 18, 2010. Located between the Lost Continent and Jurassic Park, it replaced part of the Lost Continent area. It's not as detailed as Diagon Alley, but has more rides and iconic landmarks. It re-creates Hogsmeade Village, a small wizarding settlement outside Hogwarts castle; students

A beverage cart, Hogsmeade.

take trips there a few times each year. Rooftops of the quaint little town are coated with sparkling snow. Detailed storefronts line High Street, the main path through the area.

Hogsmeade Station stands in front of the village; its Hogwarts Express train chugs off to Diagon Alley. The Dragon Challenge roller coaster is next to the station. At the end of High Street is a stage for performances. Past it is the massive Hogwarts castle, home of the Harry Potter and the Forbidden Journey attraction. Across from the castle, the small Flight of the Hippogriff coaster swoops around Hagrid's hut.

The handful of shops are nicely detailed; a couple are straight from the series. The first shop on the left is Honeydukes, a popular candy shop famous for its store-made Chocolate Frogs. Halfway down High Street is Dervish and Banges, which has apparel, toys and Ollivanders wands. Connected to it is The Owl Post; it mainly sells stationery and owl plushies. At the foot of Hogwarts castle is Filch's Emporium of Confiscated Goods, which offers a wide range of merchandise. The Forbidden Journey attraction exits through it, so it tends to be packed.

The Three Broomsticks is a counter-service spot; in the series this popular eating establishment serves foaming mugs of butterbeer and bottles of oak-matured mead. Connected to it is The Hog's Head, a dim bar with a shady reputation. The Magic Neep fruit cart sits out front.

DIAGON ALLEY.

A play on "diagonally," this area opened in Universal Studios Florida on July 8, 2014. Located between the park's San Francisco and World Expo areas, it replaced the space taken up by the "Jaws" ride. It's more detailed and immersive than Hogsmeade, though it only has one ride as opposed to three.

It re-creates Diagon Alley, a magical shopping center hidden in London where Hogwarts students buy school supplies. Its entrance is bordered by a pleasant waterfront plaza decorated with London landmarks. The triple-decker Knight Bus is parked outside; to the left is King's Cross Station, where the Hogwarts Express transports people to

Diagon Alley.

and from Hogsmeade. People enter Diagon Alley through the red archways of Leicester Square Station; to the right is a side entrance under Wyndham's Theater.

At the end of Diagon Alley is Gringotts Wizarding Bank, which is topped with a huge fire-breathing dragon; inside is the Harry Potter and the Escape from Gringotts attraction. To the left is Horizont Alley (a play on "horizontally"); to the right of the bank is a covered walkway, Carkitt Market. Knockturn Alley ("nocturnally") is a barely-marked side street, a dark enclosed area where ominous stores specialize in dark magic. It has three entrances: one off Diagon Alley, two at the end of Horizont Alley.

Live performances take place on a stage in Carkitt Market.

The whole area is lined with detailed shops; most are straight from the series. The first one on the right side of Diagon Alley is Quality Quidditch Supplies, which sells quidditch-themed apparel, toys and merchandise for specific teams. Weasleys' Wizard Wheezes is a bustling joke shop filled with tricks, toys and novelty items; in the series, it's owned and run by Fred and George Weasley, the older twin brothers of Ron. Madam Malkin's is a clothing shop that sells wizards robes and other apparel. At Shutterbutton's Photography Studio, you can create and purchase an animated photo of yourself.

Magical Menagerie is a colorful pet shop that sells animal plushies; in the series it stocks all sorts of domesticated creatures and pet-care products. Wiseacres Wizarding Equipment is a starry blue building next to Gringotts; in the series, it sells astronomy equipment such as lunascopes, star charts and celestial globes. Scribbulus, a small shop connected to Wiseacres, sells stationery and writing utensils. Gringotts Money Exchange converts muggle currency into spendable Gringotts bank notes; inside the shop an animatronic goblin answers questions from people in line. Wands by Gregorovitch is a tiny purple shop next to Weasleys' Wizard Wheezes; it sells wands made by a famous European wandmaker who competes against the more popular Ollivanders. Sugarplum's Sweetshop, the newest store in the area, is a pink candy shop that opened in 2016. Borgin and Burkes is the only shop in Knockturn Alley; it sells merchandise related to dark magic, evil creatures and the Death Eaters.

Florean Fortescue's Ice-Cream Parlour, Diagon Alley.

A handful of places sell food and drinks. Only one place has full meals: the counter-service Leaky Cauldron; in the series, this old, famous restaurant and inn serves as the entrance to Diagon Alley. At the corner of Diagon Alley and Horizont Alley, the cheerful, pastel-colored Florean Fortescue's Ice-Cream Parlour offers all sorts of odd but delicious flavors. The Fountain of Fair Fortune and The Hopping Pot serve wizarding drinks such as butterbeer. In Carkitt Market, Eternelle's Elixir of Refreshment adds vials of flavored "potions" to bottles of plain gillywater.

OLLIVANDERS.

This ancient shop makes and sells wands; it's where many witches and wizards get their first one. In the books it's in Diagon Alley; here there's also a branch in Hogsmeade. The main shop offers samples to try out and wand keepers who answer questions. Each store hosts a wand-choosing experience that's separate from its main shop.

THE HOGWARTS EXPRESS.

This scarlet train runs between Hogsmeade and Diagon Alley (i.e., between Scotland and London). Since in the real world that means the train runs between the two theme parks, Universal visitors need a two-park ticket or annual pass to ride it. While it's primarily used for transportation, it's also an attraction in its own right. Each trip—from Hogsmeade to Diagon Alley and visa-versa—has unexpected sights and sounds.

HISTORY.

J.K. Rowling originally went to the Disney company with the idea for a Harry Potter-themed area; Disney at first offered her only a single ride, one in which guests would use wands to cast spells at interactive screens. When she turned that down, the concept was revised to become Toy Story Mania at Disney's Hollywood Studios. Rowling was encouraged to work with Universal by the widow of Dr. Seuss. Audrey Geisel told Rowling that she was very happy with the company's respect for the integrity of her husband's books—their consistent themes of tolerance and responsiblity, their focus on spiritual values, their joyous wit and their artistic sense of using no straight lines—when it developed the Seuss Landing area at Islands of Adventure.

The planning process was rough, with long back-and-forth discussions between Rowling's book agents, the Warner Brothers film team and the designers at Universal Creative, Universal's Orlando-based version of Disney Imagineering.

Rowling had veto power over everything. Many of the ideas Universal proposed didn't measure up to her standards; its early plan for Hogsmeade was to simply redo part of the park's Lost Continent. Some of that plan survived; it led to that area's Dueling Dragons roller coasters becoming Dragon Challenge and its Flying Unicorn becoming Flight of the Hippogriff. When designing the Potter areas, the content in the books always trumped what's shown in the movies. Other than the Forbidden Journey attraction, neither Daniel Radcliffe nor Emma Watson reprised their roles as Harry and Hermione. Other actors did, however, including Rupert Grint (Ron), James and Oliver Phelps (Fred and George) and Robbie Coltrane (Hagrid).

Mike Aiello (Universal Orlando's director of entertainment) led the creation of Diagon Alley's live entertainment, but before that he spent years working as a boat captain on the theme park's "Jaws" ride. When it closed, he honored his fond memories of that time by sneaking in references to Jaws throughout Diagon Alley.

SOCIETY & MEDIA

AZKABAN PRISON.

A foreboding stone fortress for criminals convicted by the Ministry of Magic. *In the parks: Wanted posters for escaped criminals hang in the Leaky Cauldron, outside the Three Broomsticks and in Knockturn Alley. Newspaper articles in the queue of Harry Potter and the Escape from Gringotts warn of a mass break-out from Azkaban.*

CURRENCY.

Consists of three coins: the small bronze knut, the silver sickle and the fat gold galleon. There are 29 knuts to a sickle; 17 sickles to a galleon. *In the parks: A statue of Gringott stands atop a stack of galleons outside Gringotts bank. Galleons line shelves at Gringotts Money Exchange. Honeydukes coin-operated machines are labeled "sickles only."*

THE DAILY PROPHET.

This newspaper is the main source of wizarding news in Great Britain, but is nevertheless often quite skewed and biased. The Death Eaters seized control of it when they took over the Ministry. *In the parks: Its headquarters is on Diagon Alley. Issues are in the queues of Harry Potter and the Forbidden Journey and Escape from Gringotts.*

THE DARK MARK.

The symbol of the Death Eaters: a human skull with a hissing snake emerging from its mouth. They cast it into the sky above crime scenes, where it floats in a green fog. *In the parks: It's expelled from the basilisk's empty skull in Forbidden Journey.*

THE FLOO NETWORK.

A transportation system that allows travel between fireplaces. To access it, witches and wizards toss a handful of Floo powder into a lit fireplace (turning its flames green and painless), step into the fire and clearly say the name of the place they want to go.

The flames swell, sending the traveler speeding through a fiery green tunnel. *In the parks: Forbidden Journey begins and ends with a trip through the Floo Network.*

GRINGOTTS WIZARDING BANK.

Owned and operated by goblins, this financial institution is in Diagon Alley; it was founded by a goblin named Gringott in 1474. Underneath its elegant main hall, stone caverns lead deep underground to its vaults, which are accessed by riding fast, rickety carts. The deepest vaults are the most heavily guarded; some are protected by chained dragons. Other security measures include the Thief's Downfall, a charmed waterfall that lifts enchantments. See also Goblins in the section Creatures & Plants. *In the parks: It's the centerpiece of Diagon Alley; it houses the Escape from Gringotts attraction.*

THE KNIGHT BUS.

A purple triple-decker that acts as quick emergency transport for stranded witches and wizards. They hail it like a cab, holding out their wands in their dominant hands. Once ready to depart it takes off like a rocket, traveling at nauseating speeds while squeezing, squashing and sliding through traffic, under bridges and between buildings. Jamaican shrunken head Dre Head (say it quickly) dangles from the front mirror. See also Shrunken heads in the section Objects & Potions. *In the parks: The bus is parked outside Diagon Alley; Dre Head and the conductor answer questions about it. It weaves and squeezes through London outside the Hogwarts Express train to Diagon Alley.*

Gringotts Money Exchange. An imposing animatronic goblin sits at a desk overseeing this shop, which converts cash into Gringotts bank notes (in $10 and $20 denominations) that are accepted as currency throughout Universal. Also for sale is wizarding currency (galleons, sickles and knuts) and candy coins. The goblin talks directly to people waiting in line, answering questions. Ask how old he is and he'll answer "Old enough." Ask if Gringotts offers a dental plan and he'll stare at you for a moment then look back down, silently shaking his head.

MOVING PICTURES.

Animated pictures appear as newspaper photos, posters, framed portraits and snapshots. A photograph acts like a looping animated gif with no audio; the subject of a painting can move freely and speak with the viewer. When multiple photos or paintings appear in one area, their subjects can often move between images and interact. *In the parks: Talking portraits hang in the queues of Forbidden Journey and Escape from Gringotts. Moving photos and drawings appear throughout Diagon Alley and Hogsmeade. Visitors can make animated photos of themselves at Shutterbutton's Photography Studio.*

THE MINISTRY OF MAGIC.

The wizarding government for Britian and Ireland, abbreviated "M.o.M." It's run by the Minister of Magic and divided into seven departments. When it fell under the Death Eaters' control, it began distributing propaganda promoting blood purity and calling for Harry's arrest. Headquarters are hidden beneath London; the entrance is disguised as a normal red phone booth. Visitors dial "62442" ("MAGIC") into the phone, tap it with their wand and state their business; then the booth sinks underground and deposits them inside the ministry's atrium. *In the parks: The phone booth entrance is outside Diagon Alley, but doesn't go anywhere; dialing the code prompts a message explaining that the atrium is temporarily closed. It supplies the safety notices for all of the rides. Ministry propaganda litters the queue of Escape from Gringotts.*

THE QUIBBLER.

Published by Xenophilius Lovegood, this monthly tabloid is filled with conspiracy theories about the Ministry of Magic and ridiculous stories of imaginary creatures. Some issues come with colorful 3-D glasses called Spectrespecs. *In the parks: Issues are stored in the rafters of Filch's Emporium.*

QUIDDITCH.

Played on flying brooms, this popular sport has seven players per team: three chasers, a keeper, two beaters and a seeker. The chasers throw a red ball called a quaffle into a hoop; each successful shot is 10 points. The keeper defends hoops from quaffle throws. The beaters distract the other team by batting around two bludgers, flying black balls that try to knock players off their brooms. The seeker searches for the golden snitch, a tiny winged ball that zips around the field; it's 150 points and ends the game once caught. The game is as popular as football is in the United States; teams include the Chudley Cannons, the Holyhead Harpies, the Montrose Magpies and Puddlemere United. The Quidditch World Cup includes teams from other countries such as Ireland and Bulgaria. Hogwarts has organized intramural matches between its houses. *In the parks: A big Gryffindor/Slytherin match is the main event of Forbidden Journey; Harry wins by catching the golden snitch. Quidditch equipment, team pennants and World Cup tickets decorate the windows of Spintwitches in Hogsmeade and Quality Quidditch Supplies in Diagon Alley. Quality Quidditch Supplies displays a keeper's uniform and a team photo of the Chudley Cannons.*

THE TRIWIZARD TOURNAMENT.

A competition consisting of three life-risking tasks. Three student champions compete, one from each of the largest wizarding schools in Europe: Hogwarts (in Scotland), Beauxbatons Academy of Magic (in France) and Durmstrang Institute (in Bulgaria). The winner is awarded the Triwizard Cup. The tournament was held at Hogwarts during Harry's fourth year. As part of a Death Eater plot, he was forced to compete as a fourth champion alongside Fleur Delacour, Cedric Diggory and Viktor Krum. In the

© Universal Orlando Resort

Hogwarts castle.

First Task, each champion faces off against an angry mother dragon and tries to collect an artificial golden egg from her nest. A formal dance, the Yule Ball is held on Christmas night as part of the tournament festivities; Hermione wore a beautiful pink dress for the occasion. See also The Goblet of Fire in the section Objects & Potions; Cedric Diggory, Fleur Delacour, Victor Krum in Characters; Dragons in Creatures & Plants. *In the parks: Dragon Challenge is based on the First Task; its queue displays the Triwizard Cup and the golden dragon eggs. In Hogsmeade, the Triwizard Spirit Rally celebrates foreign schools participating in the tournament. Hermione's Yule Ball dress hangs in the windows of Madam Malkin's in Diagon Alley and Gladrags Wizardwear in Hogsmeade.*

HOGWARTS

THIS BOARDING SCHOOL in Scotland teaches young wizards and witches about the wizarding world and how to use magic. Students eat, sleep and go to class inside a sprawling stone castle; meals are served inside the Great Hall, where mail is delivered every morning via owl post. School grounds include greenhouses for herbology classes, a quidditch pitch and Hagrid's hut. Each September students travel there aboard the Hogwarts Express train to Hogsmeade; they stay at the castle for the school year. Before each term, Hogwarts sends invitation letters to eligible 11-year-olds. They take classes for seven years. Students wear black robes adorned with their house crest and trimmed with house colors; underneath they wear simple black uniforms with colored ties. To help keep its students safe, the school has protective enchantments that repel muggles and prevent apparition. Its headmaster is Albus Dumbledore; its motto is *Draco dormiens numquam titillandus*—Latin for "Never tickle a sleeping dragon." The castle overlooks the cold, dark Black Lake, home to a colony of merpeople. A dangerous woodland, the Forbidden Forest borders the castle;

Animated portraits of the Hogwarts founders, Hogwarts castle.

it's inhabited by all sorts of magical creatures, including acromantulas and centaurs. Hagrid's hut, a stone house, sits on the edge of the Forbidden Forest; a pumpkin patch grows out front. *In the parks: The castle is Hogsmeade's main focal point. Inside it is the Forbidden Journey attraction, which visits the quidditch pitch, the Forbidden Forest and the Black Lake. The Hogwarts Express train passes the lake, forest and castle. The queue of Flight of the Hippogriff passes Hagrid's hut.*

CLASSES AND ACTIVITIES.

Students take seven core classes. **Astronomy** focuses on constellations and planetary orbits. Taught by Prof. Flitwick, **Charms** teaches spells that add certain properties to an object or creature. **Defense Against the Dark Arts** trains students how to defend against dark creatures and spells. It's taught by a different professor every year; previous teachers include Quirinus Quirrell, Gilderoy Lockhart, Remus Lupin, a Death Eater masquerading as "Mad-Eye" Moody, Dolores Umbridge and Severus Snape. The magical equivalent to botany, **Herbology** is taught by Prof. Sprout in the school greenhouses. Taught by Prof. Binns, an exceedingly dull ghost, **History of Magic** lectures students about magical history. Taught by Prof. Snape (and later Prof. Slughorn) in the castle's dungeons, **Potions** teaches students how to brew magical mixtures in cauldrons. Prof. McGonagall teaches **Transfiguration,** a tricky branch of magic that focuses on changing the form and appearance of an object or creature.

Electives include **Care of Magical Creatures,** in which Hagrid teaches magical zoology in practical lessons outside the Forbidden Forest, and **Divination,** which predicts future events through crystal-gazing, tarot cards and tea leaves.

Extracurricular activities include **Frog Choir,** an a cappella group that includes fat cushion-carried toads that croak bass notes; and **quidditch** matches played between houses. *In the parks: On Forbidden Journey you're supposed to go see a lecture from Prof. Binns but instead watch a game on the quidditch pitch; in the queue you see the door to the Potions classroom, the Herbology greenhouses and the Defense Against the Dark Arts*

Hourglasses keep track of points won by school houses, Hogwarts castle.

classroom. *Flight of the Hippogriff is based on Care of Magical Creatures. The Frog Choir performs music from the series on a stage in Hogsmeade.*

HOUSES.

Hogwarts students are sorted into four houses based on how well they match up with the individual qualities of the school's founders: Godric Gryffindor, Helga Hufflepuff, Rowena Ravenclaw and Salazar Slytherin. Each house has its own common room and dorms in a distinct part of the castle. **Gryffindor** students are characterized by bravery, nerve and chivalry; the house is symbolized by a lion and the colors scarlet and gold. Most of the series' protagonists are in this house. The head of Gryffindor is Prof. McGonagall. **Hufflepuff** students are characterized by tolerance, patience and loyalty; the house is symbolized by a badger and the colors yellow and black. Its unremarkable reputation is caused by its focus on humility. The head of Hufflepuff is Prof. Sprout. **Ravenclaw** students are characterized by intellect, creativity and wit; the house is symbolized by an eagle and the colors blue and bronze in the books, though the films change this to a raven and the colors blue and silver. The head of Ravenclaw is Prof. Flitwick. **Slytherin** students are characterized by cunning, ambition and resourcefulness; the house is symbolized by a serpent and the colors green and silver. While most of the series' antagonists are in this house, Slytherins aren't inherently evil. The head of Slytherin is Prof. Snape. You can learn what house you would be in by taking a quiz on Pottermore, the official Potter website. *In the parks: Forbidden Journey's queue passes animated portraits of the founders and goes through the Gryffindor common room. The Frog Choir in Hogsmeade has members from each house.*

THE CHAMBER OF SECRETS.

This stone corridor hidden under Hogwarts was built secretly by Salazar Slytherin. He raised a basilisk there, hoping the giant snake could be used to purge the school of muggle-born students one day. Slytherin's heir reopened the chamber a thousand

The Frog Choir, near Hogwarts castle.

years later, but Harry killed the basilisk before it could do much damage. See also Basilisk in the section Creatures & Plants. *In the parks: The ride vehicle falls into the ruins of the chamber during Forbidden Journey; inside is the basilisk's bare skeleton.*

THE HOGWARTS EXPRESS.

This red passenger train transports students to and from school at the start and end of each term. Cozy cabins run its length. Candy is available from the Honeydukes Express, a food trolley pushed by a friendly witch. Each long trip runs between Platform 9¾ at London's King's Cross Station and Hogsmeade Station. Platform 9¾ is a hidden boarding area, accessed through a brick wall between platforms 9 and 10. *In the parks: The train runs between the two theme parks, connecting the two Wizarding World lands; the shadow of its food trolley passes by your cabin during the ride. In Diagon Alley, you board the train by traveling through King's Cross to Platform 9¾; the connecting station is right outside Hogsmeade. At Hogsmeade's entrance is a backup locomotive; a nearby conductor answers questions and poses for pictures.*

HOUSE POINTS.

Students earn and lose points throughout each school year; the house with the most points wins the House Cup. The running total is recorded by a set of hourglasses in the Great Hall, which are filled with red rubies (Gryffindor), yellow diamonds (Hufflepuff), blue sapphires (Ravenclaw) and green emeralds (Slytherin). *In the parks: The hourglasses stand in the queue of Forbidden Journey.*

PREFECTS.

Selected by professors, these students represent each house, carry out the headmaster's and professors' edicts and lead and discipline younger students. They wear prefect badges on their robes. *In the parks: Prefects serve as ride attendants at Forbidden Journey. A Gryffindor prefect leads the Frog Choir in Hogsmeade.*

Inside Ollivanders.

THE ROOM OF REQUIREMENT.

This secret room only shows itself to someone in real need of something; once it opens its contents are suited to match that need perfectly. *In the parks: It serves as the boarding area for Forbidden Journey.*

THE SORTING HAT.

This old talking witch's hat sorts new students into houses at the beginning of each term. Beforehand it sings a song about the school. *In the parks: The Sorting Hat poetically recites safety procedures in the queue of Forbidden Journey.*

WANDS

WITCHES AND WIZARDS control magic by channelling it through a wand. A wand chooses its own master, and refuses to work properly for strangers; its allegiance shifts if its master is killed or disarmed. They're carved from wood and implanted with a core taken from a magical creature—the most common are dragon heartstring, unicorn hair and phoenix feather. *In the parks: They're sold at Ollivanders and some street vendors. The widest selection is at Ollivanders in Diagon Alley, which has samples you can "try out" and wand keepers who answer questions.*

OLLIVANDERS WAND-CHOOSING EXPERIENCE.

This up-close-and-personal demonstration shows how a wand chooses a wizard. In this case, the wizard (or witch) is a "volunteer" that's picked out from a crowd of a couple dozen people. The crowd files into the heart of Ollivanders, inside a dark, quiet room that's lined with dusty wand boxes. The presentation begins with the wand keeper host choosing a lucky young volunteer and asking them a few preliminary questions, such as their age and Hogwarts house. As the wand keeper goes over some basic facts about wands, he uses a tape measure to determine the size of the volunteer's arm, torso and hands, as well as the space between his or her eyes. Then he hands the youngster a wand with instructions to test it out with a spell. This goes as well as it did for Harry Potter when he first tried out a wand; eventually there's a good match. The presentation takes 5 to 10 minutes. Go early morning for the most intimate experience. Get there super early and you may get a show all to yourself.

WAND TYPES.

Stores offer 34 replica character wands and three Death Eater ones. Many wands come in interactive versions. "Unclaimed" wands are associated with a time of year based on the 13-month Celtic calendar, which assigns each month a type of wood (December 23 is the Celtic "Day of Liberation" and isn't associated with any wood type): **Birch** (Dec 24–Jan 20): Favors lively, assertive people who have a knack for understanding key issues behind complicated problems. **Rowan** (Jan 21–Feb 17): Favors pure-hearted, imaginative people who help those in need. **Ash** (Feb 18–Mar 17): Favors brave, charitable people who stick firmly to their beliefs and take time to appreciate the world. **Alder** (March 18–April 14): Favors kind, cooperative people who are confident in their choices. **Willow** (April 15–May 12): Favors people who are battling inner insecurities but have high potential for success, and are able to learn and recover quickly from troubling experiences. Ron Weasley and Lily Potter have willow wands. **Hawthorn** (May 13–June 9): Favors talented but conflicted people who are intensively protective of their loved ones. Draco Malfoy has a hawthorn wand. **Oak** (June 10–July 7): Favors loyal, courageous people who are tolerant of others and have a strong affinity with nature. Hagrid has an oak wand. **Holly** (July 8–Aug 4): Favors caring, contemplative people who are good at leading others. Harry Potter has a holly wand. **Hazel** (Aug 5–Sept 1): Favors perceptive people who are good at explaining things to others. Hazel wands have the unique ability to act as divining rods. **Vine** (Sept 2–Sept 29): Favors hardworking, tireless people who feel they have a greater purpose in life. Hermione Granger has a vine wand. **Ivy** (Sept 30–Oct 27): Favors strong, forceful people who accomplish the goals they set for themselves. **Reed** (Oct 28–Nov 24): Favors bold, expressive people who care deeply for their friends and adapt well to novel situations. **Elder** (Nov 25–Dec 22): Favors clever, passionate people who are destined for greatness. Albus Dumbledore carries the legendary Elder Wand.

SPELLCASTING.

If you buy an interactive wand (about $45), you can use it to cast spells throughout both Hogsmeade and Diagon Alley. An accompanying map marks every spell, the proper wand movement for them and the location of each; visiting them all is a bit like a scavenger hunt. Each location is marked with a plaque in the pavement. To cast the spell properly, stand a couple of feet back from the plaque and face the direction it points. Use small, controlled movements in a single motion. If you have any trouble, a nearby witch or wizard will gladly help out. If a particular location isn't working, a sign posted there reads "This establishment currently has an Anti-Jinx in place. As such, all spells will be rendered ineffective." *Warning, spoilers ahead:*

In Hogsmeade. 1. In the right window of Zonko's Joke Shop, cast "Incendio" to light the fireworks on display. 2. Above McHavelock's Wizarding Headgear, cast "Arresto Momentum" at a Cornish pixie fountain to stop the flow of water into a cauldron. This tips the cauldron over, revealing a pixie that sticks its tongue out at you. 3. In the right window of Honeydukes, cast "Revelio" to open a large Chocolate Frog box; the frog inside croaks three times. 4. In the window of Dervish and Banges (to the back right under the Owlery), cast "Arresto Momentum" at a music box to freeze and silence it. Cast "Locomotor" to start it up again. 5. In the left window of Dogweed and Deathcap, cast "Herbivicus" at a red flower to make its petals grow and recede. 6. In the same window, cast the same spell at a wilted branch to turn its leaves green. 7. In the right window of Gladrags Wizardwear, cast "Descendo" at a roll of measuring tape to have it measure a set of wizard robes. Cast "Ascendio" to roll the tape back up. 8. In the window of Madam Puddifoot's, cast "Locomotor Snowman" at a snowman cake topper to make it skate across the icing. 9. In the window of Tomes & Scrolls, cast "Alohomora" at a copy of "The Tales of Beedle the Bard" to open it to the beginning of "The Fountain of Fair Fortune." 10. In the window of Spintwitches, cast "Wingardium Leviosa" at a case of quidditch equipment to levitate a quaffle.

In Diagon Alley. 1. In the right window of Weasleys' Wizard Wheezes, cast "Descendo" at a sign for "U-No-Poo" to flush it down a toilet. 2. In the window of Pilliwinkle's Playthings (in Horizont Alley), cast "Tarantallegra" to make troll marionettes dressed like ballerinas pirouette across a stage.

In Horizont Alley. 1. In the right window of Magical Menagerie, cast "Silencio" at the caged fwooper bird to silence it. 2. Above Horizont Alley's restrooms, cast "Metelojinx" at an umbrella-shaped streetlight to make it sprinkle water on the street below, trigger a rumble of thunder and make the streetlight flash like lightning. 3. At the end of Horizont Alley, cast "Incendio" at Flimflams Lanterns to illuminate the lanterns displayed in the window.

In Carkitt Market. 1. On the left side of Wiseacres Wizarding Equipment, point your wand at the orb-like Dark Detectors in the window to reveal eyes that watch your wand. 2. In the window of Wiseacres Wizarding Equipment, cast "Specialis Revelio" at a celestial map to reveal a dog and an archer in the stars; they play fetch with an arrow. 3. In the left window of Scribbulus, cast "Wingardium Leviosa" to levitate a white feather quill. 4. In the Carkitt Market courtyard, cast "Aquamenti" at a mermaid sculpture to activate the water fountain in front of it. Sometimes the spell disagrees with you and shoots a spurt of water from above the mermaid. 5. At Bowman E. Wright's Blacksmith, cast "Reparo" to assemble the top half of a suit of armor. 6. Also there, cast "Locomotor Bellows" to compress a huge pair of bellows.

In Knockturn Alley. 1. Cast "Locomotor Chimney Sweep" at a chimney-shaped sign over the street to make a little house-elf puppet scramble to escape a burst of fire. 2. At Dystyl Phaelanges, point your wand at the slideshow playing in the window to bring up a diagram of a troll skeleton that mimics your body movements. 3. At Noggin and Bonce, cast "Mimblewimble" at the window of chatty shrunken heads to temporarily muffle their voices. This prompts one of several irritated responses; one response, "You know what you can do with that wand? You can stick it where there ain't no—" is suddenly interrupted by a well-timed chorus of *"Sunshine, my only sunshine…"* 4. At Tallow and Hemp Toxic Tapers, cast "Incendio" to light a poisonous candle; a caged canary in the window gets affected by its fumes. 5. To the right of Trackleshanks Locksmith, cast "Alohomora" at a door to unlock it with a series of heavy clunks. If you try to open it, there's a sudden hiss and a blast of air from the keyhole; the door remains locked.

Hidden locations. Diagon Alley has a few unmarked spell locations. They're blotted with invisible ink on wand maps; the locations glow under blacklights if you take your map to Knockturn Alley. 1. In the right window of Scribbulus, move your wand in a triangular motion at a piece of blank parchment to reveal one of several hidden messages, such as "this is all very secret." 2. In the window of Slug and Jiggers Apothecary, move your wand in an up-and-down motion to make an orange flower bloom and wilt. 3. In the same window, point your wand at a bucket of dragon dung to make it churn; its stench fills the air.

The House-Elf Placement Agency, Carkitt Market.

CREATURES & PLANTS

Acromantula. A giant spider with a taste for human flesh. It communicates with high-pitched clicks from its venomous pincers. A huge colony lives deep within the Forbidden Forest. See also Aragog in the section Characters. *In the parks: A swarm attacks you on Forbidden Journey.*

Basilisk. Eye contact with this huge, bloodthirsty snake causes instant death. Salazar Slytherin hatched one in the Chamber of Secrets; it nearly killed Harry before he stabbed it with the Sword of Gryffindor. *In the parks: In Forbidden Journey, the basilisk's skeleton lies on the floor of the Chamber of Secrets. Eternelle's Elixir of Refreshment is topped with stone busts of magical creatures, including a basilisk.*

Boggart. This shape-shifting spook turns into the viewer's worst fear. It lurks in dark spaces. *In the parks: Borgin and Burkes keeps one locked inside a shaking trunk.*

Bowtruckle. A tiny, well-camouflaged stick-man that eats woodlice. *In the parks: A bucket of "woodlice for bowtruckles" sits next to Hagrid's hut at Flight of the Hippogriff.*

Centaur. This proud, intelligent being looks like a mix between man and horse. A herd lives in the Forbidden Forest. *In the parks: You pass by centaurs on the Hogwarts Express train to Diagon Alley.*

Cornish pixie. A blue fairy-like creature that's a notorious prankster; it speaks in shrill squeals. *In the parks: To the left of Honeydukes is a small pixie fountain.*

Crumple-horned snorkack. This imaginary beast resembles a hunchbacked purple yak with a unicorn's horn. Only the quirky Lovegood family believes it exists. *In the parks: A whimsical depiction of one is on the balcony inside Magical Menagerie.*

Dementor. This soulless creature drifts through the air feeding on happy memories. It resembles the Grim Reaper, except with a round, dark mouth and no other facial features. Its presence is accompanied by an icy chill, darkened light sources and a feeling of hopelessness. If it can, it latches onto a person's mouth and "kisses" them, devouring their soul. Since it's not truly alive, it can't be killed; the only way to fight it off is with a Patronus charm. *In the parks: A swarm attacks you on Forbidden Journey. One invades the Hogwarts Express train to Hogsmeade.*

Demiguise. Invisibility cloaks are made from the fur of this yeti-like beast. *In the parks: A whimsical depiction of one is on the balcony inside Magical Menagerie.*

Doxy. This fanged, fairy-like pest lays poisonous black eggs. A chemical called Doxycide removes infestations. *In the parks: A jar of doxy eggs tops a shelf behind the bar of The Hog's Head. A sign advertises Doxycide over Diagon Alley's restrooms.*

Dragons. These massive reptiles fly, breath fire and—given the chance—eat humans. Their byproducts have all sorts of uses: heartstrings for wand cores, hides for leather, claws and blood for potion ingredients, even dung for fertilizer. The speedy scarlet **Chinese Fireball** fights Viktor Krum in the Triwizard Tournament's First Task. Black with bronze horns, the **Hungarian Horntail** is the most dangerous species; it's named for its spiky tail it lashes at prey. It can keep pace with a Firebolt racing broom, which can reach speeds of 150 mph. One faces off against Harry in the Triwizard Tournament's First Task. The largest dragon, the gray **Ukrainian Ironbelly** can reach 60 feet in length. One escaped from Gringotts, where it had been chained up in front of the Lestrange vault. It was freed by Harry, Ron and Hermione when they broke into the bank; in a desperate move to escape security they climbed onto its back and helped it get to the surface, where it flew away with the trio clinging tight. *In the parks: In the Forbidden Journey queue, a dragon skeleton hangs in the Defense Against the Dark Arts classroom. In the Leaky Cauldron, wooden crossbeams in the rafters are carved into dragons and other magical creatures. In Magical Menagerie, whimsical carved dragons support the upper balcony. The red Dragon Challenge roller coaster represents a Chinese Fireball. A Hungarian Horntail chases you down in the Forbidden Journey; it's represented by the Dragon Challenge blue coaster. The escaped Ukrainian Ironbelly perches atop Gringotts breathing occasional bursts of fire; it's the improbable hero of Escape from Gringotts.*

Fwooper. The song of this red and gold bird eventually drives the listener insane. As a precaution, pet birds are muted with silencing charms. *In the parks: A caged one sings in the right window of Magical Menagerie.*

Goblins. Clever, greedy financiers, these short, pale beings manage Gringotts Wizarding Bank and mint the coins used for wizarding currency. They're also accomplished metalsmiths. See also Gringotts in the section Society & Media. *In the parks: The queue of Escape from Gringotts passes goblins working at desks and doors to their offices; one named Blordak co-hosts the ride alongside Bill Weasley. At the Gringotts Money Exchange, an animatronic goblin answers questions from people waiting in line.*

Hippogriff. This majestic creature combines the head, forelegs and wings of a giant eagle with the hindquarters of a horse. It's prideful and easily offended, so it's important to bow politely when encountering one; if it bows back, it's safe to approach. See also Buckbeak in the section Characters. *In the parks: Its the theme of Flight of the Hippogriff.*

House-elves. These short, meek creatures serve as unpaid servants for wealthy wizard families and are magically bound to obey their master's every command. Despite this, they're quite happy to work so long as they're treated humanely. They have bald heads, bat-like ears and squeaky voices. See also Kreacher in the section Characters. *In the parks: Shadows of cleaning house-elves are cast on the upper walls of The Three Broomsticks. In The Hog's Head, a female house-elf can be heard fretting to herself from the foot of the stairs. A facade for The House-Elf Placement Agency is in Diagon Alley's Carkitt Market. Nearby, a house-elf statue holding a lantern stands on a platform to the left of Sugarplum's Sweetshop.*

Kneazle. A large, cat-like creature with tufted ears and plumed tail. *In the parks: A golden animatronic kneazle stares down at shoppers from the balcony of Magical Menagerie.*

Mandrake. When uprooted, this ugly plant resembles a muddy infant with leaves sprouting from its head. It shrieks when disturbed; the mature plant's cry is fatal, while youngsters merely knock listeners unconscious. Hogwarts students study it in herbology class. *In the parks: Potted mandrakes shake their leaves inside the herbology greenhouses in the queue of Forbidden Journey. One wails and wiggles around in the window of Dogweed and Deathcap, in Hogsmeade.*

Merpeople. Fishy folk with thick skin, sharp teeth and wild, weedy hair. A mervillage sits at the bottom of the Black Lake. *In the parks: They're visible swimming in the Black Lake from the Hogwarts Express train to Hogsmeade. A green mermaid bust stands in the Carkitt Market courtyard in Diagon Alley. A mermaid skeleton hangs in the window of Dystyl Phaelanges in Knockturn Alley and appears in the slideshow playing there.*

Mimbulus Mimbletonia. This rare plant resembles a squirming grey cactus covered with boils instead of spines. *In the parks: One twitches in its pot inside the window of Dogweed and Deathcap, in Hogsmeade.*

Owls. Like passenger pigeons, owls are used as mail carriers to send letters and parcels. Businesses use them as couriers; they're also popular pets. See also Hedwig in the section Characters. *In the parks: You pass through a flock of owls while flying over the Black Lake during Forbidden Journey. One holding a letter in its beak flies past the window on the Hogwarts Express train to Hogsmeade. Owls perch in the rafters of Hogsmeade's Owlery and Owl Post shops, and on the wall of the Owl Post in Diagon Alley.*

Phoenix. The tears of this scarlet swan-sized bird heal wounds. When it gets old it bursts into flame, then revives from the ashes. *In the parks: Plushie phoenixes are sold at Magical Menagerie.*

Pygmy puff. A pink or purple fuzzball that coos softly when content. Fred and George bred them to sell in their joke shop. *In the parks: Plushie pygmy puffs purr inside their cages at Weasleys' Wizard Wheezes.*

Snakes. Though not inherently evil, snakes are linked with dark magic. They speak a language called Parseltongue. See also Basilisk, above; Nagini in the section Characters; Parseltongue in the section Spells & Abilities. *In the parks: The side window of Magical Menagerie displays two hissing pythons; one speaks Parseltongue to people who view it from outside the shop.*

Streeler. A poisonous, basketball-sized snail that changes the color of its shell on an hourly basis. *In the parks: Two streelers ooze in the left window of Magical Menagerie.*

Thestral. This bat-winged horse is only visible to people who have seen someone die. Despite its frightening appearance, it's gentle and shy. A domesticated herd pulls Hogwarts carriages to and from the castle; to most, the carriages appear to pull themselves. *In the parks: An invisible thestral is tethered to a Hogwarts carriage at the exit of the Hogsmeade train station. Eternelle's Elixir of Refreshment is topped with stone busts of magical creatures, including a thestral.*

Trolls. Dim-witted brutes that stand 12 feet tall. Some are trained as "security trolls." *In the parks: Security trolls attack you during Escape from Gringotts. A diagram of a troll skeleton appears in the slideshow in the window of Dystyl Phaelanges in Knockturn Alley; the skeleton itself is stowed behind the slideshow screen.*

Werewolves. These people transform into raving beasts every full moon. Though they pose no danger most of the time, they're widely feared and face harsh discrimination. See also Fenrir Greyback and Remus Lupin in the section Characters. *In the parks: Eternelle's Elixir of Refreshment is topped with stone busts of magical creatures, including a transformed werewolf.*

Whomping Willow. Any threat to this tough tree gets pummelled by its clubbed branches. It grows just outside the Forbidden Forest. *In the parks: It tries to whomp you on Forbidden Journey.*

Honeydukes, Hogsmeade.

FOOD & DRINKS

Bertie Bott's Every Flavour Beans. Advertised as "a risk with every mouthful," these jellybeans come in all sorts of tastes, including liver, grass and earwax. *In the parks: Displayed in Honeydukes windows; sold inside as well as at Sugarplum's Sweetshop.*

Butterbeer. Described as tasting like "less-sickly butterscotch," this popular drink has only a tiny trace of alcohol. It's served at the Leaky Cauldron and The Three Broomsticks. *In the parks: A nonalcoholic version tastes like butterscotch cream soda; the foam atop it is like marshmallow fluff. It's served cold, hot or as frozen slush (each version made with a slightly different recipe) throughout Diagon Alley and Hogsmeade. Florean Fortescue's Ice-Cream Parlour serves butterbeer soft-serve ice cream.*

Chocolate Frog. This sweet is charmed to croak and hop just like a real frog. It comes packaged with a trading card of a famous witch or wizard. *In the parks: They're in the windows of Honeydukes; you can buy them inside and at Sugarplum's Sweetshop. Each comes with one of five cards featuring either Dumbledore or a Hogwarts founder. The frogs also hop onto the frosted door of the Hogwarts Express to Hogsmeade.*

Edible Dark Marks. Fred and George Weasley offer these nauseating, dark-mark-shaped sweets to mock Death Eaters. *In the parks: Sold at Weasleys' Wizard Wheezes.*

Exploding Bon Bons. They blow up harmlessly when eaten. *In the parks: Sold at Honeydukes and Sugarplum's Sweetshop.*

Firewhiskey. An alcoholic drink named for the burning sensation it causes when it slides down the throat. It's sold at The Hog's Head. *In the parks: Empty Firewhiskey bottles stack behind the counters of The Hog's Head and Leaky Cauldron; both spots sell it too. It's advertised on the wall above The Hopping Pot.*

Fizzing Whizzbees. While eating these candies, people temporarily float a few inches above the ground. They're rumored to contain dried billywigs, magical insects whose stings cause levitation. *In the parks: Sold at Honeydukes and Sugarplum's Sweetshop.*

Gillywater. A drink made with water and a magical water plant called gillyweed. *In the parks: It's served as plain bottled water throughout Diagon Alley and Hogsmeade.*

Pepper Imps. Peppermint-flavored sweets that make smoke pour from the consumer's ears and nose. *In the parks: Sold at Honeydukes and Sugarplum's Sweetshop.*

Peppermint Toads. Toad-shaped creams that "hop realistically in the stomach." *In the parks: Sold at Honeydukes and Sugarplum's Sweetshop.*

Pumpkin juice. A sweet drink served in Diagon Alley, Hogsmeade and Hogwarts. *In the parks: A refreshing, cider-like drink sold throughout Hogsmeade and Diagon Alley.*

Skiving Snackboxes. Popular sweets that make the eater temporarily ill, giving them an excuse to leave boring situations (i.e., school classes). There are four varieties: Fainting Fancies, Nosebleed Nougats, Puking Pastilles and Fever Fudge. Each has two color-coded ends; one triggers the illness, the other instantly cures it. Fred and George developed them for their joke shop. *In the parks: Sold at Weasleys' Wizard Wheezes.*

Sugar Quills. Sugar-spun treats that look like feather quills. Hogwarts students in class discreetly lick and nibble on them while pretending to focus on assignments. *In the parks: Sold at Honeydukes and Sugarplum's Sweetshop.*

OBJECTS & POTIONS

"Advanced Potion-Making, Second Edition." A textbook for higher-level Potions students. An old copy annotated by "the Half-Blood Prince" came into Harry's possession during his sixth year at school. *In the parks: It's in the window of Flourish and Blotts in Diagon Alley. Other copies stack on the upper shelves of Dervish and Banges.*

Bezoar. Taken from the stomach of a goat, this stone-like mass cures most poisons. *In the parks: Jars and bowls of it are in the windows of Mr. Mulpepper's and Slug & Jiggers Apothecaries in Diagon Alley. More are stored on the second floor of Dervish and Banges.*

Broomsticks. Flying, individual modes of transportation usually reserved for quidditch games. Nimbus-brand brooms are among the most popular. The Nimbus 2000 was Harry's first broom; a gift from Prof. McGonagall. It was succeeded by the Nimbus 2001; Draco Malfoy owns one of those. The fastest broom is the Firebolt; Harry got one as a gift from Sirius Black. *In the parks: Harry flies his Firebolt and Draco his Nimbus during Forbidden Journey. A Firebolt floats in the window of Quality Quidditch Supplies. A Nimbus 2001 hangs in the window of Spintwitches in Hogsmeade. Both Nimbuses and a Firebolt float in midair inside Dervish and Banges, leashed to its second-floor balcony.*

The Deathly Hallows. These three legendary items are featured in the story "The Tale of Three Brothers," by Beedle the Bard. **The Cloak of Invisibility** completely conceals its wearer from sight; unlike other invisibility cloaks it never wears off, is unaffected by spells and can shield multiple people at once. Harry inherited it from his father. **The Elder Wand** is the most powerful wand in recorded history; most who manage to acquire it tend to be murdered in their beds by power-hungry thieves; Albus Dumbledore obtained it after defeating the dark wizard Grindelwald in 1945. Set in a gold ring, the **Resurrection Stone** (Marvolo's ring) summons the spirits of dead individuals who were dear to the Stone's holder; it was passed down to Voldemort's grandfather Marvolo and later stolen by Voldemort himself, who, unaware of its properties, turned it into a horcrux. The Hallows are represented by an eye-like symbol consisting of a vertical line (the Wand) within a circle (the Stone) within a triangle (the Cloak). See also The Tales of Beedle the Bard below. *In the parks: The Hallows are showcased by performances of "The Tale of Three Brothers" in Diagon Alley. The main trio uses the Cloak to sneak into the Defense Against the Dark Arts classroom in the queue* *of Forbidden Journey. Ollivanders sells replicas of Dumbledore's Elder Wand. Replicas of the Resurrection Stone (set in Marvolo's ring) are displayed and sold at Borgin and Burkes. The Deathly Hallows symbol appears in the Fountain of Fair Fortune in Diagon Alley.*

Fanged Flyer. A green, reptilian Frisbee with a ring of teeth along its outer edge. *In the parks: One is in a display case inside Filch's Emporium.*

"Fantastic Beasts and Where to Find Them." A comprehensive guide to magical creatures found worldwide, written by Newt Scamander and published by Obscurus Books. *In the parks: An Obscurus Books sign hangs in Horizont Alley in Diagon Alley.*

Flesh-Eating Slug Repellent. A pest-control chemical sold in Knockturn Alley. Hagrid buys some to use on Hogwarts cabbages. *In the parks: A can of it sits on a wagon by the Flight of the Hippogriff queue. A hanging sign advertises it in Knocktturn Alley.*

Flying Ford Anglia. A beat-up blue car that Arthur Weasley gave the ability to fly. It currently roams the Forbidden Forest like a wild animal, due to a mishap involving Harry, Ron and the Whomping Willow. A real car built by Ford U.K., the turquoise Anglia in the story is a 105E from the 1960s. *In the parks: It flies through the Forbidden Forest outside the Hogwarts Express train to Hogsmeade. It's smashed into a tree behind the metal detectors in the Dragon Challenge queue.*

The Goblet of Fire. Filled to the brim with blue flames, this wooden chalice impartially selects Triwizard Tournament participants. See also The Triwizard Tournament in the section Society & Media. *In the parks: It's in the queue of Dragon Challenge.*

Hagrid's motorbike. A motorcycle charmed with the ability to fly. Buttons on the dashboard trigger magical effects; a big blue one blasts a stream of dragon fire from its tailpipe, propelling it forward. *In the parks: It's parked to the left of Gringotts in Diagon Alley; you can sit on it. Hagrid flies it past the Hogwarts Express train to Hogsmeade.*

Hand of Glory. A shriveled-up severed hand that's a useful tool for thieves; candles put in its grip produce light only the holder can see. One in Borgin and Burkes tries to grab people who examine it too closely. *In the parks: In a case at Borgin and Burkes.*

Horcruxes. These dark objects anchor someone to life by storing pieces of their soul. Making one requires murder without remorse. Voldemort created six, more than anyone else, in an effort to achieve immortality, using items he considered personally valuable. He wrote in his black-bound journal, **Tom Riddle's diary,** when he was a student at Hogwarts and used his real name. Years later, the bit of his soul it contained possessed a student and reopened the Chamber of Secrets. The golden **Hufflepuff's cup** once belonged to Helga Hufflepuff; to ensure its safekeeping Voldemort had Bellatrix store it in her vault at Gringotts. Harry, Ron and Hermione later broke into the vault and stole it. Other Voldemort horcruxes are **his grandfather's ring, Salazar Slytherin's locket, Rowena Ravenclaw's diadem** and **his pet snake, Nagini.** See also The Resurrection Stone (Marvolo's ring), above; Nagini in the section Characters. *In the parks: Harry, Ron and Hermione steal Hufflepuff's cup during Escape from Gringotts, though the horcrux's identity isn't specified on the ride. Filch's Emporium displays a replica of Ravenclaw's diadem; Borgin and Burkes displays replicas of Slytherin's locket.*

Howler. A blood-red envelope used to send a loud, angry message. It bellows its message in the voice of the sender, using an abstract folded face and floating in front of the recipient. *In the parks: Howlers shout from the window of the Owl Post in Hogsmeade.*

The Marauder's Map. An enchanted, hand-drawn map of Hogwarts that shows the current location of everyone there. When not in use, it looks like a blank piece of parchment. To reveal the map, the owner taps it with their wand and says "I solemnly swear I am up to no good"; when finished, they tap it again and say "Mischief managed!" It was created by "Messrs. Moony, Wormtail, Padfoot and Prongs," the teenage nicknames of Remus Lupin, Peter Pettigrew, Sirius Black and James Potter, when they were friends at Hogwarts. *In the parks: It's on display inside Filch's Emporium.*

The Mirror of Erised. A full-length mirror that reflects the innermost, most desperate desire of the viewer; Harry sees his deceased parents standing beside him. Atop it is the inscription *"erised stra ehru oyt ube cafru oyt on wohs i,"* a backward version of "I show not your face but your heart's desire." *In the parks: In the Forbidden Journey queue.*

"The Monster Book of Monsters." This furry textbook snarls and snaps at anything that gets too close. A belt restrains its toothy binding to keep it from biting or scuttling away. Hagrid assigns it to his students for Care of Magical Creatures class. *In the parks: Snarling books are caged in the window of Flourish and Blotts in Diagon Alley. A single book is kept in a cage inside Dervish and Banges. In the queue of Flight of the Hippogriff, an empty wooden cage with a hole ripped through the top is labeled with the book's title.*

Omniculars. Fancy binoculars sold to spectators at the Quidditch World Cup. They display play-by-plays of the game, give bios of players and show events in slow motion. *In the parks: Some scatter at the bottom of the Spintwitches window in Hogsmeade.*

Opal necklace. A curse placed on this glittering green necklace has killed 19 people; it's sold by Borgin and Burkes. *In the parks: Borgin and Burkes displays replicas.*

Pensieve. This shallow dish stores silvery, fluid memories; individual memories can be relived from a third-person view. Dumbledore keeps one in an elaborate case in his office. *In the parks: Dumbledore's sits in his office in the Forbidden Journey queue.*

Polyjuice Potion. A concoction that changes the drinker's appearance into someone else for one hour. *In the parks: Its ingredients appear in labeled jars and bowls inside the windows of the Mr. Mulpepper's and Slug & Jiggers apothecaries in Diagon Alley.*

Quick-Quotes Quill. A red feather quill that takes notes without the input of its owner; it's a useful tool for journalists and reporters. *In the parks: One scribbles away in the window of Scrivenshafts Quill Shop, in Hogsmeade.*

Shrunken heads. Stitched-up human heads hung on strings as decorative items; they're often quite talkative. *In the parks: Several sing and joke in the window of Noggin and Bonce in Knockturn Alley. Silent, static heads hang inside Borgin and Burkes and behind the bar of The Hog's Head. Talkative Dre Head hangs from the Knight Bus.*

Skele-Gro. This foul-tasting potion regrows broken or missing bones. It's sold in a skeleton-shaped bottle. *In the parks: In Diagon Alley, it's advertised in a window at the end of Horizont Alley. A bottle is displayed in a glass case inside Filch's Emporium.*

The Sword of Gryffindor. This ruby-encrusted sword is a historical relic of Godric Gryffindor. It's kept in a glass case in Dumbledore's office. *In the parks: It's mounted on the wall in Dumbledore's office in the queue of Forbidden Journey.*

"The Tales of Beedle the Bard." A book of wizarding fables that include "The Tale of Three Brothers"(the story of the Deathly Hallows), "The Fountain of Fair Fortune" and "The Wizard and the Hopping Pot." See also The Deathly Hallows, above. *In the parks: A puppetry troupe performs "The Fountain of Fair Fortune" and "The Tale of Three Brothers." Flourish and Blotts and Tomes & Scrolls display the book in their windows. It provides the names for The Hopping Pot and The Fountain of Fair Fortune.*

U-No-Poo. Constipation-inducing pills sold at Fred and George's joke shop as a way of mocking the return of Voldemort, aka "You-Know-Who." *In the parks: Weasleys' Wizard Wheezes advertises it in the window and sells it as jars of novelty candy.*

Vanishing cabinets. Two of these create a passage that can be used to instantly teleport between two locations. A damaged pair forms a secret entrance into Hogwarts, from Borgin and Burkes to the Room of Requirement. To make sure this path was safe to use, Draco Malfoy sent canaries though to see if they would survive; he eventually used the cabinets to sneak Death Eaters into Hogwarts. *In the parks: One is pushed into the back corner of Borgin and Burkes; you can hear a canary faintly chirping inside.*

Wizard's Chess. Enchanted game pieces violently destroy each other when taken. *In the parks: A white queen attacks a black knight in the window of Zonko's in Hogsmeade.*

SPELLS & ABILITIES

Apparition. Gives the witch or wizard the ability to instantly disappear in one location (disapparate) and reappear (apparate) in another. The films portray an alternate sort of apparition that looks like smoke trails flying through the air; black smoke represents Death Eaters. *In the parks: Apparating Death Eaters soar over the rooftops of London outside the window of the Hogwarts Express train to Hogsmeade. The black trails of Voldemort and Bellatrix fly past you on Escape from Gringotts. At Carkitt Market, before and after performances of "The Tales of Beedle the Bard" you can hear the actors apparating just out of sight.*

Arania Exumai. Repels spiders and acromantulas with a flash of light. *In the parks: Hermione uses it to fend off a horde of acromantulas during Forbidden Journey.*

Arresto Momentum. Stops or slows a moving thing. It's especially useful for stopping falling objects in midair. *In the parks: Bill uses it to save you from some treacherous falls in Escape from Gringotts. Used with interactive wands in Hogsmeade.*

Ascendio. Raises an object. *In the parks: Used with interactive wands in Hogsmeade.*

Cruciatus Curse (Crucio). Causes the victim excruciating pain without leaving any physical marks. The Death Eaters use it to torture people for information. *In the parks: Bellatrix tries to hit you with this in Escape from Gringotts.*

Dancing Feet Spell (Tarantallegra). Makes the target's legs dance uncontrollably. *In the parks: Used with interactive wands in Diagon Alley.*

Descendo. Lowers an object. *In the parks: Used with interactive wands in Hogsmeade.*

Fire-Making Spell (Incendio). Conjures fire or lights something aflame. *In the parks: Used with interactive wands in Hogsmeade and Knockturn Alley.*

Herbivicus Charm (Herbivicus). Makes flowers bloom and speeds up plant growth. *In the parks. Used with interactive wands in Hogsmeade.*

Imperius Curse (Imperio). Puts the target in a trance, placing it under the mental and physical control of the caster. When the main trio breaks into Gringotts, Harry uses it on a goblin named Bogrod to get access to the bank's vaults. *In the parks: The trio is initially accompanied by the imperised Bogrod in Escape from Gringotts.*

Killing Curse (Avada Kedavra). An illegal spell that causes instant death. It gave Harry his lightning-shaped scar; he's the only person to ever survive it. *In the parks: Bellatrix tries to hit you with this in Escape from Gringotts.*

Levitation Charm (Wingardium Leviosa). Floats an object wherever the caster wants it to go. *In the parks: Bill uses it to fly your vehicle to safety in Escape from Gringotts. Used with interactive wands in Diagon Alley.*

Locomotion Charm (Locomotor). Makes an inanimate object move on its own. *In the parks: Used with interactive wands in Hogsmeade and Diagon Alley.*

Mending Charm (Reparo). Seamlessly repairs broken objects. *In the parks: Used with interactive wands in Diagon Alley.*

Metelojinx. Produces a small, localized thunderstorm. *In the parks: Used with interactive wands in Diagon Alley.*

Parseltongue. The language of snakes; it sounds like incomprehensible hissing to most people. Those who understand and speak it—Parselmouths—have a reputation for being dark wizards. *In the parks: Voldemort uses it to beckon Nagini in Escape from Gringotts. A python speaks it to passersby from a side window of Magical Menagerie.*

Patronus Charm (Expecto Patronum). Conjures a Patronus—a bright, silvery light in the shape on an animal—that repels dementors. Harry's is stag-shaped. *In the parks: Harry uses it to save you from dementors in Forbidden Journey and on the Hogwarts Express train to Hogsmeade.*

Revelio Charm (Revelio). Exposes concealed objects. *In the parks: Used with interactive wands in Hogsmeade.*

Silencing Charm (Silencio). Mutes a source of noise. *In the parks: Used with interactive wands in Diagon Alley.*

Specialis Revelio. Uncovers hidden spells that have been placed on something. *In the parks: Used with interactive wands in Diagon Alley.*

Tongue-Tying Curse (Mimblewimble). Curls the target's tongue, temporarily muffling their speech. *In the parks: Used with interactive wands in Knockturn Alley.*

Unlocking Charm (Alohomora). Opens locks that aren't magically protected. *In the parks: Used with interactive wands in Hogsmeade and Knockturn Alley.*

Water-Making Spell (Aguamenti). Conjures fresh water. *In the parks: Used with interactive wands in Diagon Alley.*

CHARACTERS

THE SERIES FEATURES Harry Potter, Ron Weasley and Hermione Granger, three Gryffindors who become best friends during their first year at Hogwarts. The main antagonist is the evil wizard Voldemort. His followers, the **Death Eaters,** consist of power-hungry fanatics, cowardly opportunists and eager sadists; most are pure-blood Slytherins. They conceal their identities with black hoods and elaborate metal masks. The main force of good is old Hogwarts headmaster Albus Dumbledore, who leads **The Order of the Phoenix,** a group dedicated to defeating Voldemort. Its headquarters are in London at Number Twelve, a townhouse in Grimmauld Place, which is magically protected and hidden from the surrounding muggle neighborhood.

Aragog. An ancient, blind acromantula that lives in the Forbidden Forest, where he leads a colony of his sons and daughters. See also Acromantulas in the section Creatures & Plants. *In the parks: During Forbidden Journey, he appears in a flash of lightning in the Forbidden Forest.*

Black, Sirius. Harry's godfather and one of the most passionate members of The Order of the Phoenix. In school he was close friends with Remus Lupin, Peter Pettigrew ("Wormtail") and James Potter. He was accused of mass murder, being a Death Eater and betraying the Potters to Voldemort; the real perpetrator was Wormtail, who faked his own death and framed Sirius for everything. After 12 years in Azkaban, Sirius became the only prisoner to escape without outside help. He went into hiding in his abandoned family home at Number Twelve, Grimmauld Place, which he allowed the Order to use as headquarters. The only people aware of his innocence are Harry, Ron, Hermione, the Order and the Death Eaters. *In the parks: His wanted poster appears outside The Three Broomsticks and inside The Leaky Cauldron. Outside Diagon Alley, Grimmauld Place is the row of townhouses on the right; Number Twelve is the one with the darker bricks. Ollivanders sells replicas of his wand.*

Buckbeak. A gray hippogriff, one of several specimens featured in Hagrid's first Care of Magical Creatures class. When approached by Harry, Buckbeak bowed to him and gave him a flight around the castle grounds. See also Hippogriff in the section Creatures & Plants. *In the parks: An animatronic Buckbeak rests in a nest at the Flight of the Hippogriff boarding area; he bows to riders as they take off. Outside the window of the Hogwarts Express train to Diagon Alley, he flies over the Black Lake and skims his talons through the water.*

Chang, Cho. A pretty Ravenclaw girl who Harry has a crush on for the first half of the series. *In the parks: Ollivanders sells replicas of her wand.*

Delacour, Fleur. A beautiful French girl who competes in the Triwizard Tournament as the champion from Beauxbatons Academy of Magic. See also The Triwizard Tournament in the section Society & Media. *In the parks: Hand-painted banners in the queue of Dragon Challenge support her and the other Triwizard champions. Ollivanders sells replicas of her wand.*

Diggory, Cedric. A 17-year-old Hufflepuff who's chosen to compete in the Triwizard Tournament. See also The Triwizard Tournament in the section Society & Media. *In the parks: Hand-painted banners in the queue of Dragon Challenge support him and the other Triwizard champions. Ollivanders sells replicas of his wand.*

Dumbledore, Albus. Hogwarts headmaster, founder of The Order of the Phoenix and the only wizard Voldemort ever feared. He has a long silver beard, flowing robes and half-moon spectacles. He wields the legendary Elder Wand and has a pet phoenix named Fawkes. He mentors Harry throughout the series. *In the parks: In the queue of Forbidden Journey, Dumbledore welcomes you to Hogwarts in his office; Fawkes' empty perch sits in the corner. At the end of the ride, Dumbledore congratulates you and bids you farewell. Newspaper articles in the Escape from Gringotts queue mention his death. Ollivanders sells replicas of his wand.*

Filch, Argus. The old, bad-tempered Hogwarts school caretaker. He's obsessed with catching troublemaking students and confiscating contraband items. *In the parks: At the end of Forbidden Journey, Dumbledore reminds you to pick up your stowed belongings, "lest you want them confiscated by Mr. Filch." The ride's gift shop, Filch's Emporium of Confiscated Goods, is apparently comprised entirely of items he's taken from students.*

Finnigan, Seamus. A hotheaded Irish boy in Gryffindor. He tends to accidentally make things explode when doing magic. *In the parks: He appears in a crowd of Gryffindors at the end of Forbidden Journey.*

Fletcher, Mundungus. A petty thief who reluctantly works with The Order of the Phoenix. They give him protection in return for insider knowledge of illegal wizarding activity. *In the parks: Ollivanders sells replicas of his wand.*

Granger, Hermione. A muggle-born girl who's best friends with Harry and Ron. She has an encyclopedic knowledge of magic, excels in all of her classes and has an orange pet cat named Crookshanks. *In the parks: She hosts Forbidden Journey alongside Harry and Ron. During Escape from Gringotts, she accompanies the boys during their infiltration of the bank. On the Hogwarts Express train, the trio's shadows walk and chat outside your compartment. Ollivanders sells replicas of her wand.*

Greyback, Fenrir. A sadistic, cannibalistic werewolf with a taste for children. He's allied himself with the Death Eaters; they use him to menace people into submission. See also Werewolves in the section Creatures & Plants. *In the parks: His wanted poster is on a wall in Knockturn Alley. Ollivanders sells replicas of his wand.*

Griphook. A goblin who works at Gringotts. He helps Harry, Ron and Hermione break into the bank to steal a horcrux, but betrays them once they get what they want. See also Goblins in the section Creatures & Plants. *In the parks: On Escape from Gringotts, he appears several times with the main trio, and is later seen shooting spells at them when the dragon first appears.*

Hagrid, Rubeus. The Hogwarts gamekeeper and Care of Magical Creatures professor. He's half-giant, twice as tall as an average man and three times as wide. He loves vicious magical creatures but tends to overlook the dangers they pose. He lives in a stone hut on the edge of the Forbidden Forest with his pet dog, Fang. *In the parks: His voice plays throughout the queue of Flight of the Hippogriff. In the ride's queue, Fang can be heard barking from inside Hagrid's hut. On Forbidden Journey, he stops you to ask if you've seen his escaped pet dragon. On the Hogwarts Express train to Hogsmeade, he passes by on his flying motorcycle; he shows up again with Fang at the end of the ride.*

Hedwig. Harry's pet snowy owl. *In the parks: In the boarding area of the Hogwarts Express train to Hogsmeade, she hoots and looks around from inside her cage.*

Kreacher. A very old, bad-tempered house-elf who inhabits Number Twelve, Grimmauld Place. See also House-elfs in the section Creatures & Plants. *In the parks: He peeks out of a second-floor window of Number Twelve, outside Diagon Alley.*

Krum, Viktor. A stoic 17-year-old boy who competes in the Triwizard Tournament as the champion from Durmstrang Academy. He's a famous seeker on the Bulgarian quidditch team. See also The Triwizard Tournament in the section Society & Media. *In the parks: Hand-painted banners in the queue of Dragon Challenge support him and the other Triwizard champions. Ollivanders sells replicas of his wand.*

Lestrange, Bellatrix. Voldemort's most devoted Death Eater. Deranged and sadistic, she specializes in torturing her victims into madness with the Cruciatus Curse. *In the parks: She and Voldemort are the antagonists of Escape from Gringotts. Her Wanted poster is pasted in two of the entrances to Knockturn Alley. Ollivanders sells replicas of her wand.*

Lockhart, Gilderoy. A vain, attention-seeking author with a series of autobiographies about his adventures fighting magical creatures around the world. In reality, he didn't do any of the deeds he claims; his only real skill is erasing memories of talented witches and wizards and taking credit for their accomplishments. He taught Defense Against the Dark Arts during Harry's second year at Hogwarts. *In the parks: Stacks of his books litter the Defense Against the Dark Arts classroom in the queue of Forbidden Journey. At Flourish and Blotts in Diagon Alley and Tomes & Scrolls in Hogsmeade, his books and promotional photos are displayed in the windows.*

Longbottom, Neville. A socially awkward Gryffindor boy who eventually develops into a competent fighter. He's close friends with Harry, Ron, Hermione and Luna Lovegood. *In the parks: A teacher lectures him from the other side of a door marked "Potions Classroom" in the queue of Forbidden Journey. He appears in a crowd of Gryffindors at the end of the ride. Ollivanders sells replicas of his wand.*

The Lovegoods. A little family with an odd way of looking at the world. A friend of Harry, Ron, Hermione and Neville, **Luna Lovegood** is a quirky Ravenclaw student with long blonde hair, a dreamy way of speaking and knack for reading people. Luna's father **Xenophilius** writes and edits The Quibbler. See also The Quibbler in the section Society & Media. *In the parks: Ollivanders sells replica wands for Luna and Xenophilius.*

Lupin, Remus. A compassionate werewolf who's a member of The Order of the Phoenix, Harry's friend and his favorite Defense Against the Dark Arts professor. Unlike most werewolves, he fights against Voldemort and tries his best to fit in with society. See also Werewolves in the section Creatures & Plants. *In the parks: Some of his teaching equipment is in the Defense Against the Dark Arts classroom, in the queue of Forbidden Journey. Ollivanders sells replicas of his wand.*

The Malfoys. A wealthy, pure-blood family with white-blond hair. Its elaborate mansion, Malfoy Manor, is later used as headquarters for the Death Eaters. Slytherin student **Draco** bullies and intimidates the main trio; he plays seeker on the Slytherin quidditch team. Draco's father **Lucius** is an aristocratic Death Eater; his wand is concealed within a walking stick topped with a silver snake head. Draco's mother **Narcissa** is Bellatrix Lestrange's sister. *In the parks: The Hogwarts Express train passes Malfoy Manor during a thunderstorm. Draco plays seeker on the Slytherin quidditch team during Forbidden Journey. Lucius' Death Eater mask and his snake-headed cane are displayed inside Filch's Emporium and Borgin and Burkes. Ollivanders sells replica wands for Draco and Narcissa.*

Moaning Myrtle. A gloomy ghost who haunts an unused bathroom at Hogwarts, whining, crying and flooding its stalls with water. Sometimes she explores other restrooms. *In the parks: Her voice sobs and complains in the main Hogsmeade restrooms.*

Moody, "Mad Eye." A retired auror (dark wizard catcher) who's one of the most active members of The Order of the Phoenix. He's nicknamed for his magical prosthetic eye. *In the parks: On the Hogwarts Express train to Diagon Alley, he greets you as you arrive at King's Cross Station. Ollivanders sells replicas of his wand.*

Nagini. A 12-foot venomous snake who's Voldemort's faithful companion and one of his horcruxes; he uses her like an attack dog. *In the parks: In Escape from Gringotts, she strikes at riders in the front rows of carts.*

Patil, Parvati. A popular, studious Indian girl in Gryffindor. *In the parks: She appears in a crowd of Gryffindors at the end of Forbidden Journey. Ollivanders sells replicas of her wand.*

Potter, Harry. The main character—a bespectacled, black-haired boy with a lightning-bolt scar on his forehead. He's best friends with Ron and Hermione and plays seeker on the Gryffindor quidditch team. As a baby, he was orphaned when his parents were murdered by Voldemort. But something went wrong when Voldemort tried to kill him: the dark wizard vanished and the boy was left with his distinctive scar. Witches and wizards everywhere celebrated Voldemort's disappearance, and Harry quickly became a famous wizarding icon known as "The Boy Who Lived." He was taken in by his muggle aunt and uncle, who emotionally abused him and didn't tell him anything about the magical world. He learned the truth when he was 11, when he got an invitation letter to Hogwarts. He spends the next seven years going to school, fighting against Voldemort's growing influence and struggling with adolescence. *In the parks: He hosts Forbidden Journey alongside Hermione and Ron. During Escape from Gringotts, he accompanies them during their infiltration of the bank. On the Hogwarts Express train, the trio's shadows walk and chat outside your compartment; Harry also repels a dementor that invades the train. Ollivanders sells replicas of his wand.*

Shacklebolt, Kingsley. A talented member of The Order of the Phoenix who speaks in a deep, calming voice. *In the parks: Ollivanders sells replicas of his wand.*

Scrimgeour, Rufus. The Minister of Magic elected after Voldemort's return. *In the parks: Ollivanders sells replicas of his wand.*

Slughorn, Horace. A jovial wizard who replaces Prof. Snape as potions professor at Hogwarts and later as head of Slytherin house. *In the parks: Ollivanders sells replicas of his wand.*

Snape, Severus. The soft-spoken, often cruel potions professor at Hogwarts. A former Death Eater, his motives and loyalties remain mysterious for the majority of the series. *In the parks: The queue of Forbidden Journey passes the door to his office. Newspaper articles in the queue of Escape from Gringotts announce his new position as Hogwarts headmaster after Dumbledore's death. Ollivanders sells replicas of his wand.*

Thomas, Dean. A black Gryffindor boy who's best friends with Seamus Finnegan. *In the parks: He appears in a crowd of Gryffindors at the end of Forbidden Journey. Ollivanders sells replicas of his wand.*

Tonks, Nymphadora. An Order of the Phoenix member; a spunky witch romantically involved with Remus Lupin. *In the parks: Ollivanders sells replicas of her wand.*

Umbridge, Dolores. A bigoted, sadistic witch who works for the Ministry of Magic; her girlish, heartless personality makes her one of the most fiercely hated characters in the series. She taught Defense Against the Dark Arts in Harry's fifth year at Hogwarts; while there, she instated ridiculous rules, handed out barbaric punishments and forcibly stole the title of headmaster before she was finally removed from the school. After Death Eaters took over management of the ministry, she happily produced and distributed propaganda promoting blood purity. *In the parks: Copies of her "Dark Arts Defense: Basics for Beginners" textbook are abandoned in the queue of Forbidden Journey. Desks in the queue of Escape from Gringotts are laid with her "Mudbloods and the Dangers They*

Pose to a Peaceful Pure-Blood Society" pamphlets. Several of her school "proclamations" hang on the wall inside Filch's Emporium. In Weasleys' Wizard Wheezes, she's mocked with a clockwork Umbridge that rides a unicycle and squeals "I will have ORDER!"

Voldemort. A powerful dark wizard and the main antagonist of the series. As the heir of Salazar Slytherin, he inherited the ability to speak Parseltongue. His main goal is to achieve immortality by splitting his soul into horcruxes. His real name is Tom Riddle; most people refer to him as "He-Who-Must-Not-Be-Named" or "You-Know-Who" out of fear, still shaken by the deeds he committed when he first rose to power. When he murdered James and Lily Potter and tried to kill their son Harry, something went wrong and Voldemort disappeared. It wasn't until 13 years later that he returned, having regained his body and his faithful group of Death Eaters. See also Horcruxes in the section Objects & Potions; Parseltongue in the section Spells & Abilities. *In the parks: He is the main antagonist of Escape from Gringotts; Ollivanders sells replicas of his wand.*

Warbeck, Celestina. A famous diva who sings jazzy, romantic hits. She performs with a backup group of witches known as the Banshees. Celestina is J.K. Rowling's favorite minor character in the series; her only "appearance" is in passing mentions of songs that Mrs. Weasley loves to listen to. Her appearance and persona are based on Shirley Bassey, a famous Welsh vocalist best known for singing the themes for the James Bond films "Goldfinger," "Diamonds are Forever" and "Moonraker." *In the parks: She performs with her Banshees on the Carkitt Market stage in Diagon Alley.*

The Weasleys. A red-headed family of nine, all Gryffindors and members of The Order of the Phoenix. **Arthur** and **Molly Weasley** act as parental figures to Harry. Their son **Ron** is a gangly redhead who's best friends with Harry and Hermione; he plays keeper on the Gryffindor quidditch team. Prankster twins **Fred** and **George** run a joke shop in Diagon Alley, Weasleys' Wizard Wheezes. Oldest son **Bill** works at Gringotts Wizarding Bank. He used to be a curse breaker who uncovered magical

artifacts from Egyptian pyramids but switched to a desk job when he joined The Order of the Phoenix. The youngest Weasley and the only daughter in the family, shy **Ginny** develops a crush on Harry and eventually starts dating him. *In the parks: Ron hosts Forbidden Journey alongside Harry and Hermione; during Escape from Gringotts, he accompanies them during their infiltration of the bank; on the Hogwarts Express train, the trio's shadows walk past and chat outside your train compartment. Bill hosts Escape from Gringotts. Fred, George and Ginny appear with the rest of the Gryffindor quidditch team at the end of Forbidden Journey. On the Hogwarts Express train to Diagon Alley, Fred and George fly past on brooms; one tosses a firecracker that explodes into an ad for their joke shop, which is in Diagon Alley. Ollivanders sells replicas of the wands of Arthur, Ginny, Molly and Ron.*

Yaxley. A high-ranking Death Eater who works at the Ministry of Magic. *In the parks: Ollivanders sells replicas of his wand.*

Celestina Warbeck, Carkitt Market.

© Universal Orlando Resort

The (formerly) flying Ford Anglia, near Hogwarts castle.

FUN FINDS

SINCE THE BUILDINGS in the Wizarding World were magically constructed, their walls are crooked and their chimneys tilt. Magic makes most technology go haywire, so buildings don't rely on electricity; smoke puffs from their chimneys. The area uses British terms and phrases, such as "prams" for strollers and "public conveniences" for restrooms. Other enjoyable discoveries:

IN HOGSMEADE.

1. "Please respect the spell limits" requests a sign hanging from the archway entrance to **the grounds of Hogsmeade.** 2. Sparkling snow tops most buildings; icicles hang from rooftops. 3. During the holidays, wreathes and garland decorate shops and the inside of The Three Broomsticks. 4. Wands tuck into the belts of villagers who work in the area. 5. The first storefront on the left is **Zonko's Joke Shop,** which is known for its magical fireworks. Its hanging sign is a stylized face; its name is written inside a gaping mouth. 6. In its left window, a white queen attacks a black knight in a wizard's chess display. 7. Next to the display are colorful rockets and firecrackers, including Dr. Filibuster's Fabulous Wet-Start No-Heat Fireworks. 8. A Cornish pixie uses a leaf to pour water into a cauldron in a small fountain above the window of **McHavelocks Wizarding Headgear.** 9. A skeleton with eyes, a scarf and a top hat tops the Eyeball Bananza, a coin-operated arcade machine in a window of **Honeydukes.** When he tips his hat, a crow hidden inside it reaches down and pecks in his eyeball, which pops out his mouth, rolls down his scarf and disappears into the machine. 10. The machine's coin slot reads "Sickles Only." 11. An oversized Chocolate Frog display dominates the store's far right window; large Chocolate Frog cards show holographic portraits of Albus Dumbledore and the four Hogwarts founders. 12. A short alley behind the sweet shop leads to a colorful set of doors used by its employees.

13. House-elves pull strands of licorice hair from the head and face of an Asian wizard in Clippy's Clip Joint, a coin-operated arcade machine in a window inside Honeydukes; the machine also appears in the third Potter movie. 14. Its coin slot reads "Sickles Only." 15. The shop's upper green borders are painted with the names of popular treats. 16. A spot where you can fill a box with Bertie Bott's Every Flavour Beans is shaped like the container the beans are packaged in.

17. Across the street, a backup to the **Hogwarts Express** locomotive puffs steam and rumbles idly. 18. School trunks and luggage are stacked nearby. 19. The conductor stands in front of the train, answering questions and posing for photos.

20. **The Hogsmeade Station Ticketing Office** houses lockers for Dragon Challenge. Out front, a timetable warns that "broomsticks, wands or other wizarding artefacts are left unattended entirely at the commuter's own risk." 21. Inside, lockers are topped by wooden beams reading "The Gateway to Hogwarts." Departure times for King's Cross and Hogsmeade stations are listed below. 22. Landscapes of foreign wizarding schools decorate the locker area. 23. The Ministry of Magic's Department of Magical Games and Sports supplied the **Dragon Challenge** safety signs. 24. A golden egg from the Triwizard Tournament's First Task is displayed in the center of a stone archway over the ride's entrance. 25. The archway is bordered by flags representing Gryffindor (for Harry), Hufflepuff (Cedric), Durmstrang (Viktor Krum) and Beauxbatons (Fleur). 26. Hand-painted banners and signs that support each Triwizard champion decorate the first part of the queue. 27. The flying Ford Anglia has crashed into a tree behind the queue's metal detectors. It has cracked windows and glowing headlights; it honks at people passing it. 28. Glowing blue light fills the Goblet of Fire in the center of the champions' tent; fire crackles from within it. 29. The silver Triwizard Cup stands on a pedestal in the next room. 30. Farther down the queue, a glass case holds three golden eggs from the First Task. 31. Lit candles float above a dark room. 32. Dragons roar and snarl from behind a set of closed wooden doors on the left. 33. The Hungarian Horntail trains resemble blue ice dragons; Chinese Fireball trains resemble red fire dragons.

34. At the very top of **The Owlery** an owl occasionally pops out from a cuckoo clock-like door. 35. The front is adorned with a huge, two-faced clock. Its creaking gears and ticking pendulum are visible from behind. 36. Peering down from the rafters, owls hoot, ruffle their wings and turn their heads to look around. 37. Droppings stain the beams.

38. Packages fill the window of **The Owl Post** at the back left of The Owlery; they hold broomsticks, cauldrons, a witch's hat and a violin. 39 and 40. Between them, projected Howlers pop up and yell angry messages. Two examples:—

> How dare you go to Hogsmeade without a permission form! I don't even know how you GOT there! You can bet you won't be going anywhere during the summer holidays! Don't you EVER disobey your father's wishes again!

> If you want to know what's going on in the wizarding world get your OWN Daily Prophet and stop intercepting mine! Do you think I can't SEE you, tracking down my owl every morning?!

41. Inside The Owl Post, owls hoot and look around at people from perches lining the wall. 42. A plaque topped with a little golden owl marks perches reserved for The Daily Prophet's delivery owls. 43. Packaged items in the corners of the shop include broomsticks, cauldrons, skulls, wand boxes and wizard hats.

44. At the back right of The Owlery, the window of **Dervish and Banges** shows a music box topped with an elaborate model of Hogwarts. When the box is playing, a small Hungarian Horntail chases a little broom-mounted Harry around the castle.

45. On the window's back wall is a sign that reads "Ask about test-flying our brooms within." 46. Another sign advertises the Nimbus 2001.

47. Inside Dervish and Banges, a caged copy of "The Monster Book of Monsters" snores softly; occasionally it snarls and rears forward. Its forked tongue sticks out like a bookmark. 48. A sign to the left of the ordering counter lists the store's closing procedures; step 4 is "Double check the lock on 'The Monster Book of Monsters!'—YOU KNOW WHAT HAPPENED LAST TIME." The last step is "cast a security spell." 49. Three floating broomsticks leash to a second-floor balcony. 50. Stacked textbooks on the upper floor include "Advanced Potion-Making," "Unfogging the Future" and "Winogrand's Water Plants." 51. The prices of potion ingredients are listed on a shelf above the entrance to the Owl Post. It's 15 sickles for an ounce of stewed mandrake, 19 for a pint of bundimun ooze, 13 for a pint of horklump juice, only 5 knuts for a pint of flobberworm mucus. 52. Also on display are jars of bezoars, a pile of quaffles and 3-D Spectrespecs.

53. At the **Ollivanders** wand-choosing experience, a floating broom sweeps the ceiling to the left of the indoor waiting area.

54. Outside **The Three Broomsticks,** a wanted poster shows Sirius Black's animated mugshot. It asks those with information about his whereabouts to notify the Ministry of Magic's Witch Watchers Department. 55. Inside, old paintings on the walls feature subjects such as hippogriffs, owls and Hogwarts castle. 56. Shadows cast on upper walls show house-elves using magic to clean the upper floors. 57. "Inn Guests Only Beyond This Point" reads a sign next to a staircase in the back of the room. 58. Three broomsticks are stored in a case on the wall near the border to The Hog's Head. 59. A sign across from the broomsticks reads:—

> To all guests and patrons: When leaving these premises after the witching hour please leave quietly via the right hand side door. Or please leave loudly via the left hand side door. Or please don't leave at all. Thank you.

60. To the right of the restaurant, a (real) Gringotts ATM is on a path to a seating porch. 61. Porch signs read "Please do not feed the birds or other winged creatures." 62. Inside **The Hog's Head,** a mounted boar head behind the bar occasionally moves around and snorts. 63. Next to it, a sign reads "The management will not take responsibility if you lose your HEAD!" 64. Bunches of shrunken heads hang nearby. 65. Bottles of Firewhiskey, Ocky Rot Wine and White Rat Whiskey stack on shelves behind the bar. 66. A jar of doxy eggs tops the left shelf. 67. Barrels of Hog's Head Brew front a staircase in the back left corner. 68. From the foot of the stairs, you can hear objects clattering as a house-elf frets to herself upstairs. 69. A nearby Three Broomsticks chalkboard lists "yesterday's specials."

70. A potted Mimbulus Mimbletonia twitches sluggishly in the left window of **Dogweed and Deathcap.** 71. A wailing, infant-like mandrake pokes its ugly head out of a pot in the right window.

72. Frozen water fills a trough connected to a pump outside the **public conveniences.** 73. Moaning Myrtle's voice mopes and complains inside the mens' and womens' sides. 74. The walls are damaged from Myrtle overflowing the sinks. "Caution: Floor May Be Wet" signs appear inside each entrance.

75. Above the restrooms, jars of magical ingredients sit in a window for **J. Pippin's Potions.** 76. A stone mortar and pestle hangs from a pole.

77. Hermione's pink Yule Ball dress floats in the left window of **Gladrags Wizardwear.** 78. A cat made of measuring tape bats at the hem of the dress.

79. A floating Quick-Quotes Quill scribbles in a book in the left window of **Scrivenshafts Quill Shop.** 80. Two quills cross to form its hanging sign.

81. An upright cello playing itself is among the enchanted musical instruments in the left second-floor window of **Dominic Maestro's Music Shop.** 82. The instruments play snippets of "Hedwig's Theme," the iconic instrumental from the film series. 83. In the right window, pages of sheet music occasionally fly into the air. 84. The Wizarding Wireless Network logo hangs above the right window.

85. On the first floor is **Madam Puddifoot's,** a frilly pink tea parlor that's frequented by starry-eyed teen couples. A teapot and three teacups hang from its sign. 86. In its window, chicks are starting to hatch from decorative eggs that top an Easter cake. 87. A snowball-juggling snowman tops another cake that's dressed like the snowman near the Magic Neep fruit cart. 88. Inside the shop, one flowery pink table supports a tower of carefully-stacked cups and saucers.

89. In the window of **Ceridwen's Cauldrons,** a pile of cauldrons is topped with one that stirs itself. 90. You can hear the bubbling, frothy sounds of the cauldron's contents. 91. Three small cauldrons hang from a beam over the window. 92. A tower of cauldrons is stacked to the right of the shop.

93. Across the street, the sign for **Tomes & Scrolls** is an open book; a "T" and an "S" decorate the front and back covers. 94. In the shop's right window, a large copy of "The Tales of Beedle the Bard" stands atop a stack of books that includes "Secrets of the Darkest Art," "The Healer's Help Mate" and "The Decline of Pagan Magic." 95. Its left window displays a collection of Gilderoy Lockhart's works; three are packaged into a "Travel Trilogy." 96. An animated promotional photo shows Lockhart wearing adventurous clothing and posing for the camera.

97. Among the quidditch gear in the window of **Spintwitches** is an equipment box with a quaffle and two strapped-down shaking bludgers. A compartment for the golden snitch is empty. 98. A Nimbus 2000 broomstick is chained to the ceiling. 99. Also in the window are tickets to the Quidditch World Cup, Omniculars, tins of Broomcare Wax and a book, "You and Your Owl." 100. A large golden snitch and two bludgers hang from a pole over the window.

101. To the right of the Magic Neep fruit cart is a snowman in wizarding robes, a pointed hat, a Gryffindor scarf, a twiggy goatee and a carrot nose; a snow-owl on his shoulder has a carrot beak.

102. "Wait, they might have muggle cameras," the prefect conductor of the **Frog Choir** often says when posing the group for a photo at the end of its performance. She then reminds the singers to hold still and keep their eyes open.

103. Safety signs for the **Flight of the Hippogriff** come from the Ministry of Magic's Department for the Regulation and Control of Magical Creatures. 104. In the queue, Hagrid talks about hippogriffs and explains you'll be boarding a training one made of wicker. 105. A can of Flesh-Eating Slug Repellent rests atop a wagon on the left. 106. Fang barks from inside Hagrid's hut. 107. Next to its right-hand door, a hole is ripped through an empty

A snowman and snow-owl, Hogsmeade.

Hagrid's hut, across from Hogwarts castle.

"Monster Book of Monsters" cage. 108. Next to the hut's left-hand door is a bucket labeled "woodlice for bowtruckles." 109. Past Hagrid's hut are sacks of hippogriff feed and an empty trough. 110. Farther down, faint growls, shrieks and caws come from the Forbidden Forest. 111. Near the boarding area, Buckbeak sits with his forelegs crossed in a huge nest of tangled branches. He convincingly blinks, moves his eyes and turns his head. Bits of chain hang from his neck. 112. The train is woven into a hippogriff's head, wings and talons. 113. As your ride begins, Buckbeak bows to you.

114. Inside **Filch's Emporium,** stone pillars along the walls are topped with carved owls. 115. The rafters are lined with grates filled with confiscated items, including firework brands such as Phoenix Fire Lighters, Weasleys' Wildfire Wizbangs and Dr. Filibuster's Fabulous Wet-Start No-Heat Fireworks. 116. Also in the rafters are copies of The Quibbler that feature an article called "How far will Fudge go to gain Gringotts?" 117. Five proclamations and decrees issued by Dolores Umbridge hang next to the counter along the back wall. 118. A glass case below a pillar displays Filch's secrecy sensor, a device used to detect contraband items. 119. The Marauder's Map is on display below another pillar. Footsteps labeled with indistinct names move over the opened map. 120. A wizard chess set is displayed in a cage on a table. 121. A bottle of Skele-Gro ("Bone-fide Results Everytime") is in a display case on top of a merchandise stand. 122. A green, scaly Fanged Flyer is displayed on top of another stand. 123. Behind it is a replica of Lucius Malfoy's Death Eater mask. 124. Throughout the store, boxes of files hold student records for Fred, George, Ginny, Neville, Parvati, Ron and Seamus.

IN LONDON.

1. Trash cans throughout **the grounds of London** (and inside King's Cross station) are realistically beat-up and slightly rusty. 2. The first "O" on the sign for a **Record Shop** is shaped like a record. 3. In the windows of the shop, fictional albums are filled with secret references. In the left window on the bottom shelf, an album by "The Quint Trio" features the song "Here's to Swimmin' with Bow Legged Women"—a

Dialing the Ministry of Magic outside Leicester Square Station, London.

sea shanty sung by the character Quint in the 1975 movie "Jaws," which inspired the Jaws attraction at this theme park that Diagon Alley replaced. 4. The sleeve for the pop record "Katy's in Charge" at the top left refers to Katy Pacitti, Universal's resident Potter expert. 5. A sleeve for the record "Joe Sez No" on the top right shows a light-switch with "yes" and "no" options. That's a nod to J.K. Rowling ("Jo") who had total veto power over everything Potter put in the parks and notoriously strict standards. 6. In the right window on the top shelf, the record "Stuart's Folly" refers to Stuart Craig, the set designer for the movies. 7. Between the bookstore and record shop, a nondescript sign and (nonfunctional) door mark the front of the Leaky Cauldron.

8. A **telephone booth** outside Leicester Square Station is the visitor's entrance to the Ministry of Magic. Dialing "62442" (the numerical code for "MAGIC") into the phone prompts one of seven messages from the Ministry that explains the entrance's temporary closure. 9. One message clarifies that the entrance is closed because of "inclement weather in the Department of Magical Accidents and Catastrophes." 10. Behind the phone booth is the gated-off entrance to the London Underground.

11. The purple, triple-decker **Knight Bus** is parked next to the Eros Fountain, a landmark from Piccadilly Circus. 12. The bus's left turn signal blinks. 13. Inside the bus, Jamaican shrunken head Dre Head snores and twists in its sleep when the bus conductor isn't there. 14. A chandelier is visible through the second-story windows of the bus. 15. A "compression" lever is behind Dre Head. 16. Signs of the back of the bus read "All Destinations (Nothing Underwater)." 17. While you can't actually enter the bus, you can step onto the back and look inside. To the left of the barred-off entrance is a red button marked "Press Once." 18. Inside the bus are wheeled cots and stacked luggage; medicine bags hang near the driver's seat. 19. Ads for the Daily Prophet, the Leaky Cauldron, Sleekeazy's Scalp Treatment, the Nimbus Fambus and Phoenix Fire Lighters line the bus's interior walls. 20. A message near the driver's seat warns that the beds slide when the bus is in motion. 21. Another message reminds passengers to "not distract driver AT ANY TIME."

22. At **Grimmauld Place** ("grim old place"), a row of brick townhouses to the right of Wyndham's Theater, Number Twelve is the second one down; it's visibly older and dirtier than the others, with darker bricks, rusty gates and aged curtains in its windows. On its second floor, Kreacher the house-elf occasionally peeks out from behind the window's curtains. 23. At night, Number Twelve is the only Grimmauld Place townhouse with no lights on inside. Light is only visible when Kreacher looks out the window.

IN DIAGON ALLEY.

24. **As you enter** the passageway into Diagon Alley, you hear its bricks scraping against each other as they part for you (they don't really move). 25. The Leaky Cauldron's inn spans over the alley entrance; looking back you see clothes hung out to dry over a balcony's railing. The inn is painted with the words "Wayward Wizards Welcome." 26. Trains rumble as they occasionally cross over the alley on a bridge from King's Cross. 27. Black trash cans are appropriately weathered.

28. On your left a stack of cauldrons towers by **Potage's Cauldron Shop.** 29. Signs at its window lists the cauldrons it sells: copper, brass, pewter, silver, self-stirring and collapsible. 30. In the window, piles of cauldrons are topped with self-stirring ones.

31. The sign at the entrance to the **Leaky Cauldron** shows a witch brewing in a cauldron. Water leaks from a small crack in it. 32. Inside, a chalkboard lists "yesterday's specials." 33. Another chalkboard labeled "Services" reads:—

> Knight Bus request: D.I.Y. Please don't ask any member of
> staff. Room service available from midnight to a minute after.
> We don't have any owls. Many thanks.

34. In the rafters, wooden gussets are carved into magical creatures including dragons, griffins and winged horses. 35. Silver steins hang behind the ordering counter. 36. Bottles of Firewhiskey, Ocky Rot Wine and White Rat Whiskey stack above the drink taps. 37. Mismatched keys for guests staying at the inn hang on a board of hooks in the back corner. 38. A sign to the right of the exit doors ("To all guests and patrons…") is the same as the one in The Three Broomsticks.

39. Outside **Quality Quidditch Supplies,** two basement-level windows glow on and off. 40. Decorative bludgers and a golden snitch hang from a signpost above the entrance. 41. Three quaffles hang from another sign. 42. In the left window, a Firebolt racing broom levitates in midair. 43. Signs behind the Firebolt promote the broom's features, including its "unbreakable Braking Charm." 44. Another sign boasts that it was "flown by the World Cup winning team!"; a circular emblem below reads "422nd World Cup — International Association of Quidditch — I.D.A." 45. Tins of Broomcare Wax and two beater's bats are at the front of the display. 46. A red Hogwarts crest is carved above the door of the shop. 47. Inside the right window, two mannequins model quidditch equipment. One of them holds a Nimbus 2001 racing broom. They stand between two miniature quidditch towers. 48. At the front of the window is a triangular stack of quaffles and some more beater bats. 49. An immobile golden snitch hangs above the display. 50. Team pennants for the Chudley Cannons, Puddlemere United, the Holyhead Harpies and the Montrose Magpies hang in windows of the shop's second floor. 51. Inside the store, mannequins wear protective quidditch gear over the clothes they model. A mannequin in a display case models a keeper uniform; it holds a quaffle and a broom. 52. A framed poster for the notoriously bad Chudley Cannons quidditch team hangs on the wall. It's decorated with the team's slogan: "Let's All Just Keep Our Fingers Crossed and Hope For The Best!" Posing together on a windy day; the team ducks to avoid an out-of-control player shooting past on a broom. Wind from the photo blows the edges of the words "Chudley Cannons" and makes them spin.

53. Outside **Weasleys' Wizard Wheezes,** the 20-foot Weasley twin at the corner of the store tips his top hat to reveal a white rabbit underneath; when he tips it again the rabbit is gone. 54. Text trimming the windows reads "Quality Capers For The Devious"; "Disastrous Delights"; "The Best In Jesting"; "Masterpieces Of Modern Magic"; "Petrifying Products"; "Always A Wheeze Guaranteed"; and "Shenanigans For All." 55. The window closest to Quality Quidditch Supplies advertises a constipation-inducing prank pill called U-No-Poo; a sign reads "Why are you worrying about U-Know-Who? You should be worrying about U-No-Poo." 56. In a second-floor window, a line of sombrero-wearing Day of the Dead skeletons stands behind boxes of fireworks. 57. A schoolgirl vomits into a barrel in a display for Puking Pastilles in the window to the left of the giant Weasley figure. 58. Behind that ad is a flowery display of love potions, some extendable ears, a house of balanced wizard cards and caged pygmy puffs. 59. In the window above, two pumpkins sit on a shelf; they have long rubber tongues and wear springy-eye glasses. 60. The wall is painted with ads for Edible Dark Marks and Skiving Snackboxes ("Range of sweets to make you ill!!!—Free delivery on all owl post orders"). 61. The back of the shop advertises Peruvian Instant Darkness Powder, Screaming Yo-Yos, Boxing Telescopes, Decoy Detonators and love potions. 62. An elephant's face marks an ad for Dung Bombs ("Freshly delivered every third Friday"). 63. A window on the second floor has hanging rubber chickens and a cactus that wears a sombrero and pink sunglasses. 64. A third-floor window is filled with animal masks of a dalmatian, cow, lion, pig and rabbit. 65. Inside the shop a skylight over its staircase shows a constant stream of exploding fireworks. 66. A little clockwork version of Dolores Umbridge rides a unicycle above patrons' heads while balancing a pair of cauldrons; occasionally she shrills "I will have ORDER!" 67. Pink and purple pygmy puff plushies softly coo in pink cages. 68. If you buy one, the shopkeeper will have you name it, ring a bell, announce to the store that you've adopted and named it, and lead everyone in a round of applause. 69. The fireplace has silver, owl-shaped log holders; the mantle above has burn marks.

70. Above the door of **Madam Malkin's,** a pair of golden scissors slowly open and close. 71. In a second-story window, a mannequin wears Hermione's pink Yule Ball dress. 72. A hanging sign reads "School Robes Available Here." 73. Displayed inside the shop is an enchanted white dress with an animated peacock design. 74. Mannequins model outfits worn by Albus Dumbledore and Gilderoy Lockhart. 75. A talking mirror judges the fashion sense of people who stand in front of it.

76. Old cameras and rolls of wizarding film fill the window of **Shutterbutton's Photography Studio.** 77. One camera has a little golden owl at the end of a lever. 78. Above Shutterbutton's is the window of Eeylops Owl Emporium.

79. On the street's right side, across from Weasleys' Wizard Wheezes, the window for the **Jellied Eel Shop** displays a meat pie with fish heads sticking out of it and a tray filled with jellied eels. 80. A "Jellied Eel & Mashed Onion" sign hanging over the window has an ampersand shaped like an eel.

81. In the Harry Potter saga, bookstore **Flourish and Blotts** sells textbooks to Hogwarts students and hosts book signings for popular authors such as Gilderoy Lockhart. In its right window, furry "Monster Book of Monsters" textbooks snarl, shake and gnash their teeth inside an iron cage. Shredded book pages and clumps of brown fur litter the bottom of the display window. 82. A tower of books wobbles precariously to the right of the cage. The stack includes such titles as "Triwizard Tragedies, 32nd Edition," "The Decline of Pagan Magic" by Bathilda Bagshot, "The Tales of Beedle the Bard" with original illustrations by Luxo Karuzox, "Moste Potente Potions," "Omens, Oracles & The Goat" also by Bagshot, "The Healer's Help Mate" compiled by H. Pollingtonious, "Secrets of the Darkest Art" by Owle Bullock and "Advanced Potion-Making, Second Edition" by Libartius Borage. 83. In the left window a display promotes

A FIELD GUIDE

Gilderoy Lockhart's autobiography "Magical Me," as well as his other books: "Wanderings with Werewolves," "Holidays with Hags," "Voyages with Vampires," "Break with a Banshee," "Gadding with Ghouls," "Travels with Trolls" and "Year with the Yeti." An easel displays an enlarged cover of "Magical Me." 84. Lockhart poses and preens himself in an animated promotional photo propped up beneath the easel.

85. A sign hanging above the door of **The Daily Prophet** reads "The Wizarding World's Beguiling Broadsheet of Choice." 86. Clacking typewriters and harried voices are audible from a small window above the Prophet's door:—

Excited voice: "We have a big story, exclusive! Terror at Quidditch Cup! The whole front page!"
Irritated co-worker: "The whole front page's out!"
Excited voice: "How about the boggart story?"
Editor: "Leave the boggart story in! That's wizard interest."

Editor (later): "Do we have any wizard interest stories?"
Female reporter: "We have a story about Celestina Warbeck visiting patients at St. Mungo's."
Editor: "Perfect! Celestina sells!"

Editor (again): "Do we have any wizard interest stories?"
Female reporter: "We have the story of the man who turned his wife into a cat."
Editor: "Ooh! Do we know if it was Polyjuice Potion?"

The last story is also mentioned on the Wizarding Wireless Network radio program (see upcoming listing) that plays near Magical Menagerie.

87. Next to Madam Malkin's, the window of **Slug & Jiggers Apothecary** is filled with labeled potion ingredients such as dittany, dragon claw ooze, horklump juice, nightshade, porcupine quills, snakeweed, weedosoros and wormwood essence.

88. Next door, the window of **Mr. Mulpepper's Apothecary** displays materials to make Polyjuice Potion as well as potion ingredients such as beetle eyes, bezoars, bundimun ooze, dragon blood, flobberworm mucus and powdered snake fang. A bowl of runespoor eggs sits at the bottom left. Runic symbols label a few ingredients. 89. Plastic toy insects fill some jars and bins. 90. Behind a bowl of mistletoe, a set of shark jaws allude to the "Jaws" ride that Diagon Alley replaced.

91. In the window of **Spindlewarps Woolshop,** a pair of needles knit a colorful wool scarf; they click loudly against each other. 92. A hanging sign over the window is a spool of thread. 93. Above the window is a painted ad for Spindlewarps' never-tangle wool, criss-cross stitch kits, self-knitting needles and "assorted wraps and wefts."

94. In the window of **Florean Fortescue's Ice-Cream Parlour,** giggling people with whipped cream-like hair pop out of two ice-cream-cone-shaped displays. 95. A spinning cone tops the corner rooftop, covered with rainbow sprinkles that light up. 96. A tiny green table and chairs are beneath the spinning cone. 97. Inside the Parlour, flavors from the books include Strawberry & Peanut Butter and Chocolate & Raspberry. 98. Near the shop a sign labeled "Hobb Whistll" is a teapot; steam pours from its spout.

99. Little wand shapes separate lines of text on signs alongside the window of **Ollivanders Wand Repair and Re-Tooling.** 100. Inside the window supplies for making and repairing wands include a basket of sticks, a table set up for wand-crafting and glass vials filled with dragon heartstrings, phoenix feathers and unicorn hairs. 101. A black sign for the Diagon Alley Arts Club hangs over the shop. 102. A nearby sign advertises 2nd Hand Brooms ("Repair, Retwigge, Retune Here—Nearly New Brooms"). 103. Another promotes Fear of Flying Classes.

104. The small shop **Broomstix** is on the corner past Ollivanders. A pumpkin juice ad is painted on the wall above it. Higher up is an ad for Broomcare Wax.

105. The massive dragon that clings to the top of **Gringotts Wizarding Bank** is the same one seen in the Escape from Gringotts attraction. It bears the marks of heavy abuse from its former home in the bank, including scars from the cuffs it wore and holes torn through its wings. Manacles and bits of chain still hang from its neck. 106. Often (but not always) every 10 minutes, the dragon snarls and breathes fire with a deafening roar. Sometimes the delay between blasts is 30 minutes or longer. You can feel the heat from the fire from the street below. 107. The building's weather vane is crushed under the dragon's torso. 108. The front doors of Gringotts have big round handles with the faces of wrinkled old goblins on them. 109. A gold statue of Gringott himself stands on top of a pile of gleaming galleons in front of the entrance to the ride.

IN HORIZONT ALLEY.

110. **Hagrid's flying motorcycle** is parked next Gringotts. Sit on it for a cool photo op. 111. The big blue dashboard button that blasts fire from its exhaust is disabled.

112. Up the stairs of an alley behind the bike is high-end clothing store **Twilfitt and Tattings;** wealthier wizarding families such as the Malfoys prefer it to Madam Malkin's. A sign above its window says it sells custom-to-order dragonskin jackets. 113. Above Twilfitt and Tattings is a purple sign for "Strange, Staine and Seeping Healers."

114. Above the **public conveniences** is a streetlight shaped like an umbrella. A bearded, crowned face on the wall has an arm emerging from its mouth; it holds the umbrella up. 115. On a wall above, signs advertise magical goods, organizations and services. A hanging teal sign promotes the Society For the Reformation of Hags. Below are ads for a tobacconist, Pumpkin Pasties and Doxycide. A yellow sign advertises taxi services by the Black Carpet Company ("Pure black Persian carpets—No place too far!"). A smaller brown sign sells "Knitted Beard Bags." A green sign sells "Mrs. Skower's All-Purpose Magical Mess Remover." A painted ad on the wall promotes Pepper Imps ("Smoke at the Mouth! Available at Honeydukes in Hogsmeade Village"). Others market Droobles Best Blowing Gum and Tolipan Blemish Blitzer (with dragon claw).

116. The Wizarding Wireless Network broadcasts from a speaker to the left of Magical Menagerie; it switches between segments in bursts of static. Breaking news includes "A local vampire has been admitted to casualty to a garlic bread overdose," "Muggle mistakes wand for chopsticks and causes mayhem at Chinese restaurant," "A global shortage of newt's tails sends wizards into tailspin" and a report of "two flying pigs that apparently interfered with muggle air traffic." 117. A female reporter says "Have you ever wanted to turn your spouse into a cat? Well, this man *did*. News story, coming up." 118. A commercial urges you to open a Gringotts Junior Wizard Savings account. 119. "Next on our program, our very exciting Witching Hour hosted by Glenda Chittock, with the popular 'Singing Sorceress' Celestina Warbeck." 120. Another commercial promotes the Owl Correction Facility, an "owl training and conditioning camp":—

> Have you had enough undelivered mail? Are there pecking issues at home? Are you tired of endless squawking, toilet problems or bad behavior? Don't despair—it's not too late! All is not lost! Fix your owl with Owl Correction!

121. An ad for the Black Carpet Company markets its "fully-insured pure black Persian carpets." 122. The program is sponsored by Gladrags Wizardwear: "dressing for discerning wizards since 1750." 123. After a snippet of a warbling female voice, the host says "That was Celestina Warbeck, performing her sensational hit, 'A Cauldron Full of Hot, Strong Love.'" 124. The Sports Report's host asks a question for the day:

"Which quidditch player has pled guilty in the Firebolt case? ...Why, that'd be Appleby Arrows' Shrake Wakefield!" He also talks about different quidditch teams: "Atop the Quidditch League, the Tutshill Tornados take the lead, but for how long? Can the Montrose Magpies survive another long-fighted loss?" 125. Another commercial:—

> Are you seeking a challenging career involving travel, adventure and substantial danger-related treasure bonuses? Then consider a position with Gringotts Wizarding Bank! Gringotts is currently recruiting curse breakers for thrilling opportunities abroad.

126. On the left side of the street, a sign for Obscurus Books, the publisher of the book "Fantastic Beasts and Where to Find Them," hangs over **The Fountain of Fair Fortune.** 127. Mirrored walls inside are etched with images of the eponymous artifact from "The Fountain of Fair Fortune" story from the book "The Tales of Beedle the Bard." 128. The symbol of the Deathly Hallows decorates the etched fountains.

129. Cats, dogs, rats and toads form the painted letters of the sign for **Magical Menagerie.** 130. The shop entrance is bordered by bizarre creatures with the front ends of hippos, the rears of snakes, cat-like eyes and forked tongues. 131. Inside the left-hand window, two huge green snails called streelers ooze inside glass orbs. Glowing ridges in their shells slowly change color. 132. Occasionally a streeler will get startled, causing its light to flash quickly between colors before it calms back down. 133. A hand-written label at the front of the window reads "Streelers: M.o.M. classification: XXX. Guaranteed hourly color change. American raised... Imported. Venom reported to kill horklumps." Horklumps are mushroom-like pests that overrun gardens. 134. Inside the right-hand window, a red and gold fwooper sings inside a birdcage. It whistles "The Carnival of the Animals" by Camille Saint-Saëns. 135. At the bottom of the cage is a nest filled with vividly colored eggs. 136. A hand-written label at the front of the window reads "Fwooper: M.o.M. classification: XXX. From darkest Africa. Silencing charm included. License required." 137. To the right of the cage, two massive purple toads croak inside a terrarium; the one on the right occasionally lurches forward.

138. Inside the shop, a balcony is bordered by golden poles shaped like coiled snakes. 139. A upper colorful mural shows a forest filled with magical beasts. 140. In the balcony's back-left corner is a crumple-horned snorkack, a purple creature that looks like a strange yak. This is the only place it's seen; it not fully described in the books. 141. Also on the balcony are whimsical depictions of a blue griffin, a silver unicorn and some purple cats. 142. Next to the griffin is a demiguise, a white yeti-like creature. 143. A golden, cat-like kneazel swings its tufted tail and looks down on shoppers. 144. It sits on a box labelled "Dancing Doxy" ("The Clockwork Novelty Doxy—Drives Cats Crazy!"). 145. Toothy dragon beams support the balcony. 146. A huge covered cage hangs from the middle of the room; shadows cast from within reveal magical rats doing cartwheels and playing jump-rope with their tails. They squeak. 147. When you buy a plushie, the clerk refers to your payment as an "adoption fee." 148. Two huge pythons rest in a window on the shop's left side. One faces inside, hissing and flicking out its tongue. 149. Outside the shop, a short path leads to the window, where the other snake stares at onlookers as it hisses and speaks Parseltongue in an eerie, distorted voice:—

> Snakesss make spectacular petsss... We are ssso easssy to care for... A comfy basssking place and a few rabbitsss each day will sufficcce... A Parssselmouth... a desssscendant of Sssalazar Ssslytherin perhapsss? Isss Parssseltongue your firssst language?

150. Across the pathway from the python, the words "Magical Menagerie" are spelled out by painted animals.

Borgin and Burkes, Knockturn Alley.

IN KNOCKTURN ALLEY.

151. In the **entrance to the Alley** next to the Leaky Cauldron, an animated wanted poster for Bellatrix Lestrange is on the left wall (it's also on a wall inside the alley's left-most entrance off Horizont Alley). 152. High above the poster is a projected red ad for Phoenix Fire Lighters. Every now and then it bursts into flames and burns to gray ashes; it regenerates a moment later. 153. Clouds move across the alley's dark sky. 154. Along the left wall, the window of Shyverwretch's Poisons and Venoms is lined with green and gold vials lit by flickering candles.

155. In the right window of the shop **Borgin and Burkes,** a rubber snake winds through a skull's eye socket. 156. Two basement-level windows pulse with green light. 157. Inside the shop, a Hand of Glory is displayed in a glass case in the front right corner; the hand reaches forward every now and then. 158. Above the hand, an opal necklace has a warning label that reads "CAUTION: Do Not Touch—Cursed. Has claimed the lives of nineteen muggle owners to date." 159. What look like torture implements hang on racks from the ceiling in the front corners of the room. 160. On top of the frontmost display case is an umbrella stand made from a troll's foot. It's filled with canes and walking sticks, one of which is topped with a silver werewolf head. 161. Stacked shark jaws in the bottom corner of the front display case allude to the park's former "Jaws" ride. 162. Death Eater masks are shelved behind the counter. 163. A boggart locked inside a shaking trunk under a table on the left makes soft, eerie moans that sound like whistling wind. 164. A vanishing cabinet is pushed into the back right corner. A canary faintly chirps inside. 165. A birdcage with a fruit bat's skeleton is in the middle of the second-floor balcony at the front of the store.

166. The window of shop **Noggin and Bonce** is filled with shrunken heads that talk, joke and sing; it's to the right of the shop Shyverwretch's. One song is "Show Me the Way to Go Home," a shout-out to a scene in "Jaws" where it's sung by Quint, Hooper and Chief Brody. 167. Other tunes sung by the heads were written by English music hall singers and entertainers more than a hundred years ago. "She Sits Among the

Cabbages and Peas" is an 1895 song written by Marie Lloyd, the infamous "Queen of the Music Hall" known for her use of innuendo and double entendre. 168. "Our House is Haunted" was performed by George Formby Sr., one of the greatest music hall performers of the early 20th century. Formby's character John Willie inspired Charlie Chaplin's Little Tramp character, including his signature cane twirl and duck-foot walk. 169. "With Her Head Tucked Underneath Her Arm" is a darkly comedic song about the ghost of Anne Boleyn, who haunts the Tower of London after being beheaded by Henry VIII. The song was originally performed in 1934 by Stanley Holloway, an English actor and singer known for his portrayal of Alfred P. Doolittle in the 1964 movie "My Fair Lady." 170. "There's No Toad in the Toad in the Hole" is about a traditional English dish of sausages sticking out of Yorkshire pudding batter, which supposedly look like toads poking their heads out of holes in the ground. The song was written by music hall entertainer Ernie Mayne, who wrote music that poked fun at his 280-pound weight.

171. The heads also tell jokes, most of which are head-related. An example:—

"I went to the hair salon and sat on the chair.
The stylist said, 'Your hair needs cutting badly.'
I said 'I don't want it cut badly,' and I walked out."

172. A sign for "E.L.M. and Wizards Undertakers & Embalmers" ("Cross over in mesmerizing style") hangs above an emergency exit sign in the back corner of the alley. 173. An ad projected on the wall above reads "To Let Or Lease—Reptiles/Arachnids Allowed." 174. A sign to the right advertises Flesh-Eating Slug Repellent.

175. In the main window of **Dystyl Phaelanges,** a slideshow projects diagrams of the skeletal structures of a mermaid, a thestral and a troll; the troll skeleton mimics the movements of viewers with interactive wands. 176. The window's ceiling is decorated with an intricate pattern of human skulls and bones. 177. The ancient projector and its huge focusing lenses move when the slides change. 178. The skull of a transformed werewolf sits on a shelf to the left. 179. Next to it is a skeletal, taloned hippogriff foot. 180. A mermaid skeleton with tattered fins hangs to the right of the projector. 181. A table on the right side of the window displays skulls of a giant, a house-elf, a human and a pixie. 182. Behind the screen is the troll skeleton shown in the slideshow.

183. An ad that reads "Finest Malodorous Preparations To Repel Most Foes" is projected on the building over the walkway to Dystyl Phaelanges.

184. To the right of Dystyl Phaelanges, a wrought iron gate blocks access to an alleyway. On its right wall is an animated wanted poster for Fenrir Greyback. 185. A sign for The White Wyvern tavern hangs midway down the alleyway. 186. Sounds that echo from the alley include rattling chains, clattering and snarling.

187. To the right of that alleyway, **Markus Scarr's Indelible Tattoos** specializes in animated tattoos. Text across its window reads "Ornate Designs To Impress Or Menace." 188. Inside is a chair and an old tattooing device filled with colored inks. 189. The shop's back wall is decorated with tattoo concept sketches that move and interact with each other. At the bottom left, a drawing of a hand holds a wand that balances a ball of light on its tip; the back of the hand is tattooed with a skull and crossbones. 190. Above that is art of a skull with mad rolling eyes, fluttering green tufts of hair and a forked orange tongue. 191. Another sketch shows a man's portrait; his head and neck tattooed with an animated spider and a scorpion. 192. Above the room's door is a drawing with beetles, ladybugs and a bat, which all fidget and flutter their wings. 193. Occasionally the sketch of the wand bounces its ball of light away into the drawing above the door; the light scares ladybugs in that drawing, making them fly into the face of the mad-eyed skull drawing below. After a moment of confusion, the ball of light returns to the wand and the ladybugs fly back into place. 194. To the right of the door are sketches of a masked

Dr. Filibuster's Fireworks. At left, the entrance to Carkitt Market.

Death Eater and a stylized dragon; occasionally it breathes fire, forcing the Death Eater to shield itself with a dome of blue magic. This echoes the climax of Escape from Gringotts, when Voldemort and Bellatrix face the escaped dragon.

195. A path to the right of the tattoo shop leads to a courtyard. Above the street there, a sign advertises the services of a house-elf chimneysweep.

196. At **Ariadne Spinner's** a sign reads "Arachnids available—Nocturnal, venomous, bird-eating, world's largest—Good for pets." 197. Another sign is shaped like a tarantula. 198. Shadows of gigantic spiders crawl over the shop's window. 199. The window is papered with pages of The Daily Prophet, visible are an article titled "Wizard Life Expectancy Reaches 137¾," a Sudoku-like Runokk game written in runic symbols, and a table of contents listing topics such as Abracadabra, Hocus-Pocus, Arts & Warts, Tricks & Trucks, Black Magic, Pink Magic and "Swowizbiz." 200. A loud hiss blasts from a grate beneath the window whenever someone walks by. 201. Step-by-step lessons for how to "un-tame your tarantula" are advertised on a sign to the right of the facade.

202. "Bats & Skins—Savants in Desiccation" reads text across the window of the **Fledermaus and Tanner** shop. Leathery skins, bat wings and whole bats hang inside.

203. The window for **Trackleshanks Locksmith** has an elaborate display of locks and keys. A sign over the window reads "Expert In Confunded Locks."

204. The shop **Tallow and Hemp Toxic Tapers** sells poisonous candles.

IN CARKITT MARKET.

205. Pillars topped with feather quills border the storefront of **Scribbulus**. 206. A sign to the left of the entrance door advertises peacock, pheasant and fwooper quills. 207. In the left window is an inkwell with a golden stopper shaped like an owl's head. 208. An ad for invisible ink is in the right window; it displays a blank piece of parchment. 209. Inside the shop, glass jars on a shelf above the counter contain color-changing balls of light. 210. High above the Scribbulus entrance a sign promotes the services of a palmist for a galleon per reading.

211. Pillars that border the **Gringotts Money Exchange** are marked with small plaques that read "Gringotts bank notes available here. See a wizard teller for transaction details." 212. Inside, the goblin's pointed teeth are visible when he talks. 213. Neat piles of gold ingots are stacked behind the counter and on shelves along the walls. 214. Bank notes read "Bank Rune Credit." Runic symbols are printed along the bottom edge of each one.

215. To the right of the exchange, a green sign advertises dragon-hide boots and gloves. 216. Below that is an ad for Floo Powder. 217. Across from Wiseacres, a wall is painted with an ad for "Bulman's ultimate witch's hat liner" ("New improved model! Repels dark arts, hexes—Warranted to delight the purchaser"). 218. Another ad on the wall is for "Sleekeazy's Hair Potion." 219. Farther down is a storefront for Weevanwhisker's Barber Shop.

220. The right window of nearby shop **Cogg & Bell Clockmakers** ("Artisans in Trustworthy Timepieces") has a collection of ticking clocks that all run at different speeds; some run backward. Clocks include one with a minute hand shaped like a witch and a cat riding a broomstick and a cuckoo clock that chimes periodically. 221. In the shop's left window is a large clock face and several swinging pendulums; one designed to look like an upside-down demon is clinging to it.

222. To the left is the small **Museum of Muggle Curiosities,** its window filled with vintage electrical devices such as lamps, radios, phones and wall sockets.

223. The colorful walls of the **Dr. Filibuster's Fireworks** shop are covered in ads for firework products, including Fabulous Wet-Start No-Heat Fireworks, Super Speedy Catherine Wheels, Whistling Bottle Rockets and Thunder Snaps. 224. Text across the window reads "The Best British Fireworks!"

225. On a corner of Carkitt Market is **The House-Elf Placement Agency** ("Steadfast staff—Endorsed elves").

226. A carved stone basilisk, dementor, hippogriff, thestral, unicorn and transformed werewolf decorate the upper corners of the **Eternelle's Elixir of Refreshment** stand. 227. A weathervane shaped like a bucking winged horse tops the stand's pointed spire, which pokes through the canopy of Carkitt Market.

228. Huge gramophone-like speakers amplify the sound of shows on the **Carkitt Market stage.** 229. On the stage, travel stickers from Godric's Hollow (Harry's birthplace and where his parents died) and Little Hangleton (where Voldemort's father lived and the site of the graveyard where Voldemort regained his body) are on a Wizarding Academy of Dramatic Arts luggage bag decorated with theater masks. 230. On the right wall of the stage is an ad for Flooboost Pro Floo Powder Accelerator. 231. Its sign shaped like a candlestick, candle shop Wickermires is in an alcove behind the stage. 232. Next to it is the Stowe & Packers Magical Bag Shop. 233. A painted ad for The Gringotts Money Exchange is on the back right wall of the stage. 234. To the right is an ad for Phoenix Fire Lighters fireworks ("For an eternal fire—From ashes to blaze in a flash").

235. In the **Carkitt Market courtyard,** a carved green mermaid bust decorates a water fountain in the middle of the courtyard. She holds a trident staff topped with a glowing red lantern. 236. Above and to the left of The Hopping Pot, a stoplight changes colors for the trains that travel overhead.

237. A vertical sign over the line entrance to **The Hopping Pot** reads "The Hopping Pot—Just hop in!" 238. Ads for wizarding drinks (including Firewhiskey, Dragon Brandy, Ocky Rot Wine and butterbeer) are painted on the wall above the ordering counter.

239. The sign for the **Bowman E. Wright Blacksmith** shop is shaped like an anvil. 240. From inside the shop, metal clinks as if someone's at work forging armor. 241. A fully assembled set of security troll armor hangs from the ceiling. 242. A troll's spiked mace hangs to the right of the armor.

243. To the left of the blacksmith is an ad for Madame Glossy's Self-Polishing Shoe Polish ("Just apply with a swift swish of the arm"). 244. On the second floor, a boarded window on the right reads "Forger of Golden Snitches." 245. The words "Cauldron Repairs Carried Out" are on the third-floor wall. 246. "Specialist Tackle for Magical Creatures" is printed on a fourth-floor window.

247. To the right of the door of the **Owl Post,** a window is full of packages that are waiting to be delivered by owl. Wrapped items include a broomstick, a teapot, a witch's hat, a cauldron and two human skulls. 248. On the corner of the building, owls hoot, screech and peer around from a wall of perches. 249. Aged owl droppings stain the bottom of each perch. 250. Below them, a decorative owl holds a scroll in its talons.

251. On the wall to the right of the Owl Post, a green house-elf statue holds a lantern on a high-up platform.

252. Above **the path leading back to London,** an ad for a Nimbus-brand broomstick called the Fambus Station Wagon is painted on the wall; it shows six people riding a single long broom. 253. A sign on the third floor promotes Gladrags Wizardwear. 254. To the left of Sugarplum's Sweetshop, a blue sign decorated with a winged globe advertises Travel Agents Globus Mundi. 255. To the right of the shop's door is an aged sign for Concordia and Plunkett Musical Instruments.

256. A sign in front of **Wands by Gregorovitch** lists some of the woods the company uses, including cherry, elm, hawthorn, holly, rosewood, walnut and willow. 257. Around the corner, a wall is painted with an ad for the Daily Prophet ("Over 200 years in print—To subscribe send us an owl—Ask D. Shaman—Unravelling your innermost conundrums every Wednesday").

WIZARDING WORLD FUN FACTS.

1. In **Hogsmeade,** the Ford Anglia in the Dragon Challenge queue is a real movie prop; it appeared in the 2002 film "Harry Potter and the Chamber of Secrets." 2. Dragon Challenge is the highest coaster in the park, at 125 feet. Its largest drop, 115 feet, is on the Chinese Fireball track. 3. While the Hungarian Horntail has black scales in the films, the Horntail coaster is blue and ice-themed. The discrepancy is because the previous iteration of the attraction—"Dueling Dragons," a part of the Lost Continent area of the park—featured tracks based on fire and ice dragons. 4. The design of The Three Broomsticks was created for the park before it was re-created for a set seen in the 2009 movie "Harry Potter and the Half-Blood Prince." 5. The Hog's Head pub is named after a hogshead, a unit of measurement for alcoholic drinks. 6. Its Hog's Head Brew is made exclusively for the Wizarding World of Harry Potter by the Florida Beer Co. 7. The Ceridwen's Cauldron storefront is named after Ceridwen, a legendary mythological Welsh enchantress with a magical cauldron. She used it to brew a potion that would make her son wise and grant him poetic inspiration. The first three drops of the resulting liquid gave wisdom; the rest was a lethal poison. 8. The Magic Neep fruit cart is named after the Scots word for "turnip."

9. In **London,** the Knight Bus is an actual prop used in the filming of the 2004 movie "Harry Potter and the Prisoner of Azkaban." When the Hogsmeade area of Islands of Adventure debuted, the bus carried Harry Potter film stars to the opening ceremony. 10. The London building facades were created in real-world London, then shipped to Orlando in pieces.

11. In **Diagon Alley,** many of the astronomical devices on the second-floor balcony of Wiseacres Wizarding Equipment were constructed using parts of the boats from the "Jaws" ride, as well as old camera lenses from the studio. One microscope is the one used by Bill Weasley in the pre-show of the Gringotts attraction. 12. The statue of Gringott the goblin is gilded with real gold.

Index